DREAMS DO COME TRUE

Decoding your dreams to discover your full potential

LAYNE DALFEN

Adams Media Corporation
Avon, Massachusetts

Published by Adams Media Corporation
57 Littlefield Street, Avon, MA 02322. U.S.A.
www.adamsmedia.com

ISBN: 1-58062-636-X

Printed in Canada.

J I H G F E D C B A

Library of Congress Cataloging-in-Publication Data
Dalfen, Layne,
Dreams do come true : decoding your dreams to
discover your full potential/ by Layne Dalfen.
p.   cm.
Includes bibliographical reference.
ISBN: 1-58062-636-X
1. Dream interpretation. 2. Self-actualization (Psychology) I. Title
BF1091.D32   2002
154.6'3—dc21   2001056184

This publication is designed to provide accurate and authoritative information with regard to the subject matter covered. It is sold with the understanding that the publisher is not engaged in rendering legal, accounting, or other professional advice. If legal advice or other expert assistance is required, the services of a competent professional person should be sought.
— From a *Declaration of Principles* jointly adopted by a Committee of the American Bar Association and a Committee of Publishers and Associations

Cover illustration by Daniel Nevins/Superstock

*This book is available for quantity discounts for bulk purchases.
For information call 1-800-872-5627.*

Contents

LEVEL FOUR: TAPPING YOUR SPIRITUAL STRENGTH

" . . . *in the midst of ordinary outer life,*
one is suddenly caught up in an exciting
inner adventure; and because it is unique
for each individual, it cannot be copied
or stolen."

—M.-L von Franz

This book is dedicated to my father,

Joseph Dalfen, z'l 1911–1991

and to my mother, Celia Dalfen

Acknowledgments

Thank you Andy, Lisa, Chelsea, little Emma-Jo, Mummy, and Josh too for believing in me, and to Karen, my sister-in-law, who saved the mandala discussion at the eleventh hour! Thank you also to Hainya, my sister, and to my dear, sweet, mother-in-love Mildred, both of whose consistent support and optimism helped make this dream come true.

To Deborah Joy Cafiero, my editor extraordinaire; whose patience, hard work, humor, persistence, opinionated opinions, honesty, brutality, and intelligence many times inspired me.

Thanks to the people at Adams Media. My editor Claire Gerus, who even though she picked up this ball in the middle of a play, ran with it all the way across the goal line as if it was hers in the first place. Laura MacLaughlin, Copy Chief, whose trustworthy manner sets a calmness over me. And Carrie Lewis McGraw, who seems so well able to handle my energy and intensity level! Thank you.

Carol Mann, my agent, my teammate.

I value the people who helped me appreciate the advantages of seeing things from many perspectives: Susan Saros, Mary Lippman, Dr. Zavie Brown, Dr. Leo Gold, Marla Yanofsky, the multidisciplined members of ASD, and especially the late and dear Dr. Nathan Wisebord, whose guidance taught me the great value of understanding and following my dreams.

A note to readers: Please feel free to contact me. My Web site address is *www.dreamsdocometrue.ca*.

I can also be reached in Montreal by dialing 514-481-8081, or by e-mail at *layne@dreamsdocometrue.ca*.

Introduction

This book will teach you how to interpret your dreams. In doing so, it will show you how to access the tools you need to change your life. I have tremendous faith in the power of dream work, for I have seen its positive effects on my own life and the lives of others. To convince you of this power, I'll start by telling a little bit about who I am and how I came to dream work.

My name is Layne Dalfen. I have been interpreting my own dreams for many years, and have helped others do so as well. As you will discover through reading my book, like most people, I have had my fair share of adversity. I am now a happily married mother of four: Tina, twenty-six, Lisa, twenty-five, and Chelsea, twenty-three, from my first marriage to Murray z'l; and Emma-Jo, who is six, from my present husband Andrew. But circumstances in my life have not always been as pleasant as they are now.

One of the difficult circumstances in my life, and the one that triggered my study of dreams, happened two weeks after my twenty-first birthday. My first child Tina was born with Down's Syndrome, a condition I had never heard of. My general practitioner advised Murray and me against bringing Tina home, and he recommended we start trying to have another baby right away. Because he had been our family doctor since before I was born and I had tremendous respect for him, I had Tina placed in special care. Although I afterwards met Tina's foster mother and now have a wonderful relationship with her and Tina, at the time I felt like I was giving up my child.

Not surprisingly, a few months after Tina was born I became depressed. I was fortunate to obtain the care of a very intelligent psychiatrist, and for the next eight years I underwent Freudian analysis. During that time I had difficulty articulating my feelings but often recalled my dreams; about 80 percent of my analysis revolved around dream interpretation. The experience gave me my first inkling of the power of dream work.

With this taste of self-examination, I was hooked. I enrolled in The Gestalt Counseling and Training Center, and in my early thirties I earned my Certificate in Gestalt Counseling. Through my studies at the Center, I learned to interpret dreams from a Gestalt perspective. But I still wasn't satisfied with the limited perspectives of Freudian and Gestalt dream interpretation, so I took courses at The Alfred Adler Institute in Montreal and studied dreams from an Adlerian perspective under the American Dr. Leo Gold. I later became a member of The C. G. Jung Society of Montreal and an international organization called The Association for the Study of Dreams (ASD). ASD comprises doctors, researchers, and dream workers from all over the world, each with a different philosophy and approach to understanding dreams. Our annual conferences, regular correspondence, and magazine give us the opportunity to learn from one another.

I have found over the years that there is no single, "right" approach to understanding dreams. Each different school of dream theory has had something new to teach me, some new opportunity for me to change and grow through dream work. When I created The Dream Interpretation Center in 1997, I felt it was important to teach other people how to use different approaches to dream interpretation. I encourage my clients to try out many avenues, because this leads to greater flexibility in behavior, increased self-awareness, and, ultimately, enhanced fulfillment and life satisfaction.

After years of seeing the benefits of dream work for myself, my clients, my family, and friends, I decided it was time to write this book. *Dreams Do Come True* will show you how our dreams help us think through the different issues and conflicts we face as we move through life. As I have passed through the different phases of my own life, I've perceived new attitudes, feelings, and strengths as they appear in my dreams. Viewed as a whole, dreams have enhanced my personal growth. I believe that although personal growth comes to most of us anyway, working with and understanding our dreams can propel us there that much faster.

How exactly can dreams help us achieve a better existence? One way is by creating scenarios that mirror the feelings and events we are experiencing in our current lives. When this happens, our dreams present solutions to our problems or reveal strengths we can draw on. For example, when you have a nightmare, it is your subconscious letting you know that you are more preoccupied with a given issue than your conscious mind is letting you believe. The nightmare may be scary, but it also shows you how to deal with your problem. Often the solution comes in the form of a picture or situation you have created in the dream. You can see things more clearly in your sleep.

In the introduction to Carl Jung's book *Man and His Symbols*, John Freeman relates the story of how Jung—who'd been asked to write a book on dreams for the general public rather than for scholars—had initially refused, only to change his mind in the aftermath of a dream. In the dream, Jung saw himself delivering a lecture in a crowded square. The enthusiastic response of the dream-crowd persuaded him to write his book. He claimed he consulted not only his conscious mind, but also his unconscious.

This story defines the essence of my never-ending enthusiasm for dream work. Like the Jungians, I believe that the ability to understand our dreams provides us with the opportunity to be completely in touch with our whole selves when making decisions. Interpreting our dreams is not only fun and interesting, it is important.

Our dreams are important because they show us how to live and respond more flexibly to the situations that come up. Dreams allow us to pinpoint what is missing in our response to a given situation, so we can learn new ways of behaving. Our dreams shine a spotlight on those parts of ourselves that we aren't using to their fullest extent. Sometimes dreams reveal aspects of ourselves we are not using at all.

In our dreams, we try out these new reactions to current or impending issues. Our dream provides a safe place to practice, until we feel ready to take our new behaviors or emotions out into the conscious world. Like muscles that are being exercised for the first time in a gym, underinvested character traits must be developed. At first, each time you exercise you are sore for days. You are putting unfamiliar muscles to work and it feels strange. After a time though, the movement comes easily and feels natural. The same thing happens with our behavior. We begin by practicing new behavior in dream stories. After a while, we bring the new behavior out of the dream scenes and exercise it in real life. Before long, it becomes comfortable. And with this newfound comfort, we gain flexibility and adaptability to the different situations we face. We become less predictable in our approach to solving life's problems. We increase our potential.

In dreaming we can access our deepest source of creativity. Paul McCartney's song "Yesterday," Robert Louis Stevenson's *The Strange Case of Dr. Jekyll and Mr. Hyde,* and Samuel Taylor Coleridge's poem "Kubla Khan" were all inspired by dreams. Friedrich August Kekule, a founder of organic chemistry, hit on the ring structure of benzene after a bizarre dream in which he saw a snake curled into a loop, eating its own tail. Jack Nicklaus, the professional golfer, said that the solution to a problem he was having with his swing came to him in a dream. When he applied the lesson from the dream to his game, he improved by ten strokes, overnight. And Elias Howe had almost given up on inventing a machine that could sew, until he dreamed he was captured by lance-carrying enemies. He noticed that one of the lances had a hole near its point. This dream image inspired him to rework the needle, and the sewing machine was born.

Interpreting your dreams not only helps you solve your immediate problems—whether creative, work-related, or personal—but can lead you to a richer, happier life. If you choose to look more deeply into a dream, you will learn that we gather material from our past, present, and sometimes even the future to solve all kinds of issues. In reading this book, you will discover that we tend to repeat the same self-defeating behaviors over and over. This probably comes as no surprise, but what most people don't realize is that dreams hold the key to escaping from the harmful patterns that hold us back. From our dreams we can obtain release to a freer, fuller existence.

Dream research and analysis is one of the few scientific areas in which each of us can become as knowledgeable as any professional. All you need to do is begin recording your dreams, learn several simple frameworks to help you decipher the meanings and, with a little commitment on your part, you can become adept at analyzing your own dreams. You will learn to recognize and use your own personalized set of dream symbols to solve your problems and reach your goals.

Overview

In Part I of this book, I will show you how to decode a dream so that you can attach it to a specific current situation. Are you having problems at work? Is there a difficult situation with your family? Are you facing a tough decision? Whatever issues you are thinking about (or trying not to think about) in waking life will also appear in your dreams. This is the first layer of meaning. Once the code is broken, you will find that you can actually superimpose the dream story onto your current life story. At this stage, dreamers often see for themselves the solution to a particular problem. Sometimes the solution is obvious. Sometimes it is not. I will provide you with ways to discover different strengths or solutions to an issue from your dreams.

You will find that unlocking the immediate context and its solution from a dream usually takes very little time and effort. However, if you want to look a little further, I will teach you additional exercises in Part II to point you towards the deeper patterns underlying your behavior. Dreams can reveal qualities of our own personality we didn't know we had. These less familiar character traits find means of expression in our dreams. Dr. Frederick Perls, the Gestalt master, called these "unpracticed" characteristics *disowned*. I like to call them *underinvested*.

One of the most powerful tools to access our underinvested qualities through our dreams was invented by Perls. It is highly interactive, and also happens to be a lot of fun. Think of your dream as your own personal play or movie. You are the writer, the director, and all the players. In this exercise, you pick any aspect of the dream you want—a house, a person, an animal, a rock, anything in the dream at all—and pretend you *are* that thing. You speak in its voice, you imagine its reactions, and you feel its emotions. Then you pick another aspect of the same dream—again, anything you want—and imagine a conversation between these two dream-characters. You will find that these dream-characters start to argue with each other, reason with each other, and eventually learn something from each other.

This dream conversation is your own underutilized personality traits finally getting the chance to communicate with your conscious mind. And just as your dream-characters can learn from each other, *you* can learn about using underinvested personality traits to respond to situations in new ways. Soon you become more comfortable with adopting different reactions and approaches to different situations. Now you are no longer stuck in your patterns which, while they may be appropriate in certain situations, are working against you in others. You will find yourself exercising much more of your potential. Accepting all the different parts of yourself is what Carl Jung called *individuation*; Perls, *maturation*; and Edgar Cayce called it *the best self*, or the soul.

If you are satisfied to stop after investigating these underutilized personality traits through your dreams, I am sure you will agree, your life will be greatly enriched. But your dreams have even more to teach you. In Part III, you will learn how dreams can help you work through unresolved issues from your past. You may not think this is important in the present moment, but you should keep in mind that we learn most of our patterns of behavior as children. For example, when we are children, the significant adults in our world teach us that some behaviors are more acceptable than others. Even though some of these responses may not feel comfortable for us originally, we adopt them anyway, for as children we have little choice. Later on, as adults, we continue to repeat these behaviors without wondering whether other reactions might not be more appropriate.

As you will learn in this book, my own experience has taught me that we can still change behaviors we learned in our childhood, as long as we can isolate and recognize the unresolved issues from our past. You don't always have the luxury of being able to work out these issues directly with the adult from your childhood, but that doesn't mean you can't revisit the experience from an adult perspective and change your point of view. I am not suggesting to you that this process is always easy. I am telling you it is possible. You cannot change the past, but you can certainly change how you look at it; how you judge it. Your dreams give you the opportunity to reassess the conclusions you came to as a child.

Here is a quick example. Suppose you had the kind of mother who yelled at you and made you feel inadequate and clumsy because you spilled milk on the floor by accident. She spanked you for your clumsiness. At the age of four, you agreed with her. Her truth was your truth. Now, at forty, when you drop papers by accident at work, do you reprimand yourself with disgust at your clumsiness? Last night's dream may mirror the fact that you spilled papers on the floor at work yesterday and beat yourself up over it, but by using the techniques I will show you in this part of the book, you can discover *why* you are so hard on yourself for this simple accident.

At forty, you have the option to reassess whether you think your mother was correct. Is a four-year-old incompetent for spilling milk? Today you may realize you have a different opinion than your mother did. If you finally understand where your harsh judgment of yourself originates, you might decide to change your opinion! So maybe the first few times you spill the papers onto the floor, your initial reaction might be to curse yourself. I assure you, though, after you understand where your judgments are coming from, you will start to catch yourself when you react this way. And like I explained about working out new muscles in a gym, after a while you will find it easy to say, "Oh, I dropped the papers on the floor—no problem." You might even find yourself bending down and picking them up without attaching any blame at all.

There is a bonus from this level of dream work. The more you understand the origin of your judgments and develop a greater familiarity with your disowned parts, the less judgmental you will be of others. It will become easier for you to embrace the positive qualities of those you love and forgive their faults. You will start to understand that our most violent feelings of blame or hatred usually come from underdeveloped, rejected aspects of ourselves. And just as there are positive ways to incorporate our underinvested personality traits into our own life, there are also ways to be supportive of our loved ones' personal growth without assigning blame or judgment.

If you stop the dream work here, you can already see how much it has helped you change your life. Your dream has guided you towards the solution of a specific problem or issue, revealed your hidden strengths, helped you recognize harmful patterns in your behavior, and led you to a greater acceptance and nurturance in your personal relationships. Yet your dream has even more to offer, if you know how to decipher its message. It can lead you back to the larger human community, to the qualities, needs, sorrows, struggles, and strengths all people share.

Part IV will teach you how to tap into the universal sources of human strength and wisdom through your dreams. We are all a combination of the rational and the mystical; our dreams help us bring these two elements together and let us access the deepest part of our humanity. You will learn how to recognize your own mystical wisdom and nurture it when you share fully in this universal root. The archetypal imagery that appears in our dreams connects us to each other. It makes us timeless. You will come to know your own archetypal symbols, and use them as your link to the collective human soul.

Our experiences are not ours alone. As in the example of the person who feels frustrated and incompetent for dropping papers on the floor—haven't most of us at one time or another been particularly hard on ourselves when we don't live up to our ideal of perfection? If your dream shows you are feeling frustrated and alone in your frustration, it can also show you that all of us have experienced frustration. Moreover, if you look carefully at your dream you will discover how various universal human figures have dealt with frustration and setbacks, and you can draw on these archetypal human experiences for strength in resolving your own situation.

Annie

Let me give you an example of all the benefits of dream work, using one of my client's dreams to illustrate the peeling of layers I am discussing. Last summer, Annie was entertaining her two sisters, a brother, brother-in-law, and her one-year-old niece, all who traveled here from Europe to spend a two-week vacation at her home. On the third morning after their arrival, Annie woke with this very upsetting dream. She described the dream to me:

"I'm dreaming that I'm sleeping in my bed, and that all my brothers and sisters, except my eldest brother, Adam, are staying with me. I can somehow see Adam and his wife Jill at their home in Switzerland, discussing who is going to call me, and how they are going to inform me that our father has died. I woke, waiting for the telephone, absolutely convinced I was actually about to receive the call.

"My heart was pounding, wondering, 'How I am going to tell my siblings that our father has died?' I was also wondering, 'My God! Am I going to have to call Eric in Ireland, or will Adam do that too?'" Eric, she explained, is her youngest brother. Even though she dreamed he was at her house, he really was home in Ireland—so when she woke up and thought about calling him with the bad news, she was mixing aspects of the dream with reality.

When I heard this dream, my first concern was to link it to something that was actually going on in Annie's life. So I asked her, "Annie, has anything happened in the last day or two where you found yourself wondering how you're going to express something to someone? Do you have any news to give someone?"

The question clicked with her right away. "Yes," she said. "While I appreciate that my sisters and brother are here on vacation, and want to relax and enjoy themselves, I'm feeling an incredible tension build inside me. There is the fact that each has expressed a wish to spend time with me alone. One wants a walk together, another wants to go shopping with me alone, a third wants me to take her to the gym. And then there's the cooking. Even before they arrived, I was getting calls from each of them, one requesting I cook fish one evening and another asking for that 'lamb dish' they remember. As I fell asleep last night I was already feeling exhausted, thinking that if I added up all the meals they requested and topped the remaining time off with 'alone time' with each, and touring the city, I'll probably drop! And what about my little niece who I have only just met? You know you can't rush a jet-lagged baby! I was so looking forward to spending time with her too!

"The fact is I have been very much looking forward to having my family here with me. It is so rare that we have the opportunity to spend time together. I guess the key here will be how to bridge all the good time, and to accomplish all this in the short space of time we have! *I get the feeling there isn't enough time.*"

I will never cease to be amazed at the precision of the metaphors we choose in order to capture the exact thrust of a situation. If, for example, Annie really did get that telephone call, would she be able to hide such news from her siblings? Of course not! If your parent died, you would *have* to tell your siblings. There would simply be no alternative. And you would have to deliver the difficult message with great sensitivity too.

This dream so perfectly mirrors Annie's situation. She feels responsible for ensuring that everyone has a good time. Annie feels she has to make sure everyone's needs are met. Yet she also has her own need to relax and enjoy this precious time with her siblings. She is feeling pulled in a hundred different directions, and she knows she won't be able to enjoy a thing unless she speaks to them about her own needs. But will they understand? Can she say it without hurting their feelings? *How is she going to tell them?*

Now we have discovered how the dream is mirroring her current situation. Annie has an important message to deliver to her siblings, but it's a difficult subject and she's having trouble. There is value in this level of understanding, because the simple act of discovering the dream's meaning starts new trains of thought for her. Instead of trying *not* to think about what worries her, the dream forces Annie to deal with it. She's been putting off this conversation for three days; the dream reminds her that if she doesn't bring it up soon, the visit will be over and it will be too late. By using the extreme situation of her father's death, the dream prods her into taking immediate action.

But how exactly should Annie resolve her situation? If she's willing to do a little more work with this dream, it actually shows her the solution to her family problem. In this case, Annie examined the actions in the dream (a technique you will learn in this book) to discover that the dream-characters Adam and Jill—together—are the solution to her problem.

This is how it worked with Annie's dream. We picked an important aspect of the dream-story and asked, "Who in the dream is performing this action?" The most important action in the dream was the act of delivering bad news, and the answer was obvious: Annie's oldest brother, Adam, and his wife Jill are the ones who deliver the news. This was important, because *the act of conveying a difficult message was exactly what Annie had to do in real life.* The dream pointed her to those people who could help her in her current situation.

Since Adam and Jill were the key to solving Annie's problem, I asked her to describe her eldest brother and sister-in-law. Annie said, "Together they work, but not alone, because they are too extreme of each other. Adam and Jill," Annie continued, "are a good couple because they complement each other." When asked to describe her brother Adam, she said,

"He is the eldest. He can be dry and he has a sarcastic sense of humor. He can bug and pick on people. Adam never lets his guard down. If something is bothering him, he doesn't speak up." When I inquired about a few of Jill's characteristics, Annie told me, " Jill is very controlling, and yet very sensitive. The thing about Jill is that you can see she is serious about wanting to be a good person."

Now it was time to apply these characteristics to Annie's position. I asked her how she might imagine using the different parts of these two people to approach her siblings. Once she thought of the problem from this perspective, Annie decided she needed to "take control" of the situation (like Jill would), with an approach that is "very sensitive" and displays "wanting to be a good person" (like Jill does). At the same time, Annie thought she should not "let her guard down." She needed to allow herself to "stay in touch with her tension" (as Adam would) in order to get her point across. If Annie were a combination of Adam and Jill and she had to speak to her siblings about an uncomfortable situation, she would start by "taking control" of the conversation. While she might give the news "dryly," she would approach the matter with "great sensitivity;" at the same time she would "not let her guard down" so she could say everything she needed to say.

This "Adam-and-Jill" combination of characteristics is an *underinvested* part of Annie. Her habitual way of dealing with this kind of situation is to ask herself, "How can I tell them?" and then either carry the responsibility silently, feeling taken advantage of (like she did as a child), or reject the responsibility by running away with no explanation (like she did as a young woman). In both cases, she says nothing about how she feels or what she needs.

At close to forty, Annie now realizes that her silent anxiety is creating a negative tension in the house. And yet, this negative tension is exactly what she wants to avoid, both for her own sake and her siblings. She is caught. She can't run away. She knows she has to speak up. Using the Gestalt play-acting method I mentioned earlier, Annie can use her dream to practice the combined traits of her brother and sister-in-law and rehearse exactly what she might say to her siblings on this subject.

It is already clear that Annie has derived enormous benefit from the dream work so far. The interpretation of this dream has forced her to come to grips with an important problem in her life, shown her the solution, and given her the tools to practice its resolution. But there is a deeper level to this dream. Why is she asking herself, "How am I going to tell them?" Why does she feel so responsible for everyone else? Is this a situation she has found herself in before? To understand whether this dream reveals a pattern in her life, Annie has to ask herself where in her past these feelings originated.

When we explored this question, the answer occurred to her almost immediately. She said, "When I was young, being the oldest female, whenever my parents left the house, my mother would always say to my brother Adam and me, 'If anything happens you are responsible!' Really, though, Adam used to watch television, and it was me who looked after my sisters and brother! I remember not liking that responsibility. Of course *I never* would have told my parents how I felt. The younger ones used to like to have toast with hot butter before bed. I remember having to prepare piles of toast to feed them and often their little friends too. I had this thing about wanting them to wait until I had it all prepared perfectly on a plate before they would eat. But, of course they never waited. As fast as I put each piece down it would get gobbled up! The pressure was intense. And with no help from my brother, I might add!"

When Annie was eighteen, this feeling of responsibility affected her life in another way. She remembers, "One day, my parents and I had a discussion about how my aunt never married because she devoted her time to being the caregiver for her elderly mum. When I expressed what a shame that was, my parents said something like, 'Well, what do you think you're going to do?' While this comment was said in a joking tone, I took this thought of my destiny so seriously that I very soon after, without informing them, made arrangements to move far away from my hometown. I remember wondering, 'How am I going to tell them?' The fact is, I never did tell my parents. They found out from a neighbor, whose daughter I was good friends with!"

These memories helped Annie realize several things about her behavior. First of all, she recognized a recurring pattern: a tendency to take on too much responsibility for others; an intense feeling of anxiety surrounding that responsibility; and a paralyzing inability to express her feelings about it. When the pattern got to be too much for her, she ran away, but ultimately she didn't escape. However, the dream helped her realize that it was really her *parents* who had started this problem, not her siblings.

Having this knowledge allowed Annie to see that she was transferring the anxiety caused by her parents to her siblings. Now, she could redirect the misplaced fear of expressing herself to the right people. This wasn't enough to remove all her timidity at once, but when she felt anxious and then afraid of expressing herself, she thought of this dream. It did finally give her the courage to express herself when she felt the familiar pressure. After all, she could remind herself, her siblings are no longer little children. They are adults, and they are certainly responsible for their own good time.

Almost immediately after having this dream, Annie was able to adopt a new approach with her visiting siblings. Once she understood that her anxiety about feeling responsible for everyone didn't actually *belong* to her siblings, she took the appropriate measures to communicate her own needs and set a more rational tone for the visit. On Friday night, only two days after the dream, one of Annie's sisters felt the tension building and sarcastically suggested from another room that she'd better go help with the dishes. This time, instead of pretending nothing was wrong, Annie took control of the situation and replied, "You don't have to help me on Friday. And there is no fighting on Friday. The Sabbath is *my* day. So not tonight, but in case you're referring to the rest of the time, I can't do everything myself."

Annie found that her new "Adam-and-Jill" approach to responsibility helped her deal with another very important personal conflict in her life. This had to do with the relationship between her husband and her stepdaughter. After many years together, this relationship seemed set in stone: Annie would often listen privately to her stepdaughter's complaints about her father, and then Annie would express the daughter's views to her husband. She acted as a go-between because she *felt a sense of responsibility* to keep their relationship intact. There were countless times Annie made herself available to nurture their needs at the expense of her own.

Very close to the time of this dream, a major conflict started between her husband and his daughter. One night, Annie, hearing upsetting news about her stepdaughter through her brother-in-law, found herself thinking, "How am I going to tell him?" The sentence, now a familiar one, led Annie to take a decision. While she relayed the information she had heard to her husband, she no longer tried to fix the problems arising between these two people whom she loves. Somehow, she reached a point in her life where she felt prepared to wait while her husband and his daughter worked out their issues on their own. This decision will undoubtedly result in a healthier communication between her stepdaughter and her husband, not to mention a more respectful relationship between herself and each of them.

Annie's dream shows us how a good understanding of our dreams can lead us to make better decisions in our relationships, and give us the strength to stick to them. Our dreams can also show us not only how to live our lives more effectively, but how to live them with greater wisdom. As Annie discovered from this dream, we do better to use the little time we have here on earth by having a good time with our loved ones, rather than letting our unresolved issues get in the way of our opportunities for happiness.

Annie arrived at this conclusion from looking at the universal issues in her dream. In examining the dream together, we realized that almost every person eventually has to face a parent's death. Most of us wish to deny this possibility, even though we know it must happen. Annie is asking herself the same question human beings have asked themselves all through the ages: "How am I going to tell myself that I am going to lose my parent?"

Thinking about these issues, she sensed another dimension here. Like most people, Annie was hiding another universal worry right behind the fear of losing a parent. Her own mortality! Now, her dream question screams out at us both—"How am I going to tell *myself* that *I* am going to die one day?"

With this question, Annie has linked her dream to its deepest layer. What is the learning? She has brought her own mortality to the forefront, with an awakening and powerful impact on her life. The phrase *I have the feeling there is never enough time,* which Annie used to describe her siblings' visit, echoed back to us now. Her dream reminded Annie how thankful she is to have her parents and siblings alive to appreciate, and her own good life to grow in. This widened perspective somehow put Annie's view of her current situation in a different place. It greatly helped her maintain a level of calmness when approaching her siblings. Placing things in their proper perspective sure helps us grab on to the smaller steps we take when compared to the big ones.

The dream also forced her to confront a universal truth about life and relationships: it's so easy to spend our precious time with our loved ones feeling unnecessarily anxious or resentful. There isn't enough time in our short lives to waste on pent-up, destructive emotions. Compared to the terrifying prospect of reaching our own death without having had good relationships, it is far easier to express our feelings now, when we have a chance.

Of course, like any new perspective on our behavior or relationships, the wisdom we get from an archetypal understanding of our dreams doesn't soak in all at once. We have to practice. I can tell you though, today Annie finds herself more able to move through her fears and anxiety in the face of any situation in which she has potential to adopt too much responsibility for someone else. She recognizes this pattern in her behavior and sees how it has interfered with her closest attachments. And while it's easy to generalize about the problems in our relationships, the shock of dreaming about her father's death spurred Annie to correct those problems and grow closer to the people she loves.

When she remembers that day at eighteen, hearing her parents suggest that *she* might be the one to look after them in their old age, her anger and panic at that thought inspired Annie to run away. "What a terrible burden to put on someone," she thought. Today, a few months shy of turning forty, Annie has a new understanding and compassion for what her parents may have been feeling on that day while discussing her aunt's choices. And with her interpretation of her dream, Annie realizes that she too can easily relate to a universal fear of dying, a fear of dying alone. This helps her forgive her parents for their opinion so long ago. After all, they are only human. When she reminds herself of their humanity, her fear of her parents diminishes and so does her resentment. She is freed from the underlying emotions that motivated her self-destructive behavior. She can now start to enjoy her remaining time with her parents and other loved ones in a healthier, more constructive relationship.

So, as you can see, while each layer of interpretation of Annie's dream stands on its own, there is great benefit to looking deeper as each new insight has brought her a clearer understanding of the way her dream mirrors her reality. The full dream interpretation has allowed her to make permanent changes in the way she lives her life.

I hope this analysis of Annie's dream has helped you to see how much dream work can teach us about ourselves. Self-knowledge is the first step in building a happier, more fulfilling existence. This dream also shows how, as we enter deeper into our own souls, we come closer to the universal human soul. You have seen that the deepest source of Annie's strength in fashioning her relationships ultimately arises from her appreciation of what precious little time we have, and how we may better use it, just like the ancient civilizations who faced their own mortality.

Dream work brings us inward to our deepest unconscious, at the same time as we move outward to our broadest humanity. This is one reason why understanding our dreams can bring us together. If we are more in tune with our own hearts and souls and stay focused on what we can do to make this world a better place, the world will *be* a better place. Dream work can be an important step on the road to a better existence for you and for everyone.

Dream Work Alone or with Others

In this book I will teach you how to interpret your dream alone, if you choose to analyze it by yourself, or how to work as part of a couple or group. Whether you are interpreting by yourself or working your dreams out with a friend, partner, or therapist, solving the puzzle often requires understanding what questions to ask when, and listening to and recording the answers. I will demonstrate the steps to take in order to decipher each new level of meaning in your dream.

It is often easier to uncover a dream's meaning when working with another person. This is because the expressions we use in our speaking, conscious life appear as pictures in our dreams. For example, we commonly say, "If I don't get what I want this time, I think I am going to die!" You might say those words to yourself one day, and then you go to sleep that night and dream you have two months to live. Working with another person encourages you to say things out loud, so you or your partner can hear the crucial expression that reminds you of some recent event or issue. On the other hand, you can also follow these very same steps by yourself and simply speak the answers out loud, even though you're alone. As you practice this technique, it will become more natural.

The book will guide you in a simple, question-answer format for some exercises, while other exercises (such as Gestalt) involve more elaborate interactive play. Again, a role-playing exercise like Gestalt can be very fun and useful with another person, but it's also possible to do it on your own. Whenever you are working with another person, it's important to remember that *no one knows what your dream means except you*. You must allow yourself to feel comfortable enough to say what fits for you and what does not. And if you're helping someone else with a dream, you should respect the other person's response to your thoughts and interpretations. The dreamer always has the closest access to his or her unconscious. It would be very convenient if we could read each other's minds, but unfortunately, we cannot.

A group setting can lead to even greater opportunities for dream interpretation. As long as the members of the group remember that they can only say what the dream means to *them,* the larger number of people allows a richer interpretation. For example, one commonly used method of group work is to sit in a circle. The dreamer tells his or her dream. After the other members have a chance to ask some questions, the group takes turns beginning their sentences with, "If this were my dream it would be about . . ." The dreamer has the opportunity of hearing the dream from different perspectives. And all the while, the dreamer's uniqueness has been respected. I have participated in this kind of group work, and each and every time it has been a very rich experience for me. I always learn something new about myself and pick up another way of looking at a situation.

Whether you choose to work alone, with another person, or in a group, dream work can help you at every level of your life—from the most minute problem to your highest goals. The wonderful thing about dream work is that it always gives back more as you give more of yourself. It is not necessary to do all of the exercises and methods I give you in this book, because I have found that even doing them partly or briefly can help you use your dreams to enrich your life. But the more deeply you look into your dreams, the more helpful your dreams can be. It is that simple.

LEVEL ONE
The Mirror

CHAPTER ONE

Getting Started

"It comes about without our intention, will, deliberation. The dream is the most spontaneous expression of the existence of human being. There's nothing else as spontaneous as the dream."

—*Frederick S. Perls*

Many people believe they cannot meet the first requirement of dream work—remembering their dreams. Some investigators, for example Freud, say that we forget our dreams because we don't *want* to know what is in them. If true, this would be tough to overcome, and remembering our dreams would require professional assistance. However, this isn't the only reason we forget our dreams. Our memory just doesn't work as well when we are asleep. The events in our dreams leave a very feeble impression on our minds, but we can correct this problem by taking steps to capture the memory as soon as we wake up. Dreams are not as difficult to remember as many people think. Most of the methods for dream recall are simple and easy, and they start to work in just a few days.

For those of you who are not accustomed to remembering your dreams, let's discuss the process step by step. The first and easiest suggestion is simply to *tell yourself to remember a dream*. As you drift off to sleep, say to yourself, "I am going to remember a dream."

It is also useful to spend a few minutes visualizing this process. Picture what it will be like to wake up the next morning with the dream images in your head. Imagine what it will look and feel like to reach for a pen and paper and start writing. Leave the pen and paper beside your bed because believe it or not, you will probably remember a dream within a few days.

If you wake with a dream or even a fragment of a dream, it is important to write it down right away. Don't get out of bed. You might forget it. If you can't remember the whole dream, write down as much as you can. Don't worry about writing in complete sentences. Just try to get as many images, characters, actions, and feelings from the dream as possible. Many people find that as they start writing, more and more of the dream comes back. It won't be long before you are remembering all the details. And if you do, go ahead, write your dream down in detail.

When you're done jotting down the notes on your dream, write down how you felt when you woke up. Were you happy, sad, scared, angry? Did you feel tired or rested? Did you have some thought in your mind, or some fragment of a song? When I first started recording my dreams, I didn't get out of bed until I grew accustomed to remembering. Now I only get up after I've started writing and feel confident I can sit up and continue. Some people write the dream while their eyes are still closed. Just make sure you have a large pad!

Sometimes, if I haven't put a pad beside the bed, I sleepily ask my husband Andy if I can tell him the dream as soon as I open my eyes. Once you say your dream aloud, often more detail comes to you. And once that happens, it is remembered. Plus, you have the option of later asking that person for details (although you shouldn't be surprised if he doesn't remember). Recently I learned that vitamin B_6 (100–250 mg) taken before bed increases dream recall and vividness.

Keep a flashlight on your night table in case you wake in the middle of the night. Though it is not feasible for me to use a tape recorder at home because Andy would kill me, I recently used one on a solo trip. This was one of the best experiences with dream recording I have ever had. I kept a mini recorder on my night table, and when I woke up I pushed the record button with my eyes still closed. I got *every part* of the dream that way, and then I wrote it out later. This was ideal for capturing little details I might have missed by getting up.

There is another great value to trapping the dream this way. Later that day, or sometimes even a day or two afterwards, I sit down and play the dream back to myself. The experience becomes exactly like listening to someone else's dream. I have the advantage of *hearing* what I am saying, catching the movement and plot of the dream. The experience is different than if I had just written it down. It's also a great way to hear any play on words or puns I may have used.

These are the basics of dream recording. Other dream workers have come up with various additional ideas for enhancing dream capture. For example, Patricia Garfield, Ph.D., suggests, "Lie still and let the dream images flow through your mind. The last scene of a dream often lingers; use it as a hook to reel in previous scenes. If no images occur, think about the important people in your life; visualizing them may trigger associations to a recent dream."[1] Gayle Delaney, Ph.D., in her new book *In Your Dreams,* suggests writing down whatever is on your mind when you wake. "Ask yourself, 'What was just going through my mind?'

"Jot down anything that comes to mind—a little piece of a dream, one solitary image or feeling, or just the fact that your mind seemed blank and that you are frustrated not to have caught a dream. By writing down just a line or two each day, you will teach yourself to notice what is in your mind upon awakening. And since we almost always are dreaming just before we wake, soon you will be able to remember plenty of dreams."[2]

I particularly like Dr. Robert Bosnak's suggestions for dream recall in *A Little Course in Dreams*. First, start with a small object, like your watch. Take it off. Turn it around in your hand, observing it carefully. Now sit back and close your eyes. Try to imagine the watch in your mind's eye. When you think you've mastered the feeling of remembering the image, try this one. Walking around a room (which is like a dream "space"), slowly scroll your eyes all around, taking careful note of how the furniture and objects sit in the room. This is not like looking at a page or watching television because you are *in* this space. After you've looked around several times, close your eyes and try to retrace the room in your imagination. A third exercise is trying to picture the house you are in. Imagine walking through each room, seeing and touching the walls, the furniture, and all the other objects. When you feel skilled, try this with the house you grew up in. These exercises hone the skills you need for dream recall.[3]

Dream Incubation

I know this might sound outrageous to some of you, but if there is a problem you have on your mind, you can ask yourself or a higher power to dream a solution. Here's how it works: first you write out your problem, formulated as a question. In this note, you should ask for a dream with a solution in symbols you can understand. For example, if your problem is deciding whether or not to sell your home, your note might look like this:

> *Is this the right time to sell the house? Do I really feel right about selling? Am I comfortable moving on to a new space? Am I ready? Tonight I will have a dream that gives me the answer to these questions.*

You might use similar kinds of questions about a relationship you are in or a job that you're thinking about changing.

It also helps to sit for a few minutes and conjure up the mood you have when you think about your problem. For example, while writing out my questions about whether to sell my house, I closed my eyes and let the feeling of confusion, dashed with a fear of the unknown, surround me.

Read the note before you go to sleep each night and spend a few minutes bringing that feeling forward. Glance at the note during the day. Then write down or record every dream you have afterwards, and interpret it according to the methods in this book. You will find that many of your dreams during this period deal specifically with your question.

As far back as 2,000 years ago, the Kabbalah described these steps to what we now call dream incubation. If you dream about a problem, your dream will also suggest an answer. Many dream workers ask you to evaluate if the answer makes common sense once it has been interpreted.

Keep a Dream Journal

Keeping a dream journal is a terrific way to track your emotional progress. If you are passing through a crisis or life transition, if you are trying to change a relationship, or if you just want to keep track of who you were and who you've become, your dream journal will give you new perspectives on your life's path. And you'll find that after a while, writing in your dream journal turns into a fun and relaxing occasion rather than a chore. In fact, I know from experience that it's possible to get *too* involved with your dream journal.

Many people find it more pleasant to keep a journal when they have a special, beautiful book to write in. I love stationery stores, so picking a dream journal is always an enjoyable experience for me. My daughters know I love blank writing books, and they often buy me one for Mother's Day or birthdays.

You can buy a lined book if you prefer to simply write out your dreams, or you can draw your dreams in an art book. You can do both. Some people write out the dream with drawings to illustrate different scenes or objects. I did a whole cut-and-paste picture about my Emma-Jo dream (which you will read about) during a workshop in Asheville, North Carolina. Feel free to record your dream, with its feelings and symbols, using any kinds of illustrations or graphics you like.

Include the date on the morning of a dream. Patricia Garfield suggests that before you turn out the lights at night, ". . . jot down what you have done and felt during the day. This paragraph of 'facts' needn't be long but should include the salient events and emotions you experienced. This may hardly seem necessary but two months or two years from now you will find it invaluable. Be sure to include the pleasurable flavors of your day, however small, as well as the dregs."[4]

I know someone who keeps a dream journal in his computer. He takes advantage of different fonts and spacing and includes plenty of colorful graphics. The result is a beautiful document several hundred pages long. Keeping a journal in your computer also gives you the advantage of very easily looking up what certain images mean to you. You can create your own personal dictionary. By hitting "find" on the keyboard, you can see where and how a certain metaphor or symbol was used.

Take me, for example. I have always used the symbol "freight elevator" in my dreams to express feeling uncomfortable, insecure, and unsupported. For one thing, I'm uncomfortable in high places and the up-and-down movement of the elevator makes me dizzy. I also feel insecure because the space is too big, and the ground shakes under my feet. I don't feel like I "have my ground," as some people would say.

A few years ago, in 1997, this image appeared to me in a dream. I had recently started my Dream Interpretation Center and hoped to add a French division. As I am not fluent or confident in French, it took great effort for me to teach a training group. I felt very uncomfortable and unsure of my footing doing this in a foreign language. I was trying to handle everything all by myself, and I felt like I was losing control of the situation. In addition, three possible leaders changed their minds about the job at the last minute. I realized I would be forced to go with a smaller group, or change my direction and begin interviewing again.

Around that time I dreamed I was in New York City with my daughter Chelsea. The dream reads, "We stayed in a hotel that was so tall that at a certain level, we got into a tremendous freight elevator to take us to the top." My journal goes on to say, "I forgot I had booked a lunch with an accountant/controller I know in Ottawa. We were supposed to be flying home, but I had to change the reservation at the last minute, to land in Ottawa. Chelsea was not happy about this. I had to hurry her into the large elevator which took us down some floors to the hotel reception desk."

When I look back at the dream journal, I find next to the "tremendous freight elevator" the description, "We were so small and there was so much space around us." It also says, "tinny floor, unsure footing, and so high up." Finally, I wrote next to the last part that "Chelsea and I are both going through changes. The up and down motion (elevator), like change, is difficult."

At the time, I decided to look through my dream journal to see where else the freight elevator popped up. One of the earliest moments was in July 1973, a few months after I had placed Tina in an institution. One day I realized I couldn't stand to go another minute without seeing her. I resolved to wake up early the next morning, without telling anyone (not even Murray), get into the car, and go. That night I dreamed I was in a freight elevator at a construction site. I was coming down from a high floor to the ground. It was "quite a shaky ride." I had written that "the space was too big" and "the floor was wobbly." There was nothing to hold on to, and I was alone.

If we look at both these dreams, the freight elevator links to a scenario where I am trying to do the best I can in the face of a situation I can't control. Both are also situations where I have to change my game plan as I go. In both situations too, I am alone. The benefit of being able to compare these dreams about freight elevators lies in my ability to predict what this symbol will probably mean in future dreams.

Next time a freight elevator appears, I can ask myself, "What is currently happening to make me feel insecure, unsupported, alone, and ungrounded in the face of change? Am I in a situation where I feel uncomfortable about my lack of control? *Do I have to be alone?*" You see, when Tina was four months old, I certainly had the power to ask for support, yet did not. Likewise, twenty-four years later, I could have asked for support in leading the French-speaking group. While some elements of each situation were not in my control, I could have made things easier on myself by asking for help. I would have felt less alone, maybe more grounded. Here would be a possible solution to a current issue should I dream today about a freight elevator.

Entering the images from our dreams into a computer program seems very fitting to me. Our unconscious mind links data entries just like a computer, as well illustrated by this example.

How to Map Your Dream

Once you've jotted down your dream with all the detail you can remember, the next step is to create a dream map. This map will be the basis for interpretation, because it allows you to classify all the different elements in the dream and see what's going on. You can map your dream right after you have written it. Well, get a cup of coffee first. It may take a few minutes.

1. The first step is not to judge your dream. Accept it as it is.
    Do not think it is weird or perverse.

2. Write the dream down, double spaced. Leave room on the
    left side of the page.

3. Isolate your *feelings* during the dream. Write the feelings you
    had in the dream down the left side of the page. Try to
    group or attach different feelings to certain sections of the
    dream to see if there is a progression of moods. Inquire,
    "How did I feel at the beginning of the dream? And how did
    I feel in this part of the dream? Was there any change in my
    mood as the dream progressed?" If you are mapping
    someone else's dream, make sure to write down the person's
    exact words in answering these questions. Write the dif-
    ferent mood changes beside the places where they changed.

4. Isolate and circle each *symbol*. A symbol might be a cat, a
    bear, a wall, a road, a ghost, a picnic, or even a person you
    know, to name a few. When I map a dream, I write a descrip-
    tion of the symbol outside each circle. Ask yourself (or your
    partner) to say a few things that come to mind about the
    symbol. Describe the image as if to a child or to a person
    who has never seen the thing before. Ask yourself exactly
    what it is and what is its function. Gayle Delaney says to
    speak (or write) as if you are explaining the meaning to a
    person from another galaxy.[5]

    If the symbol is a person, ask yourself for two or three
    things that come to mind when you think about that
    person. Is he straightforward? Is she shy? Is this person
    especially kind or generous? Greedy or selfish? Is he acting
    in the dream the same way you would expect him to react
    in waking life? Sometimes a person doesn't necessarily
    bring to mind an adjective, but rather an incident. For
    example, when I think of Gary (a boy I went to camp with
    as a little girl), what comes to mind is that he was my first

boyfriend and gave me my first kiss under an apple tree. The thought of Gary brings up certain feelings in me, not personality traits in him.

If you are mapping someone else's dream, it is *very* important to write down the dreamer's answers verbatim, because the key to the dream might lie in the dreamer's precise words or way of speaking. In this way, you know you are not putting your own perceptions in place of the dreamer's thoughts. And if it is your own dream you are recording, speak the questions and answers out loud and write down exactly what you have just said. Don't leave words out.

5. Look at the dreamscape. Where does the dream take place? What is the first thing that comes to your mind when you think of that location? What is the second? Write these down.

6. Put a square around each action or lack of it in the dream. For example, "I started running" or "I felt stuck and couldn't move" or "I opened my mouth to say something but I couldn't speak!" What is the dreamer doing in the dream? Is the dreamer in the action, or outside the action, observing? What are other dream-characters doing?

7. Look for repetition. You can see it in repeated thoughts, feelings, actions, symbols, or characters. For example, if I am feeling scared about something, one night I might dream about a ghost. When I check my definition or feelings associated with a ghost, I find myself saying, "I feel scared." Later in the same dream, or in another dream of the same night, I may find myself standing on the abyss of a cliff. And what does it mean? It means, "I am scared." Still later in the same dream, my grade five teacher appears. And what does it mean? It means, "I feel scared!"

An example of a repeated action (or lack of action, in this case) might be if you feel *stuck* in the first part of your dream because you can't escape from your enemy, and later on you find you can't speak up to defend yourself and you feel *stuck* again. A repeating symbol might be the same object that shows up more than once, or it might be two different objects that remind you of the same thing.

As you can see from these examples, the repetition and connections in the dream often show up during the mapping process, when you ask questions about what things mean to you. When I identify thoughts and themes that I feel go together or repeat themselves, I write them outside the circles and squares. I also draw lines to connect repeating thoughts or associations. I even number repeated thoughts or symbols.

Your unconscious uses repetition to prod you into acknowledging something you don't want to admit to yourself. Hence, the main function of a recurring dream or nightmare: to grab your attention!

8. See if you notice any polarities in the dream. Do any complete opposites present themselves? For example, a wolf and a sheep? A screaming person and another who is silent? Someone who makes you happy and someone else who makes you sad? In dreams we create polarities, opposites, and extremes, in order to measure and re-evaluate our positions on people and events. Sometimes the union of these opposites can reveal the solution to the dream problem.

The details of the map itself—the circles, squares, and lines—are not so important. Some people like to draw a line under each symbol, or put a squiggle under each feeling. You can map the dream in whatever way suits your fancy. The important thing is to ask the questions and write down the answers in a nonjudgmental way, using the precise words the dreamer has used. Once you have caught a dream or two, the rhythm of how it happens feels more comfortable. You will start to know what to look for and what to expect. The more you practice, the easier it becomes.

Dream Maps

Here are some examples for you to use as a guide. I have chosen dreams you will be reading more about in this book. I have arranged the dream maps in columns to make them easier to read.

Figure 1: The Picnic Is Over: Leslie's Dream

This dreamer contacted me through the Internet. She lives in the United States.

She told her dream. "I was at a picnic. There were a few ants. At first there were not many. And suddenly there were ants everywhere spoiling the picnic. The situation was out of control. I was trying to push them away with my hands." Using the steps we discussed, I asked the dreamer to describe how she felt at the outset of the dream when she was at the picnic.

The dreamer responded, "It felt nice to be at a picnic. The weather was sunny. The ants were not bothersome, they were just part of the scene." I continued, "What about your feelings as you realized there were many ants?" She replied, "They multiplied so quickly, I suddenly realized it was out of control. I was panicked and tried to push them off with my hands. The dream ended with the ants everywhere! I was very upset." I noted, and the dreamer agreed, that her feelings seemed to escalate in the dream.

We isolated and circled each symbol. I asked her to say a few things that came to mind about each image as if to a child or to a person who has never seen the thing before. "Can you please define 'picnic' for me?" She said, "A picnic is when you eat outside of the house, in the fresh air on a blanket. There is lots of different food. It is fun and relaxing. You can play games." To that I further inquired, "Tell me what food is." She said, "Food is nour-

Figure 1: The Picnic Is Over

Feelings	The Dream	Definition of Symbols & Associations	Notes
felt nice, relaxing	I was at a picnic.	PICNIC: eating outside of the house —fresh air-blankets- lots of food —— nourishment —fun-games —feeling full and satisfied	
sunny, warm —ants were just a part of the scene	There were a few ants. At first there were not many.	ANTS: small annoying —multiply rapidly —spoil fun	
I felt unable to control them!	And suddenly there were ants everywhere spoiling the picnic.		
*VERY upset	The situation was out of control.		
panic (ESCALATED)	I was trying to push them away with my hands.		escalating situation *SUDDENLY

Key:

◯ = Symbol in the dream

▭ = Actions in the dream

ishment. When you eat good food you feel full and satisfied." Lastly, I asked what ants are. She said, "Ants are small, annoying insects. They multiply rapidly and can really spoil the fun."

Watching for the action or movement in the dream, I asked, "What action are you taking in the dream to do something about the ants?" She responded, "I am trying to push them away with my hands." I placed a square around the movement.

Figure 2: Labrador Retrievers: Johnathan's Dream

A successful advertising executive came to my office with the following dream. He was watching Labrador retrievers and other breeds of dogs come out of a bungalow. There was a European-looking couple standing outside with their little child. Also, there was a bulldog with a smile on its face.

I asked him, "How did you feel in the dream?"

He answered, "Well, I felt happy to see all those dogs. They remind me of my childhood because my parents used to take in abandoned, abused dogs."

Moving away from the feelings for a moment, I circled the word dogs and asked, "What else comes to your mind when you think of dogs?"

He said, "Well, these dogs, the ones who are abandoned or abused, need a lot of care and attention. They're like children. But when I think of dogs in general, having one is something I aspire to, but I can't accommodate right now. Labs remind me of my childhood too, because my family often had a Lab and I associate them with stability and loyalty."

I continued, "What about bulldogs?"

He said, "I perceive bulldogs as stubborn and solid. Bulldogs make me think of Winston Churchill and his statement 'We will never surrender.'" He added, "I find bulldogs fascinating because they are ugly, but cute at the same time."

Figure 2: Labrador Retrievers

Feelings	The Dream	Definition of Symbols & Associations	Notes
felt happy, reminded of **childhood**[1]	I was watching Lab Retrievers and other dogs come out of a bungalow	LAB RETRIEVERS: *stability, loyalty* DOGS: *my childhood* -abandoned, abused -very needy-care, attention like **children**[2] -aspire to have, but can't **accommodate**[1] *now* BUNGALOW: *has one floor*	ACTION: *"I was watching" dreamer is not a part of the action in the dream, he is an observer*
	There was a European couple whom I did not know standing outside with their little **child**[3].	EUROPEAN COUPLE: *foreign, unfamiliar (newness)*[4]	FEELINGS: *reminded of childhood*
felt weird	I felt weird because all these dogs were coming out of a home that did not look like they could "**accommodate**[2]" them all.		FEELINGS CHANGED: *happy, then weird*
	Also, there was a bulldog that had a smile on its face.	BULLDOG: -stubborn, solid -Winston Churchill: "not surrender" -ugly, but cute	ROTE: *child x4 can't accommodate x2*

Key: ⬯ = Symbol in the dream ▭ = Actions in the dream

Returning to the feelings, I inquired, "So, you say you felt happy when you saw the scene in the dream."

He answered, becoming more specific, "Yes, but the dream seemed weird to me because all these dogs were coming out of a home that didn't look like it could accommodate them all."

Finally, I wanted to know, "Do you know the couple who are standing outside the house with their child?"

He said, "No. They seem foreign to me. They are not even familiar. I don't know them."

When I asked about the bungalow, he pointed out that a bungalow has only one floor. Finally, wanting to draw attention to the action in the dream, we took note that he is merely an observer to this scene. In fact, he does not partake or appear in any part of the dream.

Here you will notice the repetition of symbols and metaphors, which I have marked in the map of this dream. In searching for the dream's significance using free association, the client and I found the word "child" repeat itself three times. Once was when he said that dogs in general remind him of his *child*hood because his parents used to take in abandoned, abused dogs. The second time was when he described how abandoned or abused dogs need to be cared for just like *chil*dren; and the third was the actual *child* in the dream, standing with his parents. Building on this theme of childhood, a sense of "newness" or "lack of experience" is also present in the dream as the notion of "unfamiliarity." The couple in the dream, being European, are *"foreign"* and also *"unknown"* to him. The lack of familiarity repeats itself, like the child.

Figure 3: Deborah's Dream

Deborah dreamed she was standing with her boyfriend, looking at a row of tall buildings. I asked her if they were familiar buildings. She said the one in the middle reminded her of the Radisson Hotel in Montreal, and then she added, "It was totally *leaning!*" Deborah said that she and her boyfriend were just standing there, looking at how odd it was. "Suddenly," she said, "the building in the middle toppled into the one beside it, and they all fell into one another! They fell like dominoes!"

I asked Deborah, "How did you feel seeing that?"

She answered, "We were frightened and started running, but the buildings all fell, right in front of us."

"Were you okay?"

"Oh yes," Deborah assured me. "The buildings didn't fall apart either. They fell keeping their bricks in place." Then she added, *"They didn't even hit me!"*

Exploring this new detail, I asked, "How did you feel or what did you think when you saw that the buildings fell keeping their bricks in place?"

"I felt surprised and weird. Yet, I was relieved too. I just stood there thinking how strange it felt. And the scene was so strange to me."

Turning to the dream symbols, I asked, "What are dominoes?"

"Dominoes is a game played with small chiplike squares that have dots you can connect to the same numbers. When you're done, it looks like a finished scrabble board, or cross-word puzzle, all linked together. You can also line them up close to each other, and when you topple one, it hits the one beside it, which hits the one beside it, and so on, until they all fall down."

Take a look at the dream map and see how many of Deborah's words I wrote down verbatim. In the next chapter you will learn how important the exact words of a dream can be.

Figure 4: Sarah's Uncle Dream

Sarah, a twenty-year-old woman, came to my office to share two dreams. The first was relatively simple. She was in a room

Figure 3: Deborah's Dream

Feelings	The Dream	Definition of Symbols & Associations	Notes
felt odd	I was standing with my boyfriend, looking at a row of tall buildings.	THE ONE IN THE MIDDLE: *reminded me of the Radisson*	FEELINGS: *"felt odd" being in a new city = Toronto*
	The one in the middle was totally *leaning!*	LEANING: -leaning towards moving[1] to Toronto -Pisa/Italy (parents moved[2])	ROTE: *move x2*
	We were just standing there, looking at how odd it was.		
	Suddenly, the building in the middle toppled into the one beside it and they all fell into one another! They fell like *dominoes!*	DOMINOES: *game, small squares that connect together* -link together -line them up and topple one, hits the one beside it and so on . . . = *looked for a job, interview, apt. w/mom, roommate, mover . . . and so on . . . = dominoes!*	ACTION: *progressive movement*
frightened surprised, *felt weird* being in a new surrounding-Toronto relieved!	We started running, but the buildings fell, right in front of us. The buildings didn't fall apart. They fell keeping their bricks in place. *They didn't even hit me!*	FEAR: *"It hasn't even hit me yet!"*	FEELINGS: *progressed from odd-frightened - surprised/weird relieved.*

Key: ⬭ = Symbol in the dream   ▭ = Actions in the dream

with a young man she knew years ago who used to be her boyfriend. Their relationship had not ended well, but in the dream they seemed to be friends again. She felt she could trust him. Suddenly he was trying to push her into the closet. Sarah refused to go in the closet because she knew if she went in, she wouldn't be able to get out again. She felt quite happy and satisfied in the dream that she refused to go into the closet.

In the second dream, Sarah's uncle was proposing to her. He gave her a ring with lots of diamonds, but the ring was much too big. She noticed the ring he had on his finger fit him perfectly. Sarah was also aware in the dream that he was still married to her aunt. She described this as "weirdness," saying the situation was strange and out of place. She described her feelings, telling me she was very aware that she did not want to marry him. In the dream Sarah said to herself, "I would rather marry someone else." She was feeling very uncomfortable, thinking to herself, "Oh, God! How do I say no?"

Here I will show a map of the second dream. To start off the dialogue, I asked, "What are the first two thoughts that come to your mind when you think of an engagement ring?" She responded, "A ring means commitment. Expectations are also associated with engagement rings. Anticipating when you'll meet the right person, for example."

Then we talked about diamonds. Sarah said that diamonds remind her of an aunt of hers from her mother's family, with whom she was working on a school paper that evening. Her aunt, she explained, was wearing a large diamond around her neck. Sarah considered her aunt to be committed to her, in that she was kind enough to help her with her schoolwork. She described her aunt as a workaholic, an achiever, and very accomplished in her work. "My aunt is a self-confident, assertive woman who is not afraid to speak her mind. Actually there is a regular and loving banter that goes back and forth about a host of different subjects

Figure 4: Sarah's Uncle Dream

Feelings	The Dream	Definition of Symbols & Associations	Notes
	(My uncle) was (proposing) to me.	**MY UNCLE:** *nice—not a "big" feeling* *—cousin's father—father's side* *—don't know him well* *—underachiever*	**ROTE:** *Commitment x6* *: *"commitment[5]" is too big* **: *"commitment[6]" is too small*
I felt strange and out of place	*He gave me a (ring) with lots of (diamonds) but the ring was much too big.**	**PROPOSING:** *—marriage* *—commitment[1]*	
felt confused	*I noticed the ring he had on his finger fit him perfectly.*	**A RING:** *commitment[2]* *—expectations = when will you meet the right person? = (when will you make a commitment[4]?)*	
I was aware I did not want to marry him	*I was also aware in the dream that he was still (married) to my aunt.***	**DIAMONDS:** *my aunt, mother's side* *—commitment[3] to me* *—schoolwork* *—successful, overachiever* *—assertive*	
uncomfortable	*In the dream I said to myself, "I would rather marry someone else."*		
	I was also thinking to myself, "Oh, God! How do I say no?"	**MARRIED:** *committed*	

Polarities:

↕	aunt
uncle	
↕	mother's side
father's side	
↕	overachiever
underachiever	
↕	commitment too small **
commitment too big*	

Key: ⬭ = Symbol in the dream   ▭ = Actions in the dream

that she and my uncle disagree about!"

Finally, I asked her to say a few words that come to mind when she thinks of her uncle. The first thing that came into her mind was that while watching *Late Night with David Letterman* shortly before she fell asleep, David Letterman reminded her for a split second of her uncle. When I asked what she thinks of her uncle she said, "He's nice, but I don't get a 'big' feeling when I think of him." I said, "Tell me more about him." She answered, "He's my cousin's father, from my father's side of the family. He is someone you would imagine I know well, but you know what? I really don't know him." I asked, "Is he successful?" She responded, "He has succeeded, but he's not an overachiever."

Notice the polarities described in this dream. The aunt is the opposing image of the uncle in that 1. she is the aunt; 2. she is from another "side" of the family; and 3. she is a successful committed achiever, while the uncle is described as "not an overachiever." The polarity has repeated itself three times. If you look at the map, you will also see the word "commitment" repeated three times. Once it appears in connection with the uncle's proposal, the second time in connection with the ring, and again in relation to the aunt. Two of these references to "commitment" are directly opposed to each other: the uncle's "commitment" to the dreamer (the ring) is too big, but the uncle's commitment to the aunt (his marriage) is too small.

Figure 5: The Emma-Jo Dream

The dream I refer to as my Emma-Jo dream runs throughout this book. I worked with this dream at an ASD conference, in Asheville, North Carolina. It was discussed in several group settings, using different schools of dream interpretation. While **Figure 5a** has been mapped in the usual format, **Figure 5b** presents another kind of dream map, drawn in concentric circles, called a mandala.[6] In this particular example the mandala illustrates only the second part of the dream.

Later in the book I'll discuss mandalas[7] in much more depth, because they are a particularly useful way to interpret a dream. For now, don't worry about the details of this dream map, just observe the overall circular form.

In the first part of the dream, I was walking along St. Catherine Street East in Montreal with Andy. He needed a knife. It was quite busy, and three men were walking close to us. I felt worried. Someone was supposed to have a knife for us. I found scissors on top of a low roof and held them as we walked. I remember letting one of the men walking close to us see that there was a pair of scissors in my hand.

In the second part of the dream, we were driving in a car on St. Catherine Street West. Emma-Jo, who was four years old at the time, was standing up in the back of our car. Andy was driving. I felt so upset with myself that I hadn't buckled her in. I was yelling at her to please sit down and fasten her seat belt. Next thing I knew, she was out of the car. Then she was dashing out into the street, then back into the tall grass. She was about to walk into a field. I felt like we were on an island, because the grass was so tall and there were no sidewalks. School children were walking around us. I almost lost sight of Emma-Jo while Andy was turning the car around. I begged him to please hurry up and turn the car around to get to her. She may have stepped out into the street again. I just couldn't get to her. As we were turning, I called out to her. I woke up as I was calling her name. At the end of the dream, though, I knew she was going to wait for us.

When I called home the next morning, I found out little Emma-Jo had awakened with the chicken pox. I felt helpless and I was so far away. The fact is, whenever I have traveled alone on business, Emma-Jo has come down with *some* kind of illness. It is her gift to Andy. One time she had the stomach flu. Another time it was strep throat. So, in essence, although I may

Figure 5: The Emma-Jo Dream

Feelings	The Dream	Definition of Symbols & Associations	Notes
feels risky and uncomfortable	I was walking along (St. Catherine St. East) with Andy.	ST. CATHERINE ST. EAST: *a very long street* —East = unfamiliar = **mysterious**[1] —uncomfortable, risk, **danger**[1] —*you might meet people who are doing illegal acts*	ROTE: *adventure, mystery and excitement 5x. danger 6x, child 3x*
	He needed (a knife.) It was quite busy.	A KNIFE: **dangerous**[2]	
the men make me feel nervous (incomfortable)	Three men were walking close to us. *	*: *a sense of **danger**[3] being close* = **excitement**[2]	
expectancy	Someone was supposed to have a knife for us.		
	I found (scissors) on top of (a low roof.)	SCISSORS: *something to cut with—designs, new clothes* —pointy, **I can hurt myself**[4] —*kids take them from my office drawer!* —weapon —double edged!	
I felt happy relieved, protected	I remember letting one of the men see that I had scissors in my hand. **	A LOW ROOF: *gravel = rocks, camp = my child*hood[1] **: *I was protecting myself.*	

Polarities:

```
calm, positive sense          scary negative
of adventure mystery excitment  sense of adventure, etc.
      ▲                              ▲
      │                              │
St. Catherine St West         St. Catherine St. East
comfort, familiar             discomfort, unfamiliar
      │                              
      ▼                              
dangerous                     
              Scissors
      │                              ▲
      ▼                              │
                              creative
```

Key: ⬭ = Symbol in the dream ⟋ = Actions in the dream ☐ = Actions in the dream

Figure 5a: The Emma-Jo Dream

Feelings	The Dream	Definition of Symbols & Associations	Notes
I feel myself with him; comfortable, accepted	Andy was driving. We were on St. Catherine St. West.	ANDY: *my husband* —*a man* —*unemotional, businesslike* —*confident driver* ST. CATHERINE ST. WEST: *familiar to me*	
I felt unnerved and frightened	Emma-Jo who is four was standing up in the back of our car.	EMMA-JO: *my youngest child*[2] —*4 years old* *: *dangerous*[5]	
	I had not buckled her in.*		
I was upset and angry with myself	I was yelling at her to please sit down and do up her seat belt.		
I felt out of control, edgy, uncomfortable	Next thing I knew, she was out of the car.		
panic	Then she was dashing out into the street.**	**: *dangerous*[6]	
	Then back on the grass, about to walk into a field.***	***: *mystery*[3], *excitement, hidden adventure, expectancy*	

Key: ⬭ = Symbol in the dream   ⬜ = Actions in the dream

Figure 5a: The Emma-Jo Dream, continued

Feelings	The Dream	Definition of Symbols & Associations	Notes
I feel a sense of mystery. A certain element of **calm** is entering while still I am not driving.	I felt like we were on (an island,) because the grass was so tall and there were no (sidewalks.)	AN ISLAND: *vacation,* **adventure**[4] —*unknown* —*excitement* —*Montreal*	
	There was what seemed like school **children**[3] *walking with her.*	GRASS WAS SO TALL: *island* —*mystery* —*romance* —**adventure**[5] —*freedom*	
	I almost lost sight of Emma-Jo while Andy was turning the car around.		
	I was begging him to please hurry up and turn the car around to get her.	SIDEWALKS: *safety from cars* —*marks direction* —*marks difference between land and road*	
While I am not in control I **do** have the sense that everything is okay.	She may have stepped out on to the street again. I just couldn't get to her.*	SCHOOL CHILDREN: *inexperienced* —*close, from small community*	
	Just as we were turning, I was calling out to Emma-Jo as I woke.	*: *she has movement, I am stuck*	
	I knew in the dream she was going to wait for us to get her though.		

Key: ⬭ = Symbol in the dream   ▭ = Actions in the dream

Figure 5b: The Emma-Jo Dream—Mandala

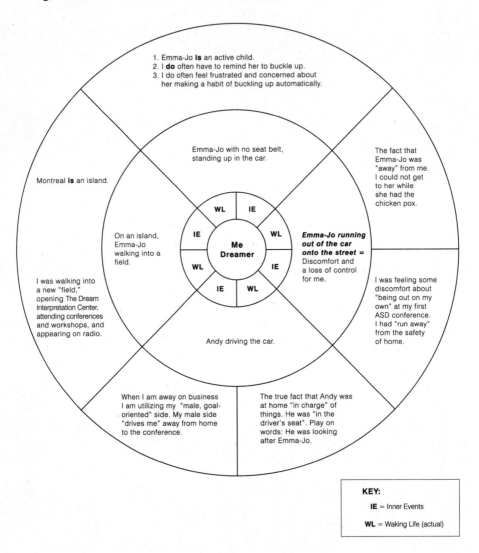

1. Emma-Jo **is** an active child.
2. I **do** often have to remind her to buckle up.
3. I do often feel frustrated and concerned about her making a habit of buckling up automatically.

Emma-Jo with no seat belt, standing up in the car.

Montreal **is** an island.

The fact that Emma-Jo was "away" from me. I could not get to her while she had the chicken pox.

On an island, Emma-Jo walking into a field.

WL | IE

IE | WL

Me Dreamer

WL | IE

IE | WL

Emma-Jo running out of the car onto the street = Discomfort and a loss of control for me.

I was walking into a new "field," opening The Dream Interpretation Center, attending conferences and workshops, and appearing on radio.

I was feeling some discomfort about "being out on my own" at my first ASD conference. I had "run away" from the safety of home.

Andy driving the car.

When I am away on business I am utilizing my "male, goal-oriented" side. My male side "drives me" away from home to the conference.

The true fact that Andy was at home "in charge" of things. He was "in the driver's seat". Play on words: He was looking after Emma-Jo.

KEY:

IE = Inner Events

WL = Waking Life (actual)

not have thought of the possibility consciously, I unconsciously suspected that she might become ill. I was obviously concerned about being away from her.

When I was with the group that made the mandala interpretation of this dream, there must have been thirty-five people in the room. Several of them were very sensitive and intelligent. Looking back, I feel extremely fortunate to have shared my dream with that particular group of people. After I read the dream aloud from my journal, I repeated it with my book closed. Relating a dream from memory allows one to recapture the mood of the dream.

When I had said my dream a second time, the group raised questions related to my symbols. As I responded using free associations, the leader wrote my initial associations inside the second circle of the mandala. Here is a transcript of the first part of our dialogue. As you read the interview, please note that each question was asked by a different person in the room.

"Where is St. Catherine Street? Is there any significant difference between St. Catherine Street East and St. Catherine Street West?"

"St. Catherine Street is one of the longest main roads that run through downtown Montreal. Since I live in the west end of the city, that part of the street is more familiar to me. Also, I associate St. Catherine Street East not only as unfamiliar to me, but I also feel uncomfortable there because there is a sense of danger or risk if walking there at night. That is because it is the section of town where you more likely find prostitutes and drugs."

"Are any of the three men familiar to you?"

"No. But I feel worried, and uncomfortable that they are watching us."

"What about scissors? What are scissors?"

"Scissors are something you can cut with. They are pointy. They can be dangerous. I can hurt myself with them. Scissors are also what I like to keep in my office drawer, and are sometimes missing! My kids take them, and forget to give them back! It annoys me. I like things to stay where they are put. What else . . . You can use them to cut designs out of paper or material for new clothes. In this case I was happy to have found them, because scissors are sharp, and if need be, can be used as a weapon as well. I felt protected having them in my hand to open and let the stranger see."

A voice from the back of the room called out, "So they are 'double-edged' then!"

The crowd reacted. "Yes," I agreed, smiling at his wit.

"What about the low roof. What can you say about that?"

"The low roof has gravel on top of it. It reminds me of a little low building from the camp I went to as a kid. I felt happy to find the scissors there."

"What about the scene when you are in the car. How did you feel?"

"I realized that actually I felt a bit unnerved and frightened by Emma-Jo's behavior in the dream. I was in touch with my lack of control about getting her to sit down. And then getting her back in the car altogether! There was even a sense of anger with myself for not getting her to buckle her seatbelt before we started to move. I felt irresponsible. I also felt edgy and uncomfortable because of my lack of control not being in the driver's seat. And Andy was not stopping to turn the car around quickly enough for me."

"Did you still have the scissors?"

"Actually, funny you mention that. The scissors were still with me, but in the glove compartment."

"Who is Andy and do you have any special associations to him?"

"My associations to Andy, aside from that he is my husband, are that he is a man, able to conceal his emotions, businesslike, unafraid, comfortable, and confident, especially when sitting behind the wheel of a car. I feel safe and comfortable with him. I have never had to play games with Andy. I can just be who I am and feel accepted."

"Who is Emma-Jo?"

"She is my youngest daughter."

Much later in the workshop, someone asked how old Emma-Jo was and I said she was four.

"What comes to your mind when you think of an island?"

I answered, "A vacation, an adventure. It is where I experience something new and unknown, something exciting." I also realized and mentioned that Montreal is an island. It is the tall grass that makes me feel as though we are on an island. There are no sidewalks through the grass. And tall grass and a field also bring a sense of mystery, adventure, and freedom. There is a certain romantic element that comes up in me, the same as a vacation. A field makes me think, "What is in the field? Is the ocean behind it? Sand dunes? It is a mystery."

"You say there are school children there who are walking into that field. What are school children?"

"School children are young and inexperienced. They are in school to learn. These seem like island children. They are close, from a small community."

"What about sidewalks? What are they?"

"Sidewalks mark the difference between the road and the land. They mark direction too. Staying on the sidewalk keeps you from the danger of getting hit by a car."

Do you see certain connections appearing? Look at the dreamscape. The scene begins on St. Catherine Street East. While I mainly associate this area with feeling uncomfortable, there is also an element of mystery and excitement. When the men follow us, I mostly feel uncomfortable again, but I also feel a little tickle of excitement. The themes of mystery, adventure, and excitement come up yet again in the images of the island, the tall grass, and the field. While I still feel uncomfortable in this part of the dream because I'm anxious about Emma-Jo, I associate an island and a field of tall grass with a positive sense of adventure. As this dream shows, the sensations of "feeling uncomfortable" and "feeling excitement" are closely related but also in some sense opposites.

They come together again and again in this dream.

A similar polarity shows up with the "double-edged" scissors, which can be used to harm or to create. Several other related polarities repeat themselves throughout the dream. In particular, Emma-Jo brings together many different emotions that seem to be at opposite ends of the spectrum: she gives me a sense of discomfort, danger, and fear, but she is in a situation filled with mystery, adventure, and excitement (surrounded by tall grass on her "island"). I'm sure if you look closely at the images and feelings in this dream, you'll be able to find other polarities dealing with discomfort, excitement, and related sensations such as the new, the unknown, or the unfamiliar.

A final, very important polarity is the one between myself and Andy. In my associations about him, he seems to be everything I'm not in this dream: he's unafraid, comfortable, and confident, while for most of the dream I am panicked and feeling completely out of control. Andy is businesslike and able to conceal his emotions, whereas I spend most of the second part of the dream yelling at Emma-Jo.

How to Decrease Dream Recall

Once you open that door and start exercising the capability of remembering your dreams, your mind gets more adept at the skill. For those of you out there who start remembering *pages* of dreams, please keep the following in mind. A Jungian analyst once told me dreams are like a field of wild flowers. If you pick a bouquet and bring it into the house, you get an idea of the field, but you don't need to gather every single flower. Just like everything else in life, we should strive for moderation. There are generally only one or two salient issues repeating themselves in people's dreams during a given period of time. The dreams may have different faces and different stories, but the issues are similar.

If you find yourself remembering too many dreams, here is

what you do. Take some deep breaths before sleep and tell yourself that you want to relax and that you *don't* want to remember
any dreams when you wake up. It works. I do it for myself and
my daughter Chelsea does it too. Then, when you *want* to, just
ask yourself to remember again and within a few days, you will.
I like to check in with myself and record a dream or two each
month. Sometimes I record more, but I don't necessarily interpret them all. This is the formula that works for me. I know
some people who record their dreams every morning. I leave you
to establish what time frame and frequency feels right for you.

CHAPTER TWO

Finding the Mirror

"What else do we have to explore but ourselves?"
—Oliver Stone

Dreams are the way you think when you are asleep. Whatever you are thinking about in your waking life, you will also ponder in your dreams. This is why your dreams can teach you so much about yourself. They reveal your inmost thoughts, feelings, and desires.

But you can't learn to know yourself through your dreams until you understand what you are actually thinking about in your sleep. This means you must find out how the dream reflects something that has been on your mind in waking life. There will be some issue in your life, a situation or a person or problem, that makes up the real subject of the dream. If the dream thoughts mirror your waking thoughts, the first step is finding the mirror.

This chapter will help you take the first step in understanding your dream. That is to say, you will learn what current issue in your life your dream is addressing. The subject of the dream is likely to be something you've been thinking about a lot lately. Or it may be something you've been trying *not* to think about, but which has occupied a lot of your unconscious thought and energy. Finding this first level is like trying to solve a puzzle. You try one piece, and if that doesn't fit, you try another. I like to call these puzzle pieces different points of entry into the dream.

To start the process, I always turn to the dream map. As you learned in Chapter 1, the dream map tells the story of the dream, but it also has the words the dreamer used to describe the different elements of the dream. A dream might show someone sitting on a large stone, and next to the word "stone" the map says, "A stone is hard and cold." Or the dreamer might be running away from a bear in his dream, and the map says, "A large animal, very scary!" The dream map will also point out the feelings the dreamer experienced, show the actions she committed or did not commit, and describe where the dream took place, all in the dreamer's own words. Any one of these pieces can give you a point of entry.

Sometimes it's the feelings in the dream that will help you attach it to a current situation or thought you had. I usually try with the feelings first because often that is the easiest way for us to make a link to waking life. For example, a friend of mine said to me over lunch one day that her husband had a dream where she was cheating on him. He felt so betrayed. She exclaimed, "Why would he dream something like that? We are so happy together. I would never betray him. I felt so sure he knew that!"

To get that initial point of entry I suggested she might ask him who, in his waking life, he might feel had betrayed him. The following day I heard back from my friend. The mystery of the dream's meaning had been solved. "Actually," she told me, "he was betrayed by the last person in the world he would have ever expected. A client who has been buying from him for years, and had come to be, he thought, a friend, had moved some of his business to a competitor." So, the dreamer used a metaphor of his wife cheating on him to conjure up the hurt and betrayed feeling he was experiencing. And he chose her because she too was the last person he would expect to cheat on him.

If the dreamer comes up blank on the feelings in the dream, I'll try a different point of entry—say, asking the dreamer about a symbol or two. When I do this I don't ask about the symbol itself, the actual object or person who appeared in the dream. Instead I look at the dream map and use the dreamer's own words in describing the symbol. So if I'm talking to the man who dreamed about a bear, I might ask him, "Is there anything that is large and very scary going on with you right now?" Sometimes I throw out different ideas as they come to me, just to jog the dreamer's mind. About the bear dream I might ask, "Do you lately have a big responsibility that you can't avoid? Has it been coming at you these days?" Another try could be, "Are you wanting to say something to someone that might be scary to come out with?" Here's another one involving a possible pun. "Have you been unable to suppress feeling hungry as a bear recently? Could that be making you feel frightened about gaining weight?"

Look for things that could fit the scenario in the dream. To the woman who sat on the stone I might inquire, "Do the words 'hard and cold' remind you of something or someone in your life?" It might be that you are feeling hard and cold towards a certain person or that you feel someone is behaving hard and cold with you. You don't want to get stuck necessarily using the feelings as the first point of entry. Some dreams call out at you to focus first on the movement, or the landscape. When I hear a dreamer tell me in describing her dream that she was trying to say something, but no sound was coming out, I will probably not go with the feelings first. Instead, I will ask, "Is there something you'd like to say to someone that you are having trouble coming out with?" Or if she says she couldn't hear in the dream, I might ask if there is anything going on in her life recently that she just doesn't want to hear about!

You know what my favorite point of entry is? I like listening to the story of the dream, the plot. As I hear the story, I love imagining different scenarios that would fit or mirror the story in the dream. It's like looking for the story behind the story. I probably have become well practiced at this because it is the method I use most often on the radio. In that venue, I must think quickly as I only have a minute or two on the line with the dreamer. This is where I can safely use the "If this were my dream . . . " technique. It is the one sure way that offers choices while at the same time separating you from the dreamer. You can show the dreamer your respect for his perceptions by leaving him room to accept or reject whatever ideas you might throw out.

Here's what I mean. A gentleman called in one night to a show I was on and described this dream: "I was skiing. We took a guide. The guide warned, 'Do not get down below me.' I soon realize that I've gone below him, not far though. And then suddenly I am caught in an avalanche. I am tumbling. I can't breathe. It feels like I am tumbling inside a washing machine. Then, the avalanche begins spreading out. I can breathe because it is getting thinner. The avalanche goes into the town weaving in between cars. Now the snow is gone, and nobody cares."

Right away I connected to a scenario that would fit for me in my life. I offered, "If this were my dream, I might have it when I find myself in a pile of trouble by not following the rules exactly the way I've been instructed. Say, for example, if I feel angry with one of my siblings, it may not be a spoken rule, but it is not a good idea for me to share my disappointment with my mum and expect her to side with me. Whenever I've tried to do this, she inevitably covers for them, by making some plausible, forgivable excuse for their behavior. Or she'll point out something that *I've* done! This is the way she tries to give me a little perspective and make me feel less angry with my sibling.

"But when she does this, I suddenly feel like I am tumbling down a hill being swallowed by an avalanche. I, too, feel as though I can't breathe. Soon after," I added, "I start realizing she had raised a few reasonable points, and the avalanche begins spreading out. I can breathe because it is getting thinner. I can even connect your dream to my life in how the avalanche goes into the town weaving in between cars, then the snow is gone, and nobody cares. That would be my weaving in and around my sibling, wanting to apologize for my part, yet at the same time elicit an apology from them for theirs. And you know what? Before I know it, the issue is gone, and nobody cares!" I ask the caller, "Can you connect to any scenario that has a similar plot?"

The answer comes back instantly! I love when that happens. This dreamer is a professional who in an advertisement mistakenly suggested that many of his colleagues are less than honest. Some registered complaints and for a while he was very concerned he might lose his license to practice. But then it turned out the board of decision-makers only gave him a slap on the wrist, and after a short time had passed, the hullabaloo was gone, and nobody cared.

You have to see with each dream what sticks out at you. And have fun with it! Be open and flexible. The act of superimposing is exactly like a dance. I move in and out of the dream. It is a back and forth motion, using the words and feelings that come out in the conversation between the dreamer and myself. This technique, called direct association, helps the dreamer connect to a meaning.

Direct association, as opposed to free association, keeps you dancing very close to the dream. In free association you move from thought to thought like links in a chain, and the dream is only the starting point for the first thought. Direct association, on the other hand, keeps returning to the dream and the words on the dream map. You take an element from the map, or the plot of the dream story, and see if you can test it as a mirror image of the dreamer's current situation. Then, you go back into the dream, searching out another point of entry. I use this back and forth motion when I am working alone with my own dreams too.

Working with the feelings sounds like this. The other day I walked in to the leasing company to renew the term on my car. When the woman going over the documents with me heard that I was a dream analyst, she was fascinated. On my way out she insisted on telling the receptionist what I do. Immediately, the receptionist asked me what it could possibly mean that she keeps dreaming she is either pregnant or has just given birth.

I asked, "How did you feel in the dream?" She said, "I feel so strange. I don't know what I am doing with this new child! Maybe a little frightened too." Just to clarify, I asked, "Do you have children?" She answered, "No!"

"Well," I explained, "very often when people dream of giving birth it could be because they have started something new. It could be anything from a new behavior to a new job. And this new thing that you're doing is making you feel strange, and wondering what you are going to do with it.

"Here's an example," I ventured. "Say you're the type of person who doesn't normally express yourself when someone says something to aggravate you. One day you hear somebody say something that really bugs you and you just come out with your reaction. That might be something that could bring on a dream like this because you'd have 'given birth' to the new behavior. And of course, whenever we try something new, we all feel a bit strange."

Both women exclaimed I had actually hit the nail on the head. That is exactly what had happened. The receptionist added, "And after I spoke up, there was me wondering what I am going to do now with what I've come out with! Plus there I was, a little frightened of the repercussion I might have to face for speaking my mind."

Of course, you don't always find the mirror with the very first question. But now that you have a "feel" for getting in touch with your feelings in a dream, let's look at Leslie's Picnic Dream.

Figure 1: The Picnic Is Over: Leslie's Dream

After Leslie said her dream out loud, and we had had a chance to map her comments, we noticed there was a progression of feelings we captured down the side of the page. Leslie described herself as feeling nice and relaxed at the beginning of the scene, then getting more annoyed, and eventually moving to a state of total panic as the ants multiplied and the situation became out of control. While Leslie described her experience and I wrote her words down, I was *in the dream* with her. Afterwards, doing the dance, I moved *out of the dream* to pose a question about her current waking life.

Forgetting the story of the dream for the moment, I looked only at her words, which I had recorded verbatim. I now repeated them back to her in the context of her life. "Is there anything that is going on in your life that started out with you feeling 'nice and relaxed,' that soon turned to your feeling 'unable to control' a situation, 'very upset,' and has recently escalated to the point where you feel panicked?" She thought for a bit, and then said, "No. I can't think of anything."

Here are two important points to note. If you are the dreamer, then when you stop to think about a question that has been posed to you, allow yourself to take time and consider your response. Mull the question over in your mind. When you try to uncover the meaning of a dream it feels like groping around in the dark when the lights have suddenly gone out. And here's something else. When a first thought comes to your mind, don't toss it away, saying to yourself, "Oh, it can't be that." Truth is, it very well might be *just* that.

If you are the interviewer, and the first method you try doesn't help the dreamer connect, you should move to another point of entry. Especially if you know the dreamer, you may be very tempted to push your ideas on to her. It is always best to allow the dreamer the respect she deserves to reach her own conclusions about a dream's meaning. After all, she is the one who had the thoughts and dreamed the dream. You can throw all the ideas you have out for her, just so long as you both realize they are only ideas. And so if you feel any resistance, that's your key to move along to the next point of entry.

Let's go through the process from my conversation with Leslie. I went back into the dream, this time reading her definitions just as she said them about two of her symbols, the picnic and the ants. Again, I stepped out of the dream and posed the question related to her waking life. I asked, "Can you think of anything that started out as 'fun and games'? Something you may have done 'outside of the house'? Is there anything that comes to mind that could have happened to 'spoil the fun'? Something that may have really 'annoyed' you?"

You don't have to be with the dreamer when she connects. I could hear Leslie *click* just by the sound of her breath over the phone. That sound has become so familiar to me. I said, "You sound like you hit on something. Did you?"

"Well," she said, sounding a bit unsure, "I had a thought."

I asked, "Will you share it with me?"

She responded, "Well, I've been seeing someone. I'm married though. And lately it has surely become annoying, because he is being transferred to another city that is over an hour away! It is going to be near impossible to see each other."

The most exhilarating and fascinating thing about discovering the link between the dream and a waking life issue is how, after you have found just one link, you can then look back at the dream and see how the whole puzzle suddenly falls into place. And when the dreamer may have been unable to connect with a point of entry at the outset, now you can go back and try again. You retrace your steps each time you go back in and out of the dream.

Here is what I mean. Once Leslie thought she may have hit on something but was unsure of herself, I danced back into the dream again. Looking at the words Leslie used to describe her feelings, I repeated them back to her a second time. But this time when she heard them, they sounded very different to her.

"So then," I asked, "do you think your feelings in the dream mirror this issue? Did your relationship start out with you feeling 'nice and relaxed,' and then soon turn to your feeling 'unable to control' the situation? That would be his being transferred to another city. This has probably made you feel 'very upset,' and has recently escalated to the point where you feel panicked, because it will become, as you say, 'near impossible to see each other.'"

"Yes," she agreed emphatically. Now we both knew we had found the puzzle. Look at the words Leslie used to define eating, and now we are able to link that to the affair. She was "feeling full and satisfied;" getting her "nourishment" "outside of the house." I mean, even the blanket suggests lying down.

The ants, only a few in the opening scene of the dream, represent the obstacles that were surmountable at the beginning and easy to control, like his wife, her husband, his children, and hers. Once he was going to be transferred, though, this would have made the annoying obstacles multiply, just as the ants did in the dream.

Later in my discussion with Leslie, we isolated her movement in the dream and took note of the action and the plot. By seeing what action Leslie did to stop the ants from ruining her picnic, we found a clue to the strength or solution in the dream.

In Chapter 3 I will show you how to superimpose these elements onto the dreamer's current waking life situation.

Rote: Noticing Repeating Themes and Images

We repeat the same thought in our dreams, and we use different symbols or faces to express that same thought. One method of learning is through rote, which is the repetition of the same phrase several times. Remember? Read. Write. Recite. Students often use rote to memorize a rule. As adults, we repeat things to ourselves when we want to make sure we remember them correctly. This phenomenon also appears in our dreams. Because the conscious mind does not always absorb the meaning of a symbol or event the first time, often two or more symbols or events in a dream point to the same message. Sometimes it takes the conscious mind a while to get the point.

When I sit down and look at the map of a dream, the repetitions often jump out at me. Think about what attracts your eye. Repeating thoughts or words in the dream map may be the quickest way to help you solve the puzzle. For example, if the element of fear has repeated itself several times, one might start by asking the dreamer if anything is causing him to feel afraid in his current life situation.

Keep your eye out for the repetition of words in the dream map. When you get good at spotting these, you can look for things in the map that repeat general ideas or categories. Say to yourself, "What is the underlying theme here?" Ask yourself, "If I take the words of the story away for a minute, what is this really about?" This exercise involves looking underneath the story line.

Here's an example. If a man feels he can't get a word in edgewise with his girlfriend and it is really starting to bug him, he might dream that he is back at school waving his hand desperately in the air, waiting for the teacher to call on him, but she doesn't. In the same night, he could dream he is driving in a slow lane filled with traffic and in the lane beside him, cars are whizzing by and he can't cut in. Maybe in the dream, he notices that the person in the car behind him is wearing a hockey suit. Once the dream is analyzed he discovers that the hockey suit links him to a memory when he was benched during the hockey finals in college. So all these stories and symbols are different, but they essentially have the same meaning. The man is feeling "unable to get in," to participate. Each of the dreams points to his genuine frustration that he can't participate. Finally, in all these scenarios he feels powerless to his circumstance.

You know we are not working on five problems we have all at once. We keep it simple. We take our time, and are generally only processing or working out one or two things at a time. Dreams of the same night belong together as part of the same whole thought. In other words you can have six dreams in a night and the stories in them might be different, but if you learn how to do a little investigating, you might find a main theme appear. And often that's how you can click in to what you are trying to say to yourself.

A client of mine, Stacey, had four dreams in the same night. Notice how connected they are beneath the surface. In the first, she was trying to "track some people down" and "get their attention," but they said they would get back to her later. She added that in waking life she had been trying to track her newspaper delivery boy down to give him a tip, and he was not getting back to her. In the second dream, there were "bad guys," "paying attention" to her. She did not want their attention. In the third dream, she was trying to "get someone's attention," but he did not even notice her. He was in a hurry. She said, "He thinks I am an insignificant person." Finally, in the last dream, she said she was a man in the mid to late 1800s. His wife was recuperating from an illness. She took a sudden turn for the worse and he (she) found himself hoping he would be able to have sex ("get some attention") soon.

These dreams are connected because they revolve around the main theme of giving or getting attention. Once we talked about the dreams I asked Stacey to think about other questions, like who is the attention coming from? Is it needed attention? One thing was for sure. Stacey was not getting the attention she wanted—not in any of the dreams.

Rote repetition not only lets us connect different dreams in the same night, but it also allows us to work with a fragment of a dream and still pinpoint what is going on. Many people think they need to remember a complete dream, one with a beginning, middle, and an end, in order to understand it. Because dreams so often repeat the same simple thoughts using different symbols, even a fragment of a dream is worth looking at. Writing down even one sentence of a dream can help you solve the mystery.

Once I dreamed I was drawing on Chelsea, using crayons. One solitary picture. One image. I discovered I had captured three daughters in one image. Chelsea, because she appeared in the dream; Emma-Jo, because I was using crayons like her; and Lisa, because Lisa is an artist. The dream showed me I was "drawing on" all my children for strength at a difficult time in my life. I even had room in the image to include my husband Andrew. I often call him "Drew."

Figure 2: Labrador Retrievers: Johnathan's Dream

In looking at the map of Johnathan's Labrador Retrievers dream (see page 17), I was struck by how the word or image of a child or childhood kept repeating itself. The word "child" appears in the dream map three times. I saw the rote.

But there was more. Dr. Ann Faraday says, "Anonymous children in dreams can represent undeveloped parts of ourselves, or parts of ourselves that have remained stuck with the conflicts of childhood, but they can also represent aspects of our total life situation where some new state of life is seen as a growing thing."[1] Keeping this in mind, I could group the "child" theme into a larger category of "newness" and "lack of experience," or "unfamiliarity." After all, a child sees the world as a totally unfamiliar place. When we feel like children, it seems like we're facing something new, unfamiliar, or unknown.

Once I opened Johnathan's child theme up to include the idea of "newness," I found four places where it repeated itself in the dream map: the repetition of the word "child," and the European couple. The European couple epitomizes this unfamiliarity or newness because they are "foreign" and "unknown." So I asked Johnathan, "What can you think of that happened to you, or that you thought about in the last day or two, that felt new to you? Do you have a new idea? Are you thinking about a new job? A new relationship, perhaps? Are you thinking of buying something new? Is there someone who you want to express something to? Do you want to say something in a new or different way than you have approached them before? Did someone else come to you with a new idea?"

Okay, well maybe I didn't throw all those questions out quite that quickly, but the point is this is what I do. I see a theme, in this case something unfamiliar or new, and think of as many questions or scenarios as I can that might fit for the dreamer. The important thing is to get the dreamer thinking; tossing different ideas around. That's how to spur an association while we're awake. He took a stab at it.

"Well. My girlfriend has, in the last few days, been talking about us getting engaged. She has been quite honest with me in expressing her eagerness about our making a commitment. Do you think it might be about that?"

Now I want to check and see if I can find a second match, another piece of the puzzle. So I moved right to the feelings. Keeping my eyes on the feelings he expressed in the dream, but moving outside it, I said, "Well! How do you feel about her honesty? And how do you feel about the idea of getting married?"

"Truth is," he said, "we've been dating for over a year. We have a wonderful relationship. I love her and I feel happy about the idea of getting married, but I felt a little weird talking about it. I don't feel ready for marriage just yet."

I said, "I wonder if we haven't found the dream. Two pieces of the puzzle have fit. So, the whole idea of marriage being 'new' or 'young' to you might explain why you have repeated that image. And your feeling happy about the idea but a little weird at the same time exactly mirrors the expressions you used when describing your feelings in the dream." The dream map showed he felt "happy" in the dream, but it also seemed "weird" to him.

Going back to the map I noticed he had said, " . . . when I think of dogs in general, having one is something I aspire to, but I can't accommodate right now." I pointed this out to him and asked, "Do you see another mirror there?" He confirmed that we had found a third match to the puzzle. Now it became Johnathan who was looking down to the map! From here on, it was he who was able to pinpoint his clever use of many of the metaphors in the dream.

"I used the definition of needy because I see my girlfriend as needy! And you know I don't think I can accommodate her in her neediness at the present time. And the house in the dream does not look like *it* can accommodate the dogs either!" Here, we can understand why he used the metaphor of "not being able to accommodate" twice in the dream.

"Finally," he confessed, "I am concerned about expressing to her how I feel about all this right now, as honestly as she did with me. I hope our relationship will remain stable." Here is where we came to discuss another phenomenon that occurs so often in dreams, as well as in our waking dilemmas. Many times the feelings we have towards someone else seem just as accurate from the other person's perspective too. Johnathan is worried about the stability of the relationship. Now *he* is the one who seems needy. He is concerned because he doesn't want to risk losing his girlfriend. On the one hand, Johnathan feels that his girlfriend is too needy. He doesn't feel ready to accommodate her needs by making a bigger commitment. Yet, the thought of her possibly ending their relationship if he doesn't accommodate her makes him feel frightened. He is afraid she will move on, and this puts him in the position of the "needy" one. His dilemma is whether to succumb to her wishes or risk being rejected.

Eventually, Johnathan traced every piece of the dream back to the mirror. In doing this he was able to clarify his feelings on the issue of commitment. He kept himself "separate" in the dream, for example, in that he was merely an observer of the scene and didn't participate in it. He identified this with the fact that he was holding himself "separate" from the idea of commitment in his life. Again, in the dream he chose a bungalow, which only has one floor. As he realized, it does not go too "deep." This symbol illustrates his shying away from anything too deep at that point in his relationship.

Play on Words and Puns

Besides being the most fun, the single most stunning way to capture the meaning of a dream lies in our use of play on words and puns. That is why it is so important to say the dream out loud. It's the way for you or your partner to hear yourself possibly using a pun. It works like this. Because we are thinking in pictures, moods, metaphors, and colors, you might use an expression and it comes into the dream in the form of a picture. You need to keep your ears open for any expressions the dreamer might use from our day-to-day language.

Last year, I had a series of dreams I came to call my "kneeling dreams." While the stories and settings of each dream were different, I was always walking around on my knees. I couldn't, for the life of me, figure out why I was always on my knees, and it was really starting to bug me. In one dream, I was clumping around a lower campus of what seemed like a familiar university (maybe Asheville, North Carolina). I seemed to be getting around okay, until I had to make it up a hill. There was snow on the ground. It was impossible to maneuver myself. I could not stand up in order to climb the hill.

A few days later, I dreamed I was on my knees again, this time in the office of a man named Neil. The pun struck me almost immediately—I was kneeling in Neil's office! In this case the pun functioned like a kind of repetition. I wasn't getting the meaning of "kneeling," so I had a dream with a "Neil" in it too.

We very frequently use this kind of wordplay in our dreams. It is the unconscious making sure it gets a message across to the conscious mind. I clicked on the meaning of my kneeling dreams only when I shared the dream with my husband one morning. I heard myself say to him, "I couldn't stand up." Hearing this, he immediately thought of another pun and asked me—who or what was I having trouble standing up to?

Another fun and quick example of play on words is the woman who told me about a dream where there were snakes all over the floor, and she "couldn't put her foot down." The dream turned out to be about her difficulty putting her foot down with her husband.

Then there was the man who described a dream where he

had to stick his hand down a garbage disposal filled with water-melon rind, in order to search for a lost key. He was trying to tell himself that he was feeling "in the pits."

Figure 3: Deborah's Dream

Deborah's dream (see page 20) provides several examples of the wonderful ways we use play on words in our dreams. Since she had used the word dominoes, I asked Deborah what in her life felt like "dominoes," or one thing leading to another. She could not connect.

I tried another entry, using an educated guess. I knew she had just moved, so I asked, "Do you think this has to do with your moving?"

She said, "No."

Deborah woke with this dream the very first day after her move. Since your dream at the first level always has to do with something that either happened to you the day before, or some-thing that you thought about the day before, I admit I wasn't ready to let go of the idea of the move. I tried again, asking, "What made you decide to move? Tell me the story."

"Well," she answered, "I moved here because my boyfriend was moving here."

"Had you been planning to move?"

"Yes," she said. "I had a few places in mind, but I was leaning towards Toronto anyway."

I remarked, "*Leaning,* did you say?" We started laughing. "So," I continued, "what happened after that?"

She replied, "Well, I started looking for a job here. Then I came here for an interview. Then I got the job. Then I came back with my mum, this time looking for an apartment. Then, I was looking for a roommate. After I found my roommate, we looked for a mover. And here I am!" She paused, thinking for a minute. *"That's the dominoes!"*

Deborah had unwittingly made another connection about the symbols in that dream. Her parents moved to Italy a while ago. One of the most enduring symbols of Italy is the Leaning Tower of Pisa. When she saw the leaning building in her dream, this conjured up the feelings of sadness, excitement, and stress that her parents' move to Italy had caused—feelings much the same as those she was experiencing with her own move now. She was using a memory from the past in order to activate the same feelings the memory induced and apply them to her present situation.

I wanted to explore some of the feelings she'd described. "You were frightened in your dream. Are you frightened about your impending move?"

She responded, "No, I'm actually quite calm. I guess it hasn't even hit me yet." Hearing her own words made Deborah gasp! Again, she used the identical expression in describing her move that she had used in describing the action in the dream. In her dream, Deborah was scared and running, but the bricks were falling in place and "didn't even hit her." This is the level of precision with which we choose our dream pictures and words.

You can see from Deborah's dream how visual puns come through in the dreamer's exact words. For example, the leaning buildings reflect Deborah's state of mind about her recent move, when she was *leaning* towards Toronto. Her final decision to move was the result of a *domino* effect. Her feelings about the move *hadn't even hit her yet* at the time she had the dream. Everything in the dream points to the move, but she didn't realize it until she heard herself using the same words to describe both the dream and the move.

Polarities

Polarities appear in your dream because you are most likely stuck in a certain belief or behavior that is off to one extreme. The polarity shows up essentially to help "pull you" away from your extreme view or behavior in your current situation. We create these opposing symbols and metaphors in order to measure and re-evaluate our positions on people and events. Sometimes the union of these opposites can reveal the solution to the dream problem. For now, we'll take a look at polarities in the dream map and see how they apply to the current situation of the dream.

Figure 4: Sarah's Uncle Dream

In looking at the Uncle Dream (see page 22), I am presenting for you a slightly more complicated example of what our unconscious can do in order to help us problem-solve. As you see from looking at the map, this dream presents another good illustration of rote repetition. But this time, we also find four polarities in the dream. Before we focus on how Sarah's use of polarities helped her connect her dream to her waking life, let me first address her uncle's appearance in the dream.

How a Dream-Symbol Gets into the Dream

Sigmund Freud said, "If I now consult my own experience with regard to the origin of the elements appearing in the dream-content, I must in the first place express the opinion that in every dream we may find some reference to the experiences of the *preceding day*. Whatever dream I turn to, whether my own or someone else's, this experience is always confirmed."[2]

When considering why they dreamed about a certain person, many people stop with the most obvious reason. So for example, when I asked Sarah what her uncle made her think of, the first thing that occurred to her was that she was watching David Letterman before she fell asleep and David reminded her of her uncle. And this *was* precisely the initial reason for how her uncle arrived in the dream story. But it is certainly *not* the only reason he is present in the dream. I refer again to our level of sophistication in how we choose our symbols. They are not random choices! Sarah needed to use her uncle, because he, in at least three ways we discovered together, is the direct antithesis of her aunt. As you will soon understand, Sarah, unconsciously, had decided to weigh out her feelings and options by way of creating a series of polarities.

Now, allow me to sidetrack here for just a minute to add another element and I promise I will return to my point. The following is an example of how we sometimes use an object in our dreams to bring to mind a particular person. When I asked Sarah what comes to mind when she thinks of diamonds, she immediately thought of her aunt. Using direct association, Sarah had discovered a double meaning and purpose for having diamonds in her dream. They brought her aunt into the dream, and they created a metaphor for commitment as seen by the engagement ring.

In the same way that her uncle came into the dream because Sarah thought of him during the *Late Show with David Letterman,* so too the diamonds appeared because her aunt was wearing a large diamond on the same evening Sarah had the dream. And again, I ask you not to toss aside your first association with any symbol in your dream. Investigate further and you are sure to find a level of precision that will astound you. Why, then, is Sarah's aunt in the dream? Same as the uncle, Sarah needed to bring in her aunt because she is the direct antithesis of someone else, namely, her uncle! Having established this metaphor, in our conversation we no longer referred to the diamonds necessarily as diamonds; but more often referred to them as the aunt.

You will notice in my discussion here that Sarah and I were able to link her dream to two completely separate issues in her life. While you read the two interpretations, look at the map and see how accurate her symbols are and how well they fit what she was pondering. We were able to superimpose her waking-life situations over her feelings in the dream, her uncle, her aunt, the ring, the fact that the ring does not fit, and the "general weirdness" of the situation she described in the story.

The First Mirror

I do not have a complete transcript of our conversation, but this is how it happened. As I began the dance, I (figuratively) found myself suddenly in the dream with Sarah, asking her how it felt to have her uncle propose to her. I asked her to try and connect to this "weirdness," as she called it.

I often ask dreamers to "add a touch of," same as you would with a recipe. Because what she described is not just "weirdness," it is weirdness with something out of place. Something is not right, or the way it should be, as opposed to, say, weirdness you might feel from seeing a grotesquely ugly face. Now hold that feeling, I told Sarah, and toss in a pinch of confusion and anger. Sarah was being put in the uncomfortable and confusing position of being asked to participate in her uncle's rejection of his wife, her own aunt!

Once she had caught and held the feeling of the dream, I asked Sarah to move away from the dream, keeping her eyes closed, and try to imagine where she may have felt a similar way in the last day or two. You want to say some of those words to yourself while you are getting in touch with the feelings. Strange, weird, out of place, confused, upset, angry, uncomfortable. Sarah had a fleeting thought. She admitted that being at her aunt's house the night before felt out of place for sure! She was there because she had decided to use an option to rewrite a term paper in which she had a C+ grade. Just the idea of having to redo that paper certainly held an element of anger and discomfort for her.

I remember looking back at the map. There, back in the dream, I saw the theme of commitment, which she had repeated or alluded to three times. The main polarity in the dream, between the uncle and the aunt, also refers to commitment in that the aunt is a highly committed overachiever, whereas the uncle is not committed enough (either to his wife in the dream, or to his work in waking life). So it was now time to step back out of the dream, but using the words *from* the dream map about commitment to see if they applied to her current situation.

Repeating Sarah's language, and adding it to her response about her feelings, I asked if she felt "committed" to rewriting her term paper. Sarah admitted that she had *really* mixed feelings about that paper.

We had found the link. This is exactly the kind of scenario where you might find yourself using polarities. She was weighing her level of commitment to the work. On the one hand, Sarah had hopes of following through and getting a higher final grade on her paper. But on the other hand she was having difficulty making the commitment. It is hard to go back over something when you thought you were finished and done with it. It feels "weird and out of place."

So, using Sarah's words in quotation marks, see now, while I say the story to you, how the dream is superimposed on her waking issue. On this level, Sarah's dream talked about how torn she was at having to rewrite the paper. The ring symbolizes her commitment to it. The commitment "doesn't fit." She didn't feel like she wanted to "marry" this project. She was feeling that the "commitment was too big." She had been working at it for a while and felt unsure whether she wanted to continue to work on it anymore. At the same time she wondered how she could "say no" to herself, and be an "underachiever." Lastly, the general "weirdness" in the dream was similar to the general "weird-ness" she felt about having to rewrite her term paper.

The Second Mirror

As we continued our session, Sarah was struck by another inci-dent that happened the day before her dream in which she also "felt strange and out of place with a touch of confusion and an element of discomfort and anger." Her long-time boyfriend had behaved in a very insensitive way. The incident had really caught Sarah off guard since he is normally very caring.

Here is how Sarah was able to make the association from the dream to her situation with her boyfriend. In addition to this inci-dent from the day before, Sarah's uncle in the dream reminded her of her boyfriend. Her uncle, like her boyfriend, was someone she had known for a long time. She had known her boyfriend for six years and they had been in a committed relationship for four. In the past she felt she could depend on him. The fact that he had disappointed her in recent weeks started Sarah wondering if she "really didn't know him at all." When we step back inside the dream now, you can really see the mirror. One reason her uncle appeared in the dream is that he represents someone she thinks she can depend on, but there he was asking her to marry him! Like the boyfriend, he was acting out of character.

In this analysis, Sarah defined the engagement ring for me as a metaphor for her uncertainty about her boyfriend's level of commitment to her. And as I have pointed out before, once you are successful in making a few links, the rest of the dream sud-denly falls into place and becomes easy to figure out. The ring was too big in the dream because when her boyfriend treated her insensitively, it "did not fit" for Sarah. She realized she was not prepared to accept this behavior. In this twist and double entendre, it is Sarah who is questioning her commitment to *him*.

The feelings she expresses, "I would rather marry someone else," and "Oh, God! How do I say no?" mean exactly what she says. "How can I speak up and say 'No!' to this behavior?" Sarah was feeling angry and yet uncomfortable about her boyfriend putting her in this awkward position. As well, she was thinking about how to express her anger, something Sarah is not very comfortable with in general. The "weirdness" in the dream was similar to the "weirdness" she felt about his unusual behavior.

So here again Sarah has used the polarities in the dream in order to measure her feelings and possible reactions to her boyfriend's behavior. She brings her aunt into the dream as a representation of someone who is quite comfortable expressing her needs, where Sarah is not really that comfortable. Here again, as in the first mirror, Sarah's natural tendency is to tilt her behavior closer to that of her uncle. She is also weighing her commitment to her boyfriend as well as wondering about his to her. She questions, just as she describes in her dream, "Is the commitment too big, or too small?" Is her commitment to her boyfriend too big? Is his to her too small?

Finally, I think it is important to point out that the underlying issue is quite similar in both mirrors. The bottom line is, how big is Sarah's commitment to *herself?* How committed is she to *herself* in terms of achieving at school, and what too is her level of commitment to *herself* in what she feels she deserves in a relationship?

Figure 5: The Emma-Jo Dream

As we look at the Emma-Jo Dream (see pages 26–27), you will be hearing from me as the dreamer rather than the interviewer. Because dream work can be so subjective, I think it is important that you have the opportunity to hear about my experience having one of my "bigger" dreams analyzed. In this instance you know for sure what impact the dream discoveries had, because you are hearing it straight from the dreamer.

You may remember that I woke with this dream on the second morning of an Association for the Study of Dreams (ASD) Conference I was attending in Asheville, North Carolina. I had tried to click on the dream's meaning. The first and most obvious event triggering the dream was Emma-Jo's illness in Montreal with the chicken pox. The dream seemed precognitive, since I didn't hear about her chicken pox until the next day. I realize that in this instance my precognition is better referred to as intuition, since, when she was younger, Emma-Jo had a tendency to become ill whenever I was away from home.

As you may have guessed by now, I did not feel satisfied with this first "mirror" of the dream. I had attended an art seminar for dream work early in the conference. So many people find the mirror to their dream by working with their hands, drawing it or creating art with the dream feelings or symbols. I admit I felt frustrated that I was not able to come up with any understanding of my dream from the art workshop. You know some dreams are what Carl Jung called "big dreams." I believe, when you have one you can sense it. I was determined to find more meaning in my dream.

I first started getting an inkling of what this dream was addressing when I heard myself repeating words like adventure, mystery, and excitement several times. Added to that, the continuous imagery of danger finally clued me in. I realized what it was that had the sense of mystery, excitement, and yet danger for me. Of course! It was the conference! Asheville was my first ASD conference. While I had gone away many times on business trips, this was my first as a dream analyst. It was truly an exciting adventure for me.

The danger I connected to was this. Some months before I arrived at the conference, I had a business idea about how to present dream work to a wide audience. My first night at the conference I made an acquaintance with a woman who seemed so nice. We got into a discussion and I mentioned what my focus was, which was in essence the business idea. I didn't present the idea as anything huge. It was more just in the course of the conversation. The thing is though, the next morning she was already after me at breakfast saying she had talked to a friend about me and could she introduce us, so I could tell him more about it. Later in the day after lunch, she actually came looking for me again, now with another woman whom she wanted me to talk to! Suddenly, I felt a serious concern for secrecy about my idea. Hence the image of danger in my dreams. Now I understood the double edge of the scissors to represent something creative, and yet they can be dangerous. And look at how precise my choice of imagery was! If you look back at my definition on the map, you will notice scissors are something that is often stolen from me by my kids. My creativity is being stolen!

The metaphor of St. Catherine Street East captures how I felt at being away from home, in an "unfamiliar" and sometimes, as in the face of my idea being stolen, quite uncomfortable place. And now look back at how three men were walking close to us and how I felt I had to protect myself in the dream. The dream suddenly became easy for me to superimpose over my waking experience.

And just then the polarity between Andy and me came up. Now I could add another totally different dimension to my understanding of the dream. The emotional/businesslike polarity between Andy and me certainly was relevant to my situation at the time I had this dream. Because I am not an academic, I often feel a certain degree of professional insecurity when attending an ASD conference, being completely surrounded by Ph.D.'s. Sometimes it seems to me like everyone else is more legitimate in this "business" than I am. In North Carolina, at my very first ASD conference, this actually made me feel panicked and out of control.

The dream with Emma-Jo dates to the period when I was

first establishing the Dream Interpretation Center. My dreams had salient themes as different issues and decisions arose. As I discovered in the mandala workshop, I was the little girl in the dream whom I couldn't seem to get a hold of. That child represented the little girl in me. Just like Johnathan's dream, where the "newness" of marriage was represented by images of children, so the public exposure to my dream work was "new" to me. In the dream I used the child as a symbol of my inexperience. Her "walking into a field" was a play on words, similar to my work in a "new field."

Accepting Yourself

If you look back to Chapter 1, where I list for you the steps to use when mapping a dream, the first rule of thumb is not to judge your dream. Accept it as it is. Do not think it is weird or perverse.

After reading this chapter about finding the mirror, I hope that you have realized why you should accept your dream just as it is. I love watching the relief appear on a dreamer's face once he has analyzed and understood his dream. I guess it is a relief to discover you are not so weird after all! But besides finding out that you're not weird, you look at your dream and accept it as it is because you yourself have designed each metaphor, symbol, mood, and story to address your issues. You have created the dream story in the unique way that only you can decode. I can't think of a nicer way to begin the process of accepting yourself, than by revealing the beauty and marvelous cleverness of your own mind each time you discover meaning through your dream.

CHAPTER THREE

Finding the Solution

"A dream is a bridge that connects the problem which con-fronts the dreamer with his goal of attainment."
—Alfred Adler

Once you have successfully attached or superimposed the dream onto a current issue in your waking life, you can look back for the solution or sometimes the strength in the dream. I mention these two options because very often your unconscious gives you the actual solution to your problem. And when it doesn't, it *does* at the very least offer metaphors that point you to strengths you may not realize you had. Then you can tap into these strengths in your given situation.

When I use the word "solution," what I mean to say is that your unconscious lets you know what you are most comfort-able doing. It gives a solution tailor-made for you. This is very different from what somebody else might tell you to do. The truth is, the best person to let you know what is good for you *is* you! And while we humans can be very adept at lying to our-selves and denying how we feel about the situations in our lives, there is one thing you can depend on. Your unconscious never lies to you. This is another of the many reasons why I love dream work. So now, I would like to point out several methods for discovering the solution to the problem presented in your dream.

What Is Missing in the Dream Story?

One of the most valuable ways your dream might point you towards a solution to your current problem is by showing you something that is missing from the story. If you realize what might be missing in the dream, this can spur you to fill in the space in your waking life. I always tell my clients not to be impatient with themselves if in fact they find something missing in the dream and do not yet feel ready to fill the gap in their waking life. That's okay. The main thing is, once something comes into your awareness, it won't be too long before you consciously decide to alter your behavior. There is bound to be some movement, even if it's small at first. Awareness is a very powerful tool for change.

For example, say you dreamed you were trying to yell at someone, and no sound came out. Your voice is missing! When you have a dream like that, you may want to ask yourself if you want to express something to someone, but for some reason you can't. Say it is your mum. You may decide you are too uncomfortable at the present time to speak up. But now that you understand why you had the dream, and what was missing, you can think about saying just something small to her. Sometimes an expression as small as, "I felt really uncomfortable about what you said to me last week," can be enough to free the energy tied up in the conflict. It lets some air out of the balloon.

Now, suppose you decide to say nothing. The problem is with your boss, and you are not going to say a word. But if this is an ongoing problem, just the awareness of why you had the dream can ease your tension. And the awareness may even get you thinking about changing your job.

I remember dreaming I was poisoned and had to get to the hospital for the antidote. Once I had analyzed my dream, and I mean in depth, a teacher of mine pointed out a most obvious piece I had missed. Throughout the dream, I was alone! Considering the size of my family, my relationship with them, and that I was dying in the dream, it was interesting to notice what was *missing*. No one from the family came with me to the hospital. The "missing" part of the dream was significant because during that period of time, I was feeling very alone and removed from one of my sisters. The dream really brought that feeling home to me. Getting me in touch with the feeling motivated me to do two things to remedy my situation: I asked my husband and children for their support, and I started approaching my sister to be friends.

Using Active Imagination to Finish the Dream

Sometimes the end of a sentence or phrase is missing in the dream. A dentist dreamed she was walking on a boulevard to her father's wedding. She was wondering why he was marrying for the third time. She arrived at the church to find her dad there, but without a bride. The families were sitting on opposite sides of the chapel. She noticed that her father sat down on the side of the bride's family. This made her feel uncomfortable and rejected. She walked up to her father and asked him why he was sitting with the bride's family. Just as he opened his mouth to answer, the dream ended.

I asked her to finish the dream.

"Just make it up," I said. "Pretend. What do you think he could have said?"

She responded, "I'm going to sit with the other side of the family, but I still belong to this family."

At the time, she was working with her father at his clinic. In the last few weeks, the dreamer had spoken with a long-time friend of hers about the possibility of opening a much-needed clinic for children in another city. Very concerned that her father might feel rejected, and in turn reject her, she had been waiting for the right moment to discuss her departure with him. Once she discovered the mirror, this dreamer was amazed at how accurately her choice of metaphors fit her dilemma. I have italicized her use of metaphors here.

In this instance, she would be staying in the same *"church"* or *field* as her dad, but she would be *"sitting with the other family,"* or in *another place* or *city*. With the phrase, "I'm going to sit with the other side of the family, but I still belong to this family," she is saying, "I am going to work at another clinic, but I am still your daughter. I still love you." The dream gave this young dentist a safe place to practice how she would break the news to her father that she wanted to stop working at his clinic. She was also helping *herself* adjust to her impending move. Is the decision to move away from a parent a rejection of that parent? I think when we separate ourselves from our parents, we not only worry about how *they* may react—often we have to convince *ourselves* that when we move away from family, we are still a part of the family! When this young woman took the opportunity to finish her dream, she gave herself a positive answer to this question, and with it more confidence in approaching her dad.

Using Active Imagination to Change the Dream

Active imagination can be used very effectively in changing a dream to have a more satisfactory ending. Just the act of picturing a different ending or a revised dream can inspire the dreamer to take a different approach in her waking life problem. For example, a few years ago, my daughter dreamed she had three weeks to live. In the dream she came to me and became very upset when the one person in the world who she can depend on was unable to help her. The next morning, we solved the puzzle of the dream by realizing that her exams were beginning in three weeks. Of course I couldn't help her in the dream—I was unable to help in waking life! So, let's say that after my daughter had this dream, she imagined herself finding a cure while researching on the Internet. If she re-enters her dream through active imagination and *sees* herself discovering the cure to her disease, this could give her the impetus to take action with her exams. The fact is she wouldn't even necessarily have to re-enter the dream. Just having the thought sets a new train of ideas in motion.

Since your dreams are your sleeping thoughts, you should be able to change the dream. After all, you change your mind while you're awake, don't you? How many times did you leave your house with the intention of buying yourself a shirt? Then you arrive downtown, and next door to the clothing store, you see a pair of shoes in the window, and decide to buy them instead of the shirt! Well, what about finishing the dream? You can rethink a dream, and continue it. Explore your options. Give the dream new ideas. Earlier, I compared exercising unfamiliar behaviors to getting in shape in a gym. After a while, it comes naturally. The same is true here in relation to "exercising your imagination." Have fun. It doesn't all have to be serious.

A young woman who called me on a radio show dreamed she was attending her boyfriend's cousin's wedding. She bought the newlyweds a book as a wedding present. When she arrived, she saw that all the other guests had brought books too. They were in a big pile in the middle of the room. She added hers to the pile. Later, she wanted to see her present again, but of course could not find hers because all the gifts were wrapped.

"Tell me in one or two words what comes to mind when you think of books," I said.

"I love books. They are escape and adventure."

I tried paraphrasing. "Are you saying you are having trouble finding 'escape' and 'adventure' in your life?"

"That's it!" she cried. "My friends have all left town. They have all moved away to new jobs in new cities. Here I am and I am out of work, stuck in this city, and I can't find a job!"

As we went on to discuss her use of symbols, I glanced down at my notes and realized the answer to the dream we had just heard. Insinuating that she might be blocking her chances in some way, and hoping to release that energy, I offered, "Why don't you take the paper off the books, and you will find your adventure!"

A suggestion you make to yourself while awake can spur the action in the dream. In an example Dr. Faraday describes an exercise she used to face her pursuers in nightmares. She successfully changed the nightmares by imagining herself turning around in the dream and saying to the strangers, "You have no power over me." When the nightmares actually did change, this made her think about how dream manipulation might affect her real, waking self.

"There are two puzzling philosophical questions arising out of this experiment: how does the waking mind, which makes this resolve, know that it is *dream* strangers and not real ones I am meant to confront, and what is the relation between the dream self, which carries over the resolve from waking life, and the elements in the dreaming personality which actually produce the strangers? On the psychological plane, if we accept, as I am sure we must, that dream strangers after my blood are symbols of emotional forces in my own mind, what is the significance, in terms of my inner psychological balance, of my learning to confront them as *strangers in sleep* rather than to come to terms in waking life with the emotions producing them?

"There seem to be two completely opposite possibilities. On the one hand, it may be that this kind of dream manipulation, however useful as a temporary expedient in dealing with nightmares, is treating the symptom rather than the real problem, postponing still further the day when we come to terms with some emotional conflict that has already been thrust aside in waking life. On the other hand, it may be that the process of suggestion sets in motion some process in the sleeping mind which actually alters the 'circuitry' of the brain from which the monster-producing program comes, and that the person who learns to tackle a conflict at the symbolic level during sleep is thereby, without knowing it, actually dealing with the emotional conflict itself."[1]

Here is a final example of how active imagination can set the dreamer to act on a solution in her waking life by changing the dream's ending. A young artistic director shared a dream in a workshop led by Dr. Leo Gold, an Adlerian psychologist who was one of my teachers. The dreamer was twenty years old. She dreamed she was at a party and had two pictures with her. One was of her aunt and her cousin, and one was of her father. A friend wanted to see them, so she gave them to him. Later in the dream, she went looking for the pictures, especially the one of her father, which was precious to her. (She had lost her father eight years before.) She found the friend who said he had put the pictures on top of the fridge. She tried unsuccessfully to reach the pictures. Her taller friend reached up, but only managed to retrieve one picture, the one of her cousin and her aunt.

The young woman awoke with the thought that she simply could not reach her father's picture. When Dr. Gold asked if she had pictures of her dad, she remarked that her aunt had many, but up until then the dreamer had not felt comfortable asking for some. In fact, she had recently been thinking about broaching the subject, but she was afraid that putting up pictures of him might make her feel sad. Recently, she was beginning to feel so far away from her father, even starting to forget what he looked like. Dr. Gold must have wondered if having pictures of her father around might help her feel more connected to him. Maybe that was the answer in the dream.

He suggested the dreamer pull a ladder over to the fridge, climb up, and take the picture of her father down with her. The truth is you can spend time with a departed loved one, any time you like. I also lost my father ten years ago. Perhaps I can't see him, but I speak to him in my mind all the time.

By bringing a ladder into the dream, Dr. Gold succeeded in "freeing" the trapped feeling the dreamer was experiencing. Through the use of new imagery, she was able to "reach" her father. After the interpretation, she went to her aunt and obtained some pictures of her father to hang in her room.

Are the Dreamer's Actions Appropriate to the Situation?

One more area to investigate while looking for the solution to a dream is noticing when the dreamer's actions in the dream are inappropriate. At this point, the reader can connect these actions to his real-life situation. One way to make this connection is by asking, "Is this action typical of your response to your current situation?" If it is, the dreamer can decide whether he wants to continue this kind of response, or choose another type of behavior to deal with the problem. Such was the case with Leslie's Picnic Dream.

Figure 1: The Picnic Is Over: Leslie's Dream

Now that Leslie had discovered the meaning of her dream, it was time for her to step back into the dream again, this time searching for the solution or strength related to her problem. In this dream, we discovered the answer by looking at the action in the story (see page 15).

I asked Leslie, "What are you doing in the dream to get rid of the ants?"

She repeated, "I am trying to push them away with my hands!"

Stepping back outside the dream, I wondered out loud, "But in waking life, would that work? Would you be able to stop ants from multiplying by trying to push them away with your hands?"

"No," she realized.

I offered, "Maybe some Raid might do the trick."

We laughed. And you know what? I received a call from Leslie a few weeks after she had this dream. She was calling to let me know she decided to get out the Raid, and had ended the affair.

So Leslie found the solution to her current issue by focusing on how her method for problem-solving in the dream was inappropriate and, more importantly, ineffective. We arrived at the solution by seeing what was "out of place" or what didn't fit in the action of the dream. The dream mirrored the lack of action Leslie was taking to solve her waking life dilemma too.

The idea of using Raid was a help to Leslie. The thought of how Raid really takes action in getting rid of the ants (her annoyance and panic) spurred Leslie to take action in her waking life situation.

Here's another thought about this dream. It gives a great example of how a nightmare often upsets the dreamer for the purpose of creating movement. The strong emotions in the dream gave Leslie the impetus to move forward towards her goal. This is one of the reasons why I always argue that a nightmare is really a good thing.

A Possible Solution: The Most Obscure Part of the Dream

Famous dream doctors from Freud to Erich Fromm have said that you can't always tell what the most important part of a dream will be. Often the most important piece of a dream appears as a much less important or even insignificant part of the dream story.[2] This means we can sometimes unlock the mystery of a dream by looking at what seems to be an uninteresting or unimportant detail. I saw this happen in one of my work-shops, to a young man who had just completed his master's degree in psychology.

On the weekend of the workshop he had this dream. He was in a school building, waiting by the photocopy machine near the elevator. There was a man sitting and crying. When the elevator opened, he rode down with the man. The dreamer asked the man why he was crying. The man responded, explaining that a tyrannical teacher (whom the dreamer knew) made him want to cry. She had "criticized" him because he said he didn't believe in God. They talked more about the professor and before long, the two men had a big belly laugh about her.

I asked for a general description of the teacher and he said she was too structured, rigid, and insensitive. When I asked if he was feeling too structured and rigid about anything, or if he felt anyone was behaving that way with him recently, he could only connect the feeling to the possible directions he was considering for his future. He was thinking of either completing his Ph.D. in Toronto or traveling overseas. He thought he might be able to secure a teaching position overseas while having an adventure and seeing the world at the same time. That would mean completing his Ph.D. at another time.

I questioned him about the crying man, the possibility of his feeling "criticized," the elevator, and the photocopy machine. His attempts to connect to the crying man and feeling "criticized" in some way were proving difficult. The only feeling he could come up with about an elevator was that he felt "closed in." But when I asked him to say a few things about a seemingly unimportant symbol, the photocopy machine, the mystery of the dream was solved.

"All you need to do with a photocopy machine is simply push a button and *identical copies* just keep spitting themselves out," he said. He gaped at me as he heard himself making the statement. I could almost hear the *click*. "You see," he said, "I'm afraid if I stay here to do my Ph.D., I see myself turning out to be exactly like every other Ph.D. in psychology I know who has ever graduated from this university. I realize they are distinct individuals, but there is something so *identical* about them, something so rigid and insensitive. I think I feel this way because to get there, we all follow the *exact same* courses from the same professors."

"Could you say then that you feel the students follow the structure with the same blind faith that many follow their religion?" When I asked him this, he linked to another metaphor from his dream that he hadn't thought of before. The man was crying because the teacher had criticized him for not believing in God. And so too this dreamer was concerned about being criticized for not wanting to follow blindly on the same path as everyone else in the Psychology Department.

While this student had already connected his dream to the direction his life was taking, you can clearly see the advantage there is to investigating the dream map thoroughly. Because really, it was not until we discussed the photocopy machine that he honed in on his worry so specifically. It was one thing for him to think about seeking some adventure before completing his Ph.D., yet quite a deeper frustration and concern to feel like he might turn into a blind photocopy of everyone else. And in the end this knowledge did actually give him the impetus to change direction in his life.

The Strength in the Dream

In some dreams you will find a direct solution or suggestion, like we did when we took note of missing or inappropriate behavior in the dream in order to replace it with something more appropriate. But many dreams, instead of giving a direct solution, call your attention to the strength of the dream.

Sometimes you find the strength in how the dreamer develops her story line. We saw this happen when the young woman who was looking for adventure had herself invited to the wedding in her dream. She easily might have dreamed there was a wedding that she was not even invited to! You want to get used to looking for these choices in the dreamer's story, because they make an important comment about the dreamer's attitude. Sometimes it is her attitude in general towards life, and yet other times it might indicate how she feels in a particular situation.

Sometimes the strength shows itself in how the person acts inside the dream story. It is just as important to notice when the dreamer's actions are *positive* in the dream as it is to focus on when something is missing in his approach. What is the strength in the psychology student's dream? By stopping to attend to the man crying outside the elevator, the dreamer revealed his sensitivity and caring nature. He had the openness and patience to take a moment and talk. He helped the stranger feel better by sharing a laugh with him. In the dream story, the dreamer demonstrated his ability to maintain a sense of humor and make *himself* feel better, by helping this crying stranger.

Noticing this quality and reminding the dreamer of his strengths is an integral part of good dream work. The strengths that the dreamer brings forward in his dream are the same ones he can now utilize in solving his current problem! In fact, the psychology student's decision to treat himself with the same patience and sensitivity as the crying stranger in his dream helped him proceed to source out possible opportunities abroad. Instead of *criticizing* himself in the face of his "photocopy rut," he decided to *lighten up, stay open, and have some fun.*

Some weeks later, this student called to inform me that he had accepted a position to teach English at a school in Europe.

"Now," he said, "I will be out of that closed-in, rigid, stuck feeling I experienced in the elevator." He was thrilled to be able to expand his horizons before embarking on a Ph.D. program. I liked how he brought a metaphor from his dream (the elevator) out to his conscious conversation. I do that too. It shows a new fluidity between the waking and sleeping mind.

When we are caught up in the throes of an issue, we too often miss noticing our strengths, and more often than not we focus on the scary or negative aspects of the dream. I don't, for example, recollect any clients who have ever called me to discuss a nightmare with the idea of a positive aspect to the dream. Then when we do the analysis, and I've pointed their attention to the strength in the dream, they have all been pleasantly surprised and uplifted. They have suddenly realized that the dream shows them strengths they can tap into in light of their specific situation. Again I reiterate, not by random chance!

Noticing certain characteristics or qualities you have is only one of the benefits in dream work. What about taking the opportunity to practice new, unfamiliar behaviors? And did you know your dream sometimes gives you the chance to reverse your perspective, so that you can not only reflect on how you perceive others, but also how you perceive yourself? In Chapter 4, I will show you more ways to discover and work with the strengths in your dream.

Figure 2: Labrador Retrievers: Johnathan's Dream

In the safety of his dream, Johnathan took the opportunity to see how he felt about his situation by literally watching one possible decision become a reality. By looking back to the dream map (see page 17), we can see now how Johnathan felt about accommodating his girlfriend's request. You'll remember when I inquired, "So, you say you felt happy when you saw the scene in the dream," and he answered, becoming more specific, that the scene seemed "weird" to him. If he decided to acquiesce to his girlfriend's request and make the commitment to marry her, he would be like the house that cannot accommodate the dogs. And this would make him feel weird.

His dream held its answer in the smiling bulldog, a seemingly unimportant symbol. After we uncovered the meaning of the dream, it was Johnathan who pointed to the answer.

"Here's this bulldog," he offered, "stubborn, solid, and like Winston Churchill, 'will not surrender!'"

In the final analysis, Johnathan took an active part in coming to a decision about what approach to take. His interpretation of the dream solidified for him what he kind of already knew. He was not willing to compromise his reluctance to marry for his fear of abandonment, and decided to respond to his girlfriend with the same honesty she had used in approaching him. While he knew that stubbornness was not the most flattering of behaviors, in this instance he felt satisfied with his steadfastness on the subject. That is why the bulldog is smiling in the dream.

Many dream workers believe animals might appear in our dreams when we are following our instincts. This point is well illustrated by the fact that Johnathan didn't want to be put on a leash! With this awareness, Johnathan is now facing his fear of being left or abandoned. Will his relationship turn out to be stable like the Labradors? Will his girlfriend remain loyal to him like the Labradors?

I think it is important to note here that Johnathan had positive feelings about eventually marrying his girlfriend. The dream served its function well, by familiarizing him with the idea of commitment. This dream's repeated image of a child, which illustrates inexperience, newness, or unfamiliarity, is there to help. Johnathan can see that the idea of marriage is still "new" and "weird" to him; but even though he can't accommodate the idea of marriage yet, it essentially makes him happy. Now that he understands the dream, Johnathan can be more patient with himself while embarking on this new phase of his life.

In a year from now, as Johnathan becomes more comfortable with the idea of marriage and has another dream on the subject, I would not be surprised to hear there are teenagers or young adults in his dreams. That would be a sign that he is experiencing some "growth" or movement on the issue.

Figure 3: Deborah's Dream

Ever hear the expression, "When this is all over, I'm going to sit down and have a nervous breakdown"? Deborah's unconscious was expressing the tension she felt in order to let her take care of the business of moving and settling into a new city. That is one of the important functions this dream served and another of many reasons why I believe a nightmare is a good thing. It is just one of the many ways your unconscious takes care of you (see page 20 for the dream map).

Your dreams not only give you the place to practice new behaviors, they also provide a safe environment to become familiar with emotions you are anticipating. Deborah's dream provided her with the opportunity to practice dealing with the frightened and excited feelings brought about by the move. For example, if you spend five, six, or sometimes seven nights in a row having scary dreams, it makes sense that after a while you would start feeling more comfortable with that emotion. You become a little numb. And once you have practiced and become familiar with the emotion, you can adjust more rapidly to the new experience during the day. This was what happened with Deborah.

Here's something else about her dream. The manner in which the buildings fell, without so much as a brick out of place, offers an important clue about how Deborah reacts to unsettling experiences. Besides allowing that she "needed the practice" with the pressures of the move, like most of us, Deborah is generally uncomfortable confronting the emotions inherent in change.

Two weeks after we interpreted her dream, Deborah called to give me two footnotes to this story. The first was that her boyfriend had moved to Toronto. When she arrived at his apartment, Deborah realized it was part of the same complex as the Radisson Hotel. (She is not sure if she knew that at the time she had the dream.) Deborah's dream, it turns out, had some precognitive elements in it. The second thing she told me was that, one evening on a weekend trip back home to Montreal, she went dancing with her friends at the piano bar in the Radisson Hotel. Deborah explained, "As we all left the hotel, I suddenly realized for the first time that I no longer live in Montreal! I became so overcome with sadness, I sat down and had myself a good cry. I felt great after that. Refreshed!" Deborah's understanding of the fuller meaning in her dream gave her the opportunity to acknowledge her difficulty with, as she calls it, "falling apart." And with that awareness, she allowed herself the luxury of expressing herself.

If you've ever wondered where those feelings go that "have not hit you yet," now you know! Feelings don't just disappear; they may appear in your dreams because they have to go somewhere. Dreams often provide the opportunity for us to acknowledge our real feelings and work them out. They let us deal with them using our unconscious self. In this case, Deborah was able to attend to the move in a relatively calm manner during the day, while her dream dealt with the frightened feelings her conscious, waking mind would not acknowledge.

Figure 4: The Uncle Dream: Sarah's Dream
Mirror #1

Dr. Freud wrote, "Dreams are quite incapable of expressing the alternative 'either–or'; it is their custom to take both members of this alternative into the same context, as though they had an equal right to be there."[3]

In her Uncle Dream (see page 22), Sarah expressed her dilemma about rewriting her paper by presenting both sides of the "either-or" polarity inside the dream. "Either I am going to settle for the grade I already have, which isn't the best I can do, or I am going to behave more like my aunt would in my situation and bear down into the rewrite, making sure I have done the best I can. But I don't feel like doing the rewrite!" As she well describes in the dream, these two choices made Sarah "feel confused."

It is precisely because Sarah was so far over on the uncle's side, in her temptation to accept the grade she got the first time around, that she incubated a dream with questions like, "How do I say 'no' to making a commitment to myself?" This dream presented Sarah with the two choices in order to pull her away from the extreme "Uncle" position. Your unconscious does this for you when you *yourself* know, somewhere deep inside, that you are not really doing the best thing for yourself. Sarah knew inside what she really wanted for herself. She really wanted to be there, to make that commitment to herself. That is why she created this specific dream. She had to move herself away from the part that reacts the way her uncle might react in this situation.

The aunt's appearance in the dream is twofold. She is there to solidify, to repeat, for the sake of getting the point across to Sarah's conscious mind, that this dream will help her measure and re-evaluate her position on the school assignment. We know this because Sarah was working on that very assignment with her aunt, the same night she had the dream. The aunt's *symbolic* role in terms of the rewrite was reinforced by her *actual* role in helping Sarah with the real assignment. I remember how Sarah described her aunt's attitude.

"She is so kind to have taken the time with me," she explained. "You know, she goes over everything, every point so thoroughly with you when doing something. Imagine. She didn't have to take all that time with me. You can really see how committed she is, not only as a teacher but her wanting to help *me*. She is very caring. And there is another thing too. When my aunt has marked up one of your papers, you get a very clear direction about what is missing from it!"

I asked, "Do you think there is a connection in how committed you describe your aunt feels towards you versus the level of commitment you feel towards yourself?"

When she heard this question, Sarah saw very clearly that she had to get more on the side of behaving like her aunt. The simple act of watching how her aunt works made it easier for Sarah to move in that direction. This gave her the motivation she needed to recommit herself back to the term paper. I am saying here that Sarah's aunt was the answer to her dilemma. She needed to adopt her aunt's behavior.

You will find the answer to the Second Mirror in Sarah's dream, or the situation with her boyfriend, in Chapter 4.

Figure 5: The Emma-Jo Dream

Working with this dream, I discovered two different variations on the *same* basic problem—my fear that someone might steal my business idea, and the general (and closely related) issue of my professional insecurity (see pages 26–27 for the dream map). While the Emma-Jo dream did not direct me to a specific solution, it did point me to strengths I had that could help me in my situation.

A very significant positive aspect to the dream was my feeling just as it ended. Do you remember what I said? "As we were turning, I called out to her. I woke up as I was calling her name. At the end of the dream, though, I knew she was going to wait for us." This is very important. It tells you (and me) that in the face of my worst fear of losing Emma-Jo, I feel comfortable and confident it is all going to work out okay. This is a comment not only on my attitude in relation to someone possibly stealing my business idea, but my general attitude towards life. In the face of my fears as they developed during the week of the conference, I had to tap into this positive and comfortable attitude I normally adopt. The dream brings it forward by showing how sure and confident I feel that Emma-Jo will wait while we turn the car around.

To that strength, I added another ingredient. I found a solution in my Emma-Jo dream by using active imagination. I took the opportunity to finish the dream differently. Instead of having the dream end when my husband turned the car around to get her, I imagined the dream continuing. I saw us getting to her. Then I pictured myself getting out of the car and walking together with her. I imagined little Emma-Jo and me coming through the tall grass to a long sandy beach by the ocean, with the warm sun shining on us. This ending secured a positive resolution for my dream. It spurred the confidence I had embarking on a new field, and let me really *feel* that the situation would turn out all right. It helped me substitute my panicked insecurity for a feeling of serenity.

As for my concern about someone stealing my idea, let us examine again the way in which my unconscious chose to develop the story. Was I walking down St. Catherine Street East with no weapon to defend myself? No. I had my scissors with me. Even when they weren't visible, I still had them in the glove compartment of the car. My weapon for protecting my idea is in fact my creativity! When I made this connection, I realized that my business idea would require a certain kind of talent and ability to deliver a message in a certain way. It is precisely my creativity that will allow me to make my idea a successful one. Anyone can try an idea. But your creativity and application determine the success you achieve. And my way is my own way. Someone may be able to steal my idea, but they cannot steal me! And so, I do have my scissors with me all the time. I have myself and my creativity and my potential with me all the time too, even when I pack it away where no one can see it.

The Value of Knowing
and Applying Different Frameworks

Let's recap what I discovered so far, from looking at my Emma-Jo dream. First, let me say that I specifically chose my Emma-Jo dream for this book because it is a rather involved dream with many subplots, actions, and symbols. This analysis demonstrates, and will continue to do so throughout the rest of the book, why it's worthwhile to explore many different avenues for the strength and solutions you can uncover in the dream. The different frameworks you choose to look at will bring you different kinds of inspiration. Often a different approach can point you to a new solution or strength on top of what you've already found. Or maybe trying a new framework can give you a solution where you couldn't find one before.

For example, take a look at what I call the first level of interpretation, attaching the dream to a current issue in your life. When I was able to connect all the feelings in my dream—the adventure, the excitement, the fear and discomfort—to the ASD conference, it gave me a greater awareness of my emotional reaction, which I was trying to suppress or ignore at the time. In and of itself, this awareness took away my feeling spooked, an emotion that might have stuck with me all day if I had never understood the meaning of the dream. And it also clued me in to *why* I was feeling so spooked: the dream showed me how *dangerous* it was for me to be discussing my business ideas so freely! If for no other reason than to motivate me to stop discussing my business idea, the dangerous or scary parts of the dream served me well.

In the last section of the dream, I was able to link the play on words around Emma-Jo *walking into a field* with my sense of professional insecurity. Again, I was feeling very insecure during the conference, but I was trying to push this emotion out of my conscious awareness. It would have been better for me to con-sciously accept my feeling of insecurity and then work to resolve it. This was exactly what my Emma-Jo dream helped me do, once I understood it. For one thing, the polarity between Andy and me in the dream can direct me towards a possible solution in my waking life. (As you'll recall, I am screaming and panicky in the dream while he stays calm and takes care of busi-ness.) I chose to move towards the "Andy" side of the polarity and adopt a more businesslike and confident approach to the conference and to the "dream-interpretation business" in gen-eral. This has, in fact, helped me feel more professionally secure and less concerned about what university degrees I hold. I have come to feel confident about my capabilities, and no longer equate them with having a Ph.D. or degree in psychology. As well as this solution, the dream helped me find other strengths and feel more confident during those crucial early months at the Dream Interpretation Center. It reminded me to tap into the positive attitude I usually adopt and apply it to my current situation. When I used active imagination to finish the dream on a positive note, this especially helped me visualize and achieve a sense of security, tranquility, and inner certainty about the path I had chosen. And finally, for even more reas-surance, the dream showed me with the scissors how I always have my potential and my creative edge with me. Each of these frameworks gave me a different source of strength and inner confidence that I would pull through okay, and that I had some-thing unique and useful to contribute to my new field.

You will discover in the coming chapters how I worked through deeper layers in the Emma-Jo Dream. In doing so, I not only found out *why* I was reacting to the ASD conference in the way that I was, but so too I was able to shed light on some other choices I have made in my life. My point is that, even if you just make a quick dream map and ask a few questions about the dream, this is valuable in and of itself. And if you want to look deeper into your dream, spend more time with it and explore all the different sides, your dream can reveal even more. You can take however much you want.

LEVEL TWO:

Using Your Whole Mind

CHAPTER FOUR

Listening to Your Underinvested Side

"If you hate a person, you hate something in him that is part of yourself. What isn't part of ourselves doesn't disturb us."

—Hermann Hesse

In this chapter, I will introduce a Gestalt approach to dream work. If you haven't found the solution to your problem through the methods I discussed in Chapter 3, certainly a Gestalt approach will move you closer to finding one. This wonderful method not only helps a dreamer connect with solutions to his problems, but almost always points to the strength in the dream. The concepts in this chapter are, as far as I am concerned, the most important learning one can capture from dream work.

Dr. Carl Gustav Jung said that each of us, newly born, starts out with a feeling of wholeness, a powerful and complete sense of the Self. This means we are born with all possibilities of behavior. We are giving; we are selfish. We are outgoing; we are shy. We are comfortable expressing our needs and we are not. We have the ability to feel frightened and we can be brave.

The people who bring us up send out messages. These messages might be direct or indirect, but somehow the messages ("You should do this," and, "You shouldn't do that!") reinforce that it is better to be one way than another. And so, through the years, we form "habits" for the behaviors we learn are accept-

able. Then we forget about all the other ways of responding to
events in our lives. You could say we become "overinvested" in
a particular way of reacting. And of course, we become "underinvested" in the other parts of our psyche. It was Jung who first
suggested that dreams can compensate for these distortions in
the way we see things, slanted by the overinvested parts of our
character.[1]

We all face situations in our lives where we may need to use
any number of different behaviors, depending on the circumstances. If we always respond to events in the same way, we
have little choice on how to proceed in a given situation. We
need to access our "underinvested" or alienated parts. The disowned aspects of our character appear in our dreams when we
need to use them. Generally, these character traits appear in the
dream as anyone or anything else, but not as the dreamer. The
following is an example of how this happens.

One of my teachers shared a story that really made an impression on me. She grew up with a friend who was an only child. The
"message" that friend received from her parents was that it was
okay to feel selfish. She didn't have to share. She could feel comfortable expressing her needs. This teacher of mine was brought
up in a family with a sibling, and the "messages" *she* received
were, "Don't be selfish. Share with your brother." As a result, this
woman grew up with difficulty expressing her own needs. Now,
twenty-five years later, both women were in the hospital at the
same time, recovering from surgery. When the only child's friends
called the hospital to see if there was anything they could bring
her, she felt comfortable asking for a pastrami sandwich with fries
and lots of mustard. When asked the same question by her
friends, the teacher responded, "It's okay, you don't have to bring
me anything. I'm fine." This example illustrates how one individual has become overinvested in her giving and sharing side, to
the point where even when it is quite appropriate to ask for what

she wants, she doesn't even realize she can. That part of her is too underinvested.

All the Parts of the Dream Are You

Now the stage is set for me to explain how it is possible, on the same evening as this teacher refused a sandwich from her friends, that she might have a dream with someone she considers "selfish" in it. Why? Because her "unselfish" behavior in the hospital is inappropriate. She needs to access the disowned or alienated, "selfish" part of herself. It is there! It's simply lying dormant from childhood waiting to be woken up. When a character trait is "missing" and needed in a particular situation, that trait will very likely present itself in the person's dreams.

Allow me to further explain. All the parts of the dream are you. You are the producer, the director, and all the players.[2] You are even the wall, the water, the road, the building, the snake, the monkey, and the monster. When you go to see a movie starring Julia Roberts, she doesn't play all the parts! Likewise, in our dreams, we cannot have only one face playing all the parts. For example, I am Layne the wife, the mother, the daughter, the aunt, and the friend. I am the giving person, the selfish person, the writer, the radio personality, the dream analyst, and the businessperson. I have a plethora of emotions; I can be sad, happy, weak, strong, assertive, and shy, angry and frustrated, optimistic and energetic.

In our dreams we usually take the role we most easily connect to in our waking lives, and then give out the other parts in the dream to people, animals, objects, or things. We use them as metaphors and symbols to say something to ourselves that only we can understand. The dreamer "projects" the alienated character traits that he needs onto something or someone else in the dream. So our dreams show us all the different parts we need to be fully ourselves, in every situation. This is what Perls, the founder of Gestalt dream work, meant when he said we are naturally self-reg-ulating organisms. He wrote, ". . . responsibility can also be spelled *response-ability*: The ability to respond, to have thoughts, reactions, emotions in a certain situation. Now, this responsibility, the ability to be what one is, is expressed through the word 'I.'"[3]

In situations like the one in the hospital, where it is certainly understandable and acceptable for the teacher to say, "Yes, please bring me a sandwich," we often dream about someone we think of as selfish. This is because our unconscious is trying to call our attention to that selfish part of ourselves we need.

Here's another example. When I was seven years old and my father reprimanded me, I was not exactly allowed to look up at him and say, "Excuse me, I am not comfortable with the way you are speaking to me." My father was old-fashioned European in his child-rearing philosophies, and that comment would have landed me in my room after dinner for a few days, not to mention a sore behind! So along the way I learned to keep my displeasure to myself. It became my way of being, my habit. I followed this habit and forgot about all the other ways of responding when people said things I didn't like. Perls describes what happens to us when we limit ourselves this way: "You do not allow yourself—or you are not allowed to be totally yourself. So your ego boundary shrinks more and more. Your power, your energy, becomes smaller and smaller. Your ability to cope with the world becomes less and less—and more and more rigid, more and more allowed only to cope as your character, as your preconceived pattern, prescribes it."[4]

If my husband is speaking rudely to me now, it is no longer appropriate for me to stand there shaking in my boots and take it like I might have when I was six. Now I have the power to change my reaction. My dreams can help me do this by showing me the disowned parts of myself that would speak up to Andy.

In this scenario, I might dream of someone I know who is comfortable about expressing how she feels. Now this might be my grandmother who, by the way, passed away when I was only three years old. The reason I might choose my grandmother is because, all the time I was growing up, these are the kinds of phrases I heard when my parents spoke of her: "Well, she really knew how to say what was on *her* mind! Boy! You never had to wonder about what she was thinking! She'd let you know just exactly what! And if she liked you, you'd know it, and if she didn't, you'd know it too." And my unconscious would choose her for my dream story because I need to utilize that part of myself in my current situation with my husband. I need to "become" my grandmother in order to say to him, "I am not happy with how you are speaking with me! I will not stand by and be treated like this. You are going to have to approach me with more respect when you have something to say to me."

Perls suggests, "You see how you can use *everything* in a dream. If you are pursued by an ogre in a dream, and you *become* the ogre, the nightmare disappears. You re-own the energy that is invested in the demon. Then the power of the ogre is no longer outside, alienated, but inside where you can use it."[5] I need to respond as if I were my grandmother. That is the answer the dream gives me to my current situation with Andy.

So often I hear from people who have dreamed about someone they know who has passed on. They typically ask, "Does it mean I'm going to die because I dreamed of my dead cousin last night?" I normally say to them, "Tell me a few things that come to your mind when you think of that cousin." The answer might come back, "He was so easy-going. Took everything in stride." I'm always so happy to respond to a worried dreamer that he can relax. His cousin might have just appeared in the dream to help him access that "easy-going, take things in your stride" part of himself. He is possibly taking something too seriously in his waking life.

We have some choices about how we can try on the different parts of our dreams. For one, there's what I'd call a full-blown Gestalt technique. This is when you role-play, by speaking as the different parts of the dream in order to get in touch with your disowned parts. In Chapter 5 I'll show you this technique in detail, but for now here's a quick example. During one workshop, a gentleman client described a dream in which he was on a massive jet coming in for a landing and missed the runway. He thought he was going to crash. The jet landed smoothly in a large field. He said there was no road.

I asked him to be the jet, to speak as it would speak. He said, "I am a jet. I am strong and powerful. I have a big engine. I am pointed in a direction, heading for the runway. I can see the runway. I know exactly where I am going to land. Oh my God! I have missed the runway!" He suddenly interrupted himself, having connected to the dream's meaning. "I know what the dream is about! I lost a house that I had put a bid in for. And I lost it despite the fact that I was very aggressive with my bid. I didn't *land* the deal. And I was so sure I would own that house!"

I asked him to continue with what else the jet might say. He offered, "I am scared I am going to crash! But I don't! I am landed in a field. There is no road here, no runway, and I have landed safely!"

I asked, "So then you're saying that you seem to have landed safely, but are not sure which way to go next?"

"Yes," he said. "And the truth is I was so in love with that one and only house, I *do* feel like I have no direction now."

When I asked him to speak as the field, he said, "I am the field. I have wide, open space. I have room to move. I have grass that blows in the wind and can move in any direction." He added, "Well, what a nice thought!" He had found the positive side of the dream and the answer to his problem by connecting to his ability to move in the wind and change direction. He also got in touch with his power by becoming the jet.

The most obvious advantage to speaking out as the different parts of the dream is that you are able to literally become that part of yourself. This can be extremely helpful when you need to access a certain character trait in your current situation and it is sleeping. This gentleman was so in touch with his powerful, jetlike side that he was missing the other part of himself that knows how to let go. He needed this other part to move with a situation he could not control. When he spoke up as the grass in the field, he was able to see this "move with the wind" character trait in a good sense, and find the feeling of freedom and release that went along with it.

Sometimes using a Gestalt framework with a nightmare helps you connect to what scared you in the dream and realize that the part exists in you. Like Perls said, if you know you have a strong "monster" inside, you can get a tremendous feeling of power to deal with the current problems in your life. In this case, the dreamer was able to discover a part of himself that is filled with a wonderful sense of freedom and movement. So you don't only have to use this approach in order to connect to the ogre in your dream. Any part of any dream can help you access character traits that help you respond to the events in your life.

Maybe you feel uncomfortable about role-playing your dream. That's okay. Just knowing that all the parts are you can help you feel less intimidated or separated from the parts of your dream that seem foreign to you. Interestingly, only a few days after that workshop, I came across another young man who told me he has a recurring dream of being a passenger aboard a big plane. But in his dream he is sure he is going to crash. Unlike the first dreamer who was so in touch with his powerful, jetlike side, this dreamer felt far more connected to the frightened passenger! And where the previous dreamer's main focus was on how he landed in a field, this dreamer described, "Each time the plane goes out of control and does all the things a crazy stunt plane does. And yet after being tossed around and turned upside down the plane lands safely on the ground." I pointed out to him that he is not only the passenger inside the plane but the jet too. He has the potential to toss himself around, turn himself upside down, sure he is going to "crash," and yet after all of it he is able to land safely on the ground. He looked at me stunned. He was absolutely astounded to realize this part belongs to him too! And I should add, so happy to connect with his "jetlike" side. This showed him that he has the energy, reserve, and the ability to find his "ground" all inside himself. He immediately became less fearful of the jet, and I expected this image would change for him in future dreams he might remember (if, for that matter, the dream returned again).

Just after I wrote this piece I had occasion to speak to this dreamer. He wondered why the image of the scary plane ride had gone away. Most often once you have freed up the energy tied to the dream by understanding it, the image doesn't return. So this young man didn't have to actually act out or speak as the different parts of his dream. His simple awareness about how the whole dream represented different aspects of himself helped him realize he might want to tap into the exact part of his psyche he seemed so afraid of. Either way, it's valuable to recognize that all the parts of the dream are parts of you. It opens up your choices. It helps you to understand that in each of life's situations, you have options on how you might want to proceed.

Seeing Yourself from Different Perspectives

When you look at your dreams from this point of view, you will get different perspectives on your attitudes and behavior. As we just saw, the gentleman in my workshop was able to get a new perspective on his own approach to buying a house. His first method was literally the "jetlike" approach to the runway, a single-minded attitude that didn't work. But when he recognized that the field also represented a part of his psyche, he was able to connect to a more flexible side of himself.

When you know your dream represents different parts of you, you can use the dream to give you several different perspectives on the same subject or event in your life. I mean, not just how you feel about someone else's role in your situation, but your own role too. This can help you in your relationships. Here's an example of what I mean.

An executive named Kevin called me from Florida one day, with a dream that started him wondering if he should check himself into an institution. He told me very simply that he was standing at the front of a classroom, giving a lecture about hygiene to a room full of animals. He remembered some squirrels, and a chimpanzee too. Kevin explained, "The chimpanzee had large teeth; a big broom was used to brush them." When I asked how he felt, he described himself as feeling perfectly comfortable while teaching this class in the dream. He was completely in charge.

"What comes to mind when you think of hygiene?" I asked.

"How clean you keep yourself is how people judge you," he responded. When I questioned Kevin about the chimpanzees, he said he thought they are smart. "They copy what they see and can be trained to behave the way you want them to."

"What about big teeth?" I asked.

"Big teeth," he repeated, thinking. "Well, I'll tell you that teeth in general are very important, because people often draw their first impressions of others from the appearance and cleanliness of their teeth."

Lastly I inquired of Kevin what he thinks of when squirrels

come to mind. "Squirrels are annoying! And they are ubiquitous! Also, they store their nuts for the winter."

When Kevin looked more closely at this dream, he realized
that he was in the process of re-evaluating or *judging* several issues.
For one thing, although he was in love with his future bride, he felt
concerned about certain aspects of her character and wondered
whether they would change after living together. Thinking there
might be a link to the hygiene, I asked, "Do you mean you are
concerned about, or judging how well she keeps herself?"

"Oh no! It isn't about that. But I *am* making some judgments about other things that bother me about her. And you
know, the fact is getting married is a very important decision
for me. I just wonder if those qualities she has which disturb me
will change after we have been together for some time."

So Kevin's use of hygiene pointed to the fact that he was
judging his fiancée. There were *big teeth* in his dream, because he
was saying to himself that the *something very important* was his
future. The question became, "Will she be the chimpanzee and
over time, copy the behavior I show her?" Was he *in charge*
within the relationship, as he felt in the dream?

Here was my suggestion. Knowing how difficult change is,
Kevin might have a better chance trying to change *himself*, and
his own attitudes, than to gamble his happiness on successfully
changing his future wife. I suggested he might think about the
characteristics that bother him about her, and accept that they
might never change. Once he accepted this, he then needed to
decide if he could change *himself* enough so that they no longer
bothered him. I asked, "Do you still want to marry her, even if
she is not a chimpanzee?"

During this conversation I asked Kevin whether someone or
something "was ubiquitous, and annoying" in his life at that time.

"Who or what do you think the squirrels might be?"

Kevin connected immediately to a second issue he was

facing. I was not surprised to hear this. I see this multiple problem-solving ability appear in so many dreams, especially since, in this case, his second problem ended up being related to the issue with his girlfriend. Kevin was feeling oppressed by his parents. He said exasperated, "Their *opinions* and *judgments* of me *are everywhere*! You see my parents are not so well off financially, and lately, they've been applying pressure on me. They want me to stop thinking about putting money away for my fiancée and me. Instead, they are asking me to give my savings to them."

Kevin's parents had succeeded in making him feel guilty. In this regard, he was evaluating if *he* were the chimpanzee. Would he behave in the way his parents trained him, and acquiesce to their demands?

In this dream, the squirrels serve several purposes. They represent not only Kevin's parents and their ubiquitous judgments, but himself as well, in that he had been storing money away for himself and his bride, just as squirrels store their nuts for the winter. I also wondered, did the squirrels have something to say about Kevin's own judgmental side? So I asked him, "Do you think that in the case of your trying to control your fiancée's behavior, you are the squirrels, with your opinions and judgments everywhere?" Kevin saw the connection and agreed with me.

Where is the learning in the dream? When Kevin and I applied the framework that all the parts of the dream were parts of him, we saw how all those animals in the room represented his different thoughts and feelings on the subject. They were the different aspects of his character talking with each other. He was weighing and re-evaluating how much he wants to control, and how much he feels comfortable *being* controlled.

I believe the answer in this dream lies not in the extremes, but somewhere in the middle. I asked Kevin what he thought of my idea. He admitted, "Well, in relation to my fiancée, I might practice being less of a squirrel and more of a chimpanzee. On the other hand, in relation to my Mum and Dad I'd like to get feeling more comfortable about being a squirrel and less comfortable about being a chimpanzee. I'm not suggesting that I want to horde my money, but simply that it is reasonable that I be able to put my own needs first." Dreams very often have symbols that provide you with the ability to see things from more than one perspective. Isn't it something to think how when thinking about his concerns with his future bride, it is Kevin wanting to control? He wants his fiancée to be a chimpanzee. Yet, when he looked at his dream as it mirrored his issue with his parents, now he became the chimpanzee!

After discussing his unique and intelligent use of symbols in the dream, he no longer felt his dream odd or weird at all. Kevin's dream reminds us why the use of dictionaries in dream work should be extremely limited. Our unconscious is always taking things in. Images that you don't even realize you are taking in are imbedding themselves in your unconscious in their very own personal way. Look at this dreamer's unique definition of chimpanzees and how they bring to his mind an element of hygiene!

Making Healthy Projections: Being Lucid while Awake

Typically, if you notice a particular trait in someone else that you disdain, it is usually an indication that this trait is an underinvested aspect of your own character. You see something in the other person that reminds you of a part of yourself. You (unconsciously) know it exists, but you don't like it. Interpreting and understanding a dream helps us find the parts of ourselves we need, and identifying with the various components of the dream counteracts alienation. You learn to recognize *all* the parts of yourself, even when you see them in somebody else. It is a healthy "projection" if you identify something in others that you *know* exists in you, even if you don't like that part, because at least you know who you are and what you have in common with other people. An unhealthy projection is when you have no awareness of your own character "flaws" so you get extra irritated when you see them in someone else, because you don't know that they're also a part of you. The most important message I can send is that we *all* have our strengths and weaknesses. Our weaknesses are simply underdeveloped or disowned aspects of our character. I do not equate "weaknesses" with something "bad." Weaknesses or behaviors we want to strengthen are the normal course of events for humans, I hope!

Having this knowledge helps me. When I *do* find myself feeling really aggravated with some character trait I see in someone else, I take the opportunity to turn the questions inside myself. I ask, "What is going on here with me? Why is this person making me feel this way? Does this person have something that I am missing in my behavior?" Now the judgment is no longer pointed towards the other individual. I have turned the focus on myself, which I might add, is where it belongs. The reason it belongs there is because I have a much greater chance of changing something in myself than I do attempting to change someone else. And besides, that's not what I am here to learn. I am here to learn to grow from within, not to try to control or change someone else. Don't you think the world would be a happier place if we all tried directing our focus inward more often?

Here is a great illustration of this principle at work. After not seeing or speaking with her in some thirty years, I recently have been reunited with an old camp friend who now lives in

Utah. Her name is Michelle. We now e-mail and speak regularly on the phone. For a while Michelle was tossing around the idea of joining Weight Watchers. She had been expressing real ambivalence to me about taking the plunge. On the morning of the day she was to attend her first meeting, she woke with the following dream. She was so distressed by the dream that she telephoned me in a panic to understand its meaning.

Michelle dreamed that the parents of a friend of hers were throwing a big party in honor of renewing their wedding vows. Michelle was carrying her father in the dream. "He was so sick," she said. "I think he had cancer. I was carrying him around like one of my kids. He must have only weighed about sixty pounds!"

I asked Michelle, "How did you feel in the dream?"

"I didn't want them to see me like that. I didn't want them to see me walking around carrying my father. I know what this dream is about," Michelle added.

"Oh, good. That makes things easy. And for *sure you* know what it is about."

"It is about the fact that just in the last few days, I have been involved in helping my father make some decisions about helping a family member who is in some financial need. The dream is a metaphor about how I am slowly becoming the patriarch. There is a shift taking place."

I inquired, "Is there an element of you 'not wanting to be seen' providing this help? I ask because that is what you described in the dream. You said you didn't want them to see you."

"No, actually there is no element of feelings like that at all. The whole topic is out in the open. Everyone who is involved knows we are going to help."

"I agree with you about the metaphor of a shift in the patriarchal duties taking place," I explained, "but usually at the first level of meaning, the dream will mirror all the feelings about the subject it is addressing. You may have touched on one of the deeper meanings of the dream. Would you like to see if we can find the first level of meaning?"

"Yes. I would love to!"

I continued, "Why don't you tell me a couple of things that come to mind when you think about these people who were having the party."

"They're classy, sophisticated types, you know? They run with the crowd, and what the crowd does. I don't like them."

I admit that the minute I heard Michelle say these people "run with the crowd" and she doesn't like them, I was reminded of something she had said to me earlier in that very conversation. She had said that she planned on attending a Weight Watchers meeting away from the area where she lives, because she didn't want to be around a "certain crowd." I looked down to the dream map I was creating and noticed that these people were having a party to renew their vows to each other. I asked her, "Do you think the fact that you mentioned the couple were renewing their vows to each other could have anything to do with you making a commitment to yourself about your weight loss?"

She responded immediately. "No. The fact that they were renewing their vows to each other was a very insignificant part of the dream. What was important was that my father was so sick and that I was carrying him around. He was only sixty pounds!"

"Okay. Why don't you tell me a few things about your dad. What is his character like?"

"My father is a nonconformist. He is anti-establishment. I'm like my father."

"I see a polarity. So while you describe your father as a nonconformist, you say the people who were having a party are the type who go with the crowd. There's this pull between those two energies." I confessed my suspicion. "I know this is cheating. I call it cheating when I know the dreamer, and they have shared with me what they are going through at a particular time. I can make an educated guess as to the meaning of a dream. It is an advantage I don't have with a dreamer who calls in to a radio show, or someone who contacts me over the Internet."

"Tell me what you think it's about."

"Well, but you have to say if it doesn't fit."

"I will."

"The dream at the first level is always about something that either happened to you the day before, or something that you thought about. Considering that tonight is the night you are going to a meeting about your weight, here are some thoughts I have as to why that is the subject of the dream. One is the fact that you mentioned just in this conversation that you intend on traveling to a meeting out of your area to avoid seeing a certain crowd who you say you don't like, same as you describe the couple in the dream. The second reason is because your ambivalence about joining the program would explain how the polarity appears in the dream. And the third clue you gave me is how you keep saying how many pounds your father weighs in the dream!"

Michelle was laughing. I felt comfortable continuing, even touching back to the area she had so adamantly dismissed only a few minutes before. "This subject of renewing vows. While you think it is irrelevant to the dream's meaning," I explained, "very often what you think is the most unimportant aspect of a dream turns out to be the *most* important element. And after all, isn't your making a commitment to do something good for yourself, kind of like renewing your vows to yourself?"

"Yes," she said. "I see where you are going here. And I like it. And you know what else about that couple who are having that party? They are so bloody skinny! They are totally weight-obsessed people!" Now Michelle had found the link. "But why would my father be sick in the dream?"

"Well, what do you think? Here is what you said to me

when describing how you felt in the dream. You said, 'I didn't want them to see me like that. I didn't want them to see me walking around carrying my father.'"

Michelle said into the phone, "I didn't want them to see me carrying around sixty pounds!"

"Yes!" I agreed, laughing at her use of play on words. "And maybe that is the polarity. If our society dictates to us that it is better to be thin, then we might conclude that you are conforming, or 'going with the crowd' if you are thin. And by remaining overweight, you are in a sense a nonconformist. There would be the polarity established. There's the pull. Are you going to conform or not? Is your father overweight?"

"No. He's not."

"So then, in this instance do you think behaving in an anti-establishment way is unhealthy? I mean, if you stay overweight and are then a nonconformist, it doesn't mean you are doing the healthiest thing for yourself in continuing with this behavior, does it?"

"No. And that would be how he is sick in the dream. I am carrying around not only the weight but I am also carrying this sick part of me. And also, most importantly, I don't want to be seen with this weight. Especially in front of people like them!"

My point in discussing this dream is to illustrate to you that Michelle dislikes these people precisely because she herself is like them in some ways. This is an example of what I mean when I say that we project the parts of ourselves we don't like, or don't want to acknowledge onto others. Said simply, when Michelle says that she *doesn't want to be seen* (carrying extra weight) by these people, she is really saying she doesn't want to be seen by *herself* carrying the extra weight! It is important for her to tap into the fact that she herself has a conformist side.

But why is this something Michelle needs to know? Because her conformist side is the part that is judging herself. The first step in being kind to yourself is discovering that you are being *unkind* to yourself. How can you get there if you believe it is someone else doing the judging, when really it is yourself? Michelle doesn't feel like she measures up to what *she* thinks she should look like. When she describes those people as weight-obsessed, she is saying that she herself is weight-obsessed. And the fact is that the harder we are on ourselves, the harder it is to succeed in reaching our goals. Being hard on yourself can block your success. And being hard on yourself *without even realizing it* just makes it that much harder to succeed.

Michelle needs to realize she is exactly who she dislikes. Michelle may be a nonconformist in many ways. She may even be a nonconformist in *most* areas of her life. But when the subject has to do with weight, Michelle is a conformist. This shouldn't make her feel like a worse person. It isn't something she has to be ashamed of. When she becomes less conflicted about these different parts coexisting inside her, Michelle will have opened the door to successfully renewing her vows to herself. Now that she is able to focus her task inward, she can discover that she doesn't need to hate either part of herself, or refuse to acknowledge that her conformist side exists. Hey! In this case she *needs* that conformist attitude! If she didn't have it, maybe she'd just continue to gain weight not caring a hoot for what she looks like! Michelle can celebrate her conformist side. She needs to embrace it! It will ensure her success in renewing her vow to herself.

Creating a Wholeness Within You

Developing character traits as we need them in given situations is what Perls referred to as "maturation." It is what Jung called "individuation." They were all saying the same thing. No matter whose writings I have read, everyone had his or her own way of expressing the importance of developing all our potential. Jung believed that the only sure way to maturation lies in our willingness to recognize and practice our disowned character traits. He called them our *shadows,* because they are the opposite of the way we usually are. Without them we remain fragmented.⁶ With them we not only help ourselves respond to different situations, but we also become whole.

Dream work helps you to become more flexible, unpredictable, and open in your approach to each situation as it arises. The only reason we can refer to parts of ourselves as "disowned" is because we never use them. As we saw with Michelle, we usually reject these traits at first and refuse to admit they are part of us. The next time you find yourself thinking that someone is judging you, stop. Ask yourself, "Is this really more a case of me judging myself?" Or maybe you are putting yourself in that person's place and thinking that if you were her, you *would* be judging yourself! For example, say you do something that you think will offend a friend of yours. There you are, thinking your friend is offended, when maybe she isn't at all! It is only you thinking she *must* be offended, because *you* would be offended if someone did that to you.

Either way you look at it, what you think someone else is thinking about you can sometimes say a lot more about you than it does about the other person. You are "projecting" your own stuff onto someone else. And like I said before, your projections onto other people usually come from parts of *yourself* you don't want. It is important to recognize when a judgment, or any other thought you assign to someone else, actually *belongs* to that person. If not, you are looking at your Shadow.

This is one reason why you want to catch yourself when you feel someone else is judging you. Now, you may be thinking, I'd rather not know all this! In a lot of ways, it's easier not to know when you are projecting your own thoughts onto someone else.

It means there's a voice inside you that's judging you, or maybe even dislikes you. But you know what? It's better to have that awareness. Then you can examine that voice in the open and decide whether it's right or not. If you decide that *you* are the one who is assuming you know what someone else is thinking, use the opportunity to ask the person how he feels. This process will help you realize that other people may not be thinking those things about you after all. And as we saw with Michelle, there may be a reason for that judgmental side of yourself. You can use it to help you move towards your goals, like she did, as long as you remember that it's not the *only* part of you. Especially if you're stuck in a place where you don't want to be, you might want to consider whether this side of you could help you out of your current situation. If your usual responses don't work, it's time to try something new. And I think you will find that accepting *all* the parts of your personality, even those you don't like, is the best way to start opening up all the possibilities in your life.

Don't be surprised if you feel uncomfortable with your newly discovered emotions and reactions in the beginning. It is like anything else that is new to us. As you practice, you will find yourself becoming more and more comfortable.

I know a man who always had to be the one initiating the conversation when he was first introduced to a group of people. He would put so much energy out telling people what he does, how many people in his family, asking others about themselves, and trying to get everyone, including himself, comfortable. Realizing he wanted to tap into the underinvested part of himself who is able to sit quietly and see what happens if he's not the center of attention, he took the opportunity at a conference to try it on for size. At first he found himself having to literally sit on his hands and hold his tongue from speaking out. The experience was foreign and not too comfortable for him. Over a period of months he tried this more quiet entry at several group-type experiences, and found himself becoming more and more relaxed while watching how others get comfortable, *without* his interventions. Actually, he very quickly saw the benefits of waiting and watching, especially in situations where the group members are unknown to him. Now he enjoys the luxury of hearing what people say, watching how they react to each other, and basically choosing whom he might want to get close to. In business matters he is able to assess who are the leaders when meeting new clients. This helps him devise strategies beneficial to landing accounts. So he is no longer stuck with reacting to situations in the same old way he has been doing since childhood. He has become more adult, because he has more control over his own behavior in each different situation.

When looking at the Picnic Dream, we noticed Leslie's lack of action in her waking-life situation by the fact that she is trying to get rid of the ants with just her hands. This can be seen in a new light at this level of dream work. In a Gestalt framework, it really was Leslie herself who became the Raid. After all, *she* is the one who ended the relationship! Now she was no longer handling her problem like a child with no control over her predicament. As a mature adult, she took matters and her destiny into her own hands. This is what Jung means by individuation, and what Perls means by maturation—having the ability and responsibility to take your life into your own hands.

In the Labrador Dream, Johnathan is the bulldog, smiling in his decision not to surrender to marriage before he feels ready. He's the house that can't accommodate all those dogs too! And it is Johnathan again who is all the other dogs in his dream. They represent the part of him that feels needy and vulnerable. Johnathan's awareness of this needy and vulnerable part of himself can make him a very understanding and accepting listener, not only to his girlfriend but also to anyone who expresses their vulnerability to him. He won't be judging in others what he accepts in himself. And his awareness also allows him to verbalize his ideas to his girlfriend, *all* his ideas, which include his ambivalence about the subject too. And who but a mature adult is so comfortable expressing all of what he feels, and with such clarity and no fear? Only a very young child who has not yet learned to suppress his truths for fear he is expressing what he shouldn't.

Finally, in the Leaning Dream, we can now see how Deborah played the part of that leaning building when she described she was "leaning" towards moving to Toronto. Analyzing her dream from this framework, we can see something of great importance. The building that falls without so much as a brick out of place stands for Deborah's reaction to stressful situations in her life. She more often than not holds herself too close together. She never lets herself fall apart. Was that something she learned she shouldn't do in her childhood? Maybe when she was told to stop crying as a child, Deborah got the idea that it was more acceptable to hold herself together when she feels upset. From this point of view, her dream gives Deborah the opportunity to feel. To feel the excitement, the adventure, the sadness, and even the stress related to the move. Many of us agree it is unhealthy to hold in too many emotions. That is how people get heart attacks and a host of other illnesses. Understanding her dream from this level affords Deborah the opportunity to step away from her habitual reaction that may have begun in childhood, to separate herself from her parents' idea of what is acceptable behavior and what is not. Based on this dream, now Deborah can come up with her *own* idea of how she can respond to stress.

Polarities

If all the parts of the dream are parts of our psyche, why is it so often that the extreme parts of ourselves, the two polar opposites, appear in the same dream? Why don't the gray parts stand out? What is it about the black and white that our unconscious uses to attract our attention to our behavior?

I think one answer may be that we *do* have a tendency to be over on one side of the bar. There wouldn't be a need for a polarity in the first place if we were feeling moderately about a given circumstance. If you are so far over on one side of a behavior, then its opposite will give you the rise to remember the dream. Remember, like most people you probably have certain behaviors and attitudes that are overinvested, and others that are underinvested. Well, naturally you will look at a given subject from your overinvested side—but that is not the most beneficial way for you to be looking at it! Your unconscious knows what's best for you. It never lies to you. When your unconscious wants you to look at and work on something it gives you a dream to remember, In fact, your unconscious often gives you the solution to an issue by suggesting a reaction somewhere in the middle of two polarities. We are self-regulating. We regulate ourselves through our dreams.

If you are underreacting to a given situation, the opposite overreaction will often appear in the dream. We saw this when Deborah didn't allow herself any excited feelings towards her move in waking life, but in her dream she was running away from the toppling buildings, for fear of being trampled by them. In essence, just the appearance of the complete opposite forces the reaction to "pull" itself towards the middle. We have a compensatory mechanism to balance lopsided feelings about a person or an event. If I am a person who is totally weak, I might dream of a person with great strength, a hero perhaps. In doing this, I would create the regulating balance.

During one of my recent lectures, an elderly woman shared a beautiful example to illustrate my point. She dreamed she attended Princess Diana's funeral and her late husband appeared, telling her everything was okay and she should carry on. She was feeling a great sadness at the thought of Diana's death and she presented herself with a great comfort and happiness at being with her late husband. His appearance in her dream served to move her sadness away from the extreme and closer to a middle ground.

A graphic artist described a dream in which he was observing a house flying on top of a plane. He associated the house with his wife, his mortgage payments, paying bills, and other responsibilities. He also connected the house to a colleague whom he viewed as successful. The plane, on the other hand, symbolized his youth when he used to build model planes. Planes also raised thoughts of travel, adventure, and fun. He added that there was certainly some fear associated with planes. During the interpretation, he remembered that his wife had reprimanded him the day before because she had caught him reading the newspaper in the middle of the afternoon. She felt that he should have been working. He felt he needed to escape to abate his stress level. This issue brought forth the polarity in the dream between "childhood" and "adulthood." The answer was somewhere in the middle. He realized that he needed to share his stress more with his wife and find time to be the child and have fun too.

Figure 4: Sarah's Uncle Dream
Mirror #2: The Boyfriend

When Sarah's boyfriend started acting insensitive with her, she found herself in the same predicament as I described earlier about myself, were I to stand in front of my husband shaking in my boots as if I were seven years old being reprimanded by my father. Sarah's silence in the face of her boyfriend's disappointing behavior is very limiting for her (see the dream map on page 22).

As I pointed out in Chapter 2, Sarah was feeling angry and yet uncomfortable about her boyfriend putting her in this awkward position. She was thinking too about how to express her anger, something Sarah is not very comfortable with in general. Her aunt appeared in the dream because she represents the underinvested part of Sarah's character that could express her needs and feelings openly. "Sarah," I said, "you described your aunt as an assertive woman who is not worried about speaking her mind when the need arises." I wondered out loud if she thought her aunt appeared in the dream as the solution to her problem. Once you understand the theory of how and why you might bring someone into your dream, it isn't usually long before you catch on to why you have picked out certain dream characters. Sarah needed to utilize this aspect of her character. When she became aware of the possibilities that her aunt's role in the dream gave her, Sarah took the first step towards changing an out-of-date behavior pattern.

It is interesting to note that in the first dream, Sarah didn't let her old boyfriend push her into the closet. She said she knew that if she went into the closet, she wouldn't be able to come out and she felt happy she resisted. She was practicing resisting what "doesn't fit" for her.

And just as Sarah's aunt is part of her potential to behave in a certain way, so too is her uncle. He represents the needy part of Sarah who is afraid to speak up for fear of being rejected. She just has to move from this overinvested part to the under-invested, or unpracticed, part of herself. When Sarah dreamed about her aunt, she was reminding herself that she had a real-life model for the behaviors she needed to practice. Sarah had just spent the previous evening with her aunt, so she got a chance to see exactly how a committed, successful person acts towards the things or people she's committed to. The time Sarah spent working with her aunt gave her waking practice about doing something good for herself. And the awareness she got from her dream helped her seize this model for her own life, so she was able to treat her boyfriend and *herself* in a more "aunt-like," open, and committed way.

Figure 5: The Emma-Jo Dream

Let's take a look at who (and what) in the Emma-Jo Dream represents what part of me. Andy represents my male side, taking care of business in an unemotional way. He's sitting behind the wheel driving the car. Andy represents the part of me that has the ability to feel calm and in control of my situation. In contrast, the part of me playing myself shows the way I felt at the conference, which probably explains why I took that role in the story. This is the part of me that, like many of us, feels strange and out of place, even a little panicked, in new surroundings. I was away from home and feeling lonesome. There was also, as I mentioned earlier, my feeling of panic and lack of control about my business idea, which I was afraid might be stolen by someone. And note that even in talking about the idea in the first place, I was definitely *not* acting businesslike.

You can already see some interesting polarities coming out in this dream. The three men who walk so close to us, watching us, are the part of me that *does* watch myself so closely, ready to pounce and attack at the slightest move. This is my judgmental side, and yes, I do sometimes feel nervous and need to defend myself in the face of my own self-criticism. The men are in that way my adult side too. They are the "you should" and "you shouldn't" aspect of myself. And in Emma-Jo I find my child, not only literally but figuratively too. She is everything the three men aren't when she runs freely in and out of the car. While they are watching, she is not watching. While they are sticking too close to me, she moves too far away. She is my childlike side, running to move away from the strictness of parental scrutiny.

Looking at my dream from a Gestalt framework, we can clearly see the polarities of my male and female sides, my child and my adult sides. The scissors, as you remember, are a metaphor for the creative aspect of my character at the same time as they represent my risk-oriented quality, which can sometimes be dangerous. The creative side of me takes risks, but the risks I take in my creativity will bring me to my goals. I mean, we can see this risk-oriented approach to creativity operating at this very moment by my level of self-disclosure! Do I not run the risk of being a danger to myself if and when some readers might criticize me in the face of my honesty?

When I understood the Emma-Jo Dream from a Gestalt approach, I got a very clear sense of the polarities in my own mind. Look at how Emma-Jo was playfully dancing between the more timid and risk-oriented sides of my character. The "business-like," unafraid, confident, male side of my character was driving the car forward. My male side was totally ignoring my female side by going ahead and attending the conference, being a guest on radio, being interviewed by the press, and even going so far as to write a book. Meanwhile, my female side was edgy and uncomfortable because not only was she was experiencing something new and unfamiliar, but she was having this experience alone!

Look at another very important aspect of the polarity between Andy and myself in the dream, and how this polarity so beautifully expresses the issue of maturation, or individuation. I believe one of the messages I understood while I was growing up was that it is comforting and acceptable for a child to have someone take care of her. Aside from that more obvious role I learned, I also learned that one of the roles a female plays is to be taken care of. I will touch on some of the ways I understood this in a later chapter. But the point I want to make here is that my female side at this time of my life was panicked partly because I was out there at that ASD conference and running the business on my own. No one was looking after me. I was in touch with my inner child, my *female* inner child—the part who is supposed to have someone taking care of *her.* She is not supposed to be looking after herself! And this side of me in the dream is pulling away from the side of me that knows and understands I am fully capable of looking after myself. What we are discussing here, which we are discussing in each of these dreams where a polarity appears, is what we call *ambivalence,* that human aspect inside all of us. It is a forever pull between what we learned as children and is ingrained in us, and what we have found we disagree with as adults. Ambivalence also takes us back and forth between who we feel we are, and who we want to be.

The important thing here is that there is a process taking place and that process seems to have to happen in a certain order. I use the word seems not because I insist it has to have this sequence, but because it seems reasonable to me that one step would provide the opening for the next. The way it works is, you first have to accept that all these parts coexist inside you. They are all part of the same person. In accepting this reality, we eliminate some of the ambivalence and open the door to accessing and using these different parts of ourselves, as we need them. I don't have to deny my male side exists, or judge it for that matter.

In getting in touch with the male side of myself, that calm, businesslike, move ahead side, I am not only *individuating* myself from the messages my parents sent me, but in doing so I am making a move towards *maturation.* The role I understood I should play as a woman and a child (and I might add the youngest child) is now appearing in my dream for me to seize! And when I get in touch with and behave like my male side, as represented by Andy in the dream, this is my opportunity to seize the adult in me. The best use of the Gestalt approach is more than acknowledging that these polarities coexist in me, but to begin to get the different parts to work together, as a team. My job as an adult is to go beyond the polarities I learned as a child.

For example, by becoming comfortable with my male side, instead of being judgmental, I can use it to look after my female side. I must also accept that I not only have a want-to-be-taken-care-of, childlike, female side, but that she will always exist inside me. There is no point in being judgmental of her. She is not going anywhere. The thing is that my mature side can look after the child in me. That would be the greatest benefit of capturing my dream from a Gestalt perspective, and the sure sign of my becoming an adult.

But how can I use my mature, male side to look after my female, panicked side? Is there any way to bring our polarities together or in communication so that one side is not in a panic while the other is barreling ahead? In my case, the first clue to ensuring that my "female" side does not stay in a constant panic at the things my "male" side is doing, is to acknowledge her! The Emma-Jo Dream manifests itself in the first place as a self-regulating mechanism inside me. I am overreacting in the dream, because I am underreacting in my waking life. I was judging the female, frightened, take-care-of-me side so much that I had left no room for her to exist. Hence the dream.

And let me say something more about that, besides the dream, and about the actual Emma-Jo. While she may be in fact a little girl, there is so much about her behavior that leaves you wondering how needy she really is. She acts very independent for her age. It could be all the adults around her, sisters, parents, and their friends, who have affected her personality, but truth is when you look at her behavior in or out of the dream, she is anything but needy! You see that she is small and childlike in her appearance, but in the dream she is off and running on her own. She doesn't exactly look like she needs help. And she is certainly not vying for parental approval. And I too am like her, yet my childlike side is not visible physically. While the inside of me sometimes cries out to be looked after, you'd never know it on the outside to look at me. Maybe I judge that side of myself so harshly that I must ignore she exists. Or maybe some part of me is scared that if I let her show up at all she will overtake me. I'll break down. My male side will disappear. I am discussing emotion here with you, not reality. But, you know your emotions can account for some pretty irrational and uncomfortable behavior.

How can I make this work? What is the learning here? I'd like for you to come away from this dream, not just with some abstract ideas about my or your "male" and "female" sides, or "child" and "adult" sides, but actual *learning* for your situations too. If I discover from my dream that I am ignoring or pushing down my female side to such an extent that she must cry out in the dream, the task becomes to pay attention to her. My adult, take-care-of-business side can go lift the phone and take care of the business of expressing my fears to my husband, my daughters, my friends, and any one of a number of other people who are there to lend me emotional support. My adult side knows I won't crack by admitting I am scared. I can be both. I can be frightened to death and I can move ahead and go where I need to go too. I realize what was missing in my approach was reaching out to someone, asking for help, expressing myself. Any and all of those choices would have calmed that frightened, insecure little girl who was locked up inside that dream-analyzing woman at the conference.

CHAPTER FIVE

Top Dog and Under Dog

"The sad truth is that man's real life consists of a complex of inexorable opposites—day and night, birth and death, happiness and misery, good and evil. We are not even sure that one will prevail against the other, that good will overcome evil, or joy defeat pain. Life is a battleground. It always has been, and always will be; and if it were not so, existence would come to an end."

—C. G. Jung

This chapter will illustrate what happens when you use the full-blown Gestalt method and speak up as the different parts of your dream. One common result, as you learned in Chapter 4, is to see how we project our disowned or alienated parts of ourselves onto others in the dream. We project these alienated character traits because it helps us remain disconnected from them. We're trying to deny we have these parts that we don't want.

Carl Jung called these parts of yourself your Shadow. I like that image. It's (what you consider) the dark side of you that always follows you around. I appreciate the expression Shadow for another reason. Your shadow is a part of you that is always there. It shows up every time you face a certain direction. It appears whenever you stand in a certain position too, doesn't it? Well, your Shadow, in the way that Jung means it, always stands just behind you. It's there but you usually can't see it. Actually, it behaves in your dreams exactly the way a beach ball does when you try and hold it down under the water. No matter how hard you try to keep it under, it just keeps popping up. And so your Shadow does in your dreams. It just keeps popping up, especially when situations occur that inspire you to try and keep it down. So one goal of a Gestalt approach would be to help you appreciate *all* your qualities. Keeping something hidden in your Shadow doesn't mean it's not there. It also doesn't mean that this quality secretly controls you. It's just one part among many inside you. Having none of anything is limiting. Realizing that you have some of something promotes flexibility, real power. Besides, keeping anything down and hiding is hard work, and generally will produce a host of illnesses.

From the moment you start to identify with some unfamiliar part of yourself, you immediately begin the process of feeling less alienated from that part. And you know what? It is actually kind of nice to feel that the "others" in the dream are all a part of you rather than being, say, against you, or separate from you. You get the opportunity to reown them! It's fun. In this scenario, you have the power of all the forces in the dream, the forces of the dream don't have power over you. It is the definition of real adventure!

You may also find, while speaking as the different characters in the dream, that you're having a conversation about some situation in your waking experience. Or maybe you will find yourself saying something to a dream character that you want to say to someone in waking life. Working with your dream in this way is similar to other kinds of dream work. Don't feel stuck! Stay open to the possibilities. Have fun! Go with what feels right for the dreamer! Take a point of entry that attracts *you* as the dream worker. Anything is good, and the more avenues you explore, the more you will discover.

The awkwardness that most people feel when starting this approach is an adventure too. It takes a certain kind of person to just lunge forward and do it! To just not stop yourself, or judge yourself for fear of feeling uncomfortable or foolish. I say, if you have any inclination or curiosity about the Gestalt experience, take the jump. The outcome is always worthwhile. You never know what you will learn, but I promise you, you will learn something.

Doing Gestalt

Let me describe some choices you have when applying a Gestalt approach to your dream. You can work alone or with a friend, but always remember that you can and should move in whatever direction the focus takes you. Don't feel stuck! Move wherever and however you want to move. This freedom of movement based on the direction the dreamer's conversation takes, or based on the dreamer himself, will let you practice a sense of flexibility with your environment whether inside or outside the dream. I want you to look at and work with the dream from the viewpoint that anything you say or feel is legitimate. And that means, if you are not connecting to a specific issue in your life, that's okay too. Just go with the conversation as it happens.

To begin, say the dream out loud, and in the present tense. Do this because the present tense gets you inside the experience differently than saying it in the past tense. It becomes easier to transport yourself back there and reconnect to the feelings you had. That is true when doing dream work in any framework. You might then try talking to an object or scene or person, rather than being that thing and speaking as if you are it. So, if you want to speak to the scenery, or the mood, you can! Play with it. If speaking to a rainy nighttime scene, you might ask, "Why are you so dark and dreary?" If there is a cow lying in the middle of the road, you can ask it, "Why are you blocking my path?" Maybe you want to say, "Hey! Get out of my way, you fat cow!"

Another way to enter the dream can be from the point of view of becoming the actual other person or object in the dream. Speak as it would speak. Say I dream about a ghost, and then I want to speak as if I am the ghost. I might say, "I am a ghost. I am here to frighten you! I am scary! I am transparent. I can move around so quickly and silently, you'd hardly know I'm there!" Someone else might say, "I am a ghost. I am here to protect you. Don't be frightened. I am your guardian angel. I will watch over you for always." Another choice you have is to make the different parts of the dream interact with each other. Have a conversation between the ghost and the night scene. Maybe the cow wants to say something to the path she's sitting on. Maybe she's there resting because the path has been warmed by the sun, and feels nice on her stomach!

Listen. When was the last time you pretended? This is a chance to recapture that playfulness that's been sleeping since you were a kid. You are free here to express your creativity. Move outside the dream. If you find that your dream conversation reminds you of a past event, you can go back to that event. Say your ghost dream makes you think of someone you knew when you were five years old. You can keep speaking as the ghost, but this time, talk to that person you used to know all those years ago. Or maybe you want to apply the discoveries you make in the dream work to current situations in your life. So allow your movement to take you away from the dream setting if you want, and into a role-playing experience with someone in your life. If your dream-conversation reminds you of someone you want to express yourself to in waking life, go ahead and do it! Don't hold back. A conversation that begins with a rock in a dream might turn out to be you engaging in a fantasy conversation with your husband, or your friend, or your mother! And you are playing both parts. Even though neither your mother, nor your husband or friend was even in the dream, the playing may lead you to a current issue in your life which does, in fact, involve that person.[1]

And here is something else. Take the time to notice how your body feels during these conversations and play-acting. That will tell you many things about your reactions to the dream work. Is your chest tight? Are you breathing? Breathing is important. A teacher of mine used to say that. Don't think breathing is a small thing. Are you trembling while something difficult is happening? Are your fists clenched?

When you work alone, or even with someone else, use a tape recorder. That way you get to flow with the moment and will still have the access to listen to what happened afterwards. Especially when I work alone, I want to hear again what I said later on. Besides, the tape forces you to speak out loud. Working alone really allows you the room to express what you truly want to say, no holds barred.

Adlerians do "psychodrama" to recreate a dream, and the Gestalt framework leaves you plenty of opportunity to do that too, especially if you are in a group. The dreamer can cast members of the group and direct the action. He or she can also choose to play a part. Whether dreamers watch or partake, they can use the opportunity to note their reactions to each part of the dream. There is a group in the United States called Playback Theatre. A volunteer from the audience comes up on stage and describes a dream. As with psychodrama, the dreamer chooses which actors play which parts. The dreamer can also ask someone to be an object such as a tree, a wall, water, or the sun. Whereas in psychodrama the dreamer is an active participant in the acting and directing of the play, in Playback Theatre, once the improvisation begins, the dreamer is an observer. The actors "play back" the dream to the dreamer and the audience. This experience is fun and adds insight. The important goal is to understand your dream and begin to understand yourself, regardless of the method. That is why I am presenting ideas suited to those who learn best by doing, seeing, or hearing.

Stuck Between a Rock and a Hard Place

Christine, an aspiring actress, and her husband had recently moved into a new home. The expenses associated with the house were more than they had anticipated, and while Christine had confidence she was on her way to being discovered, there were moments when she wasn't sure they'd be able to weather the storm before the money started rolling in. This dream is from that period of her life. When I met with Christine in New York, she had heard about Gestalt from a fellow actor, and was eager to play with her dream from a purely Gestalt framework. The following transcript of our session together gives a good feeling for the flow of the Gestalt process, and reveals some of Christine's insights about herself and her situation, which she was able to discover from her dream.

The Dream

"We are at a party. I am organizing a painting on these beautiful rocks. There is a girl working on the painting. I come outside, and, realizing that the painting looks so majestic and beautiful in the evening light, I ask her to leave it and say that she can go home. The painting is glistening, probably because of the waves from a wild ocean splashing it. Once she is gone, I jump in the ocean! I cannot imagine why in the world I am doing this. I would normally *never* do something like this. I am frightened of the ocean. The waves are pushing me around like crazy. I have lost control. There are only three directions I can go in. One is towards the painting. The second is back to the place that I jumped in from. And the third is towards these massive rocks that are sticking way up out of the ocean. The waves are pushing me towards the rocks. No matter how hard I swim I cannot make it back to where I jumped in from in the first place! I just can't get back there. I am sure I'm going to die when I get smashed into the rocks. They are coming closer. I start reaching under the water to feel for the rocks. I have an idea that if I can somehow feel them, I will be able to break my hit. I do it! And I make a decision and get up onto the rock. I am climbing a little bit higher and then higher still. And here I am, clinging to the rock. I am very high up in the air. I am just almost high enough for these three men to see me, but not quite. They are sitting in what looks like a control tower or a watchtower. And the way they sit is something like a cockpit, because there are two of them side by side, and the third man is behind. So he's behind where the pilot would sit on a plane. I have to reach myself up. I am straining my neck stretching myself as far as I can, hoping one of them will see me. The two up front don't see me, but I am now sure the one in the back sees me! I am mouthing the word HELP for him to see. I am afraid to scream it because I don't want to move my body and risk falling. I see him say something to the two up front. The fact that the two men up front are not looking at me is now making me wonder if that third man has seen me at all! You know what? I know he saw me, and he is calling for a helicopter. I am sure of it. I am just going to hold on here as tight as I can and wait. A helicopter will come and lower a rescue man to me. I am hanging on to this rock like crazy. The waves are crashing below me. The rock is still. Uncomfortable, but still."

Our Conversation

"What emotion do you recall, mostly?"

"What emotion did I feel when I came out of that dream? Well, it was very upsetting. I don't like high spaces and I don't like the ocean. I never go into the ocean without someone holding my hand. I don't like waves. I don't like movement."

"What is the actual emotion?"

"Panic."

"Was this the whole time?"

"Well, really I feel fear and some frustration in the water. When I start to think about what I am going to do, and reach underneath and feel the rocks, that was great. I felt some control there. I also felt some control and initiative when I climbed up there."

"A polarity."

"Yes. And then once I got up there, that was it. It was just the matter of holding on and waiting."

"Okay. One of the first images you saw was the party. You were at a party. If you can imagine the party as an entity, as a thing, can you speak as the party to Christine?"

"I am lots of people. I am lots of personalities. Some of us are comfortable at a party and some of us are not. A party . . ."

"Let me give you an example. You don't have to describe. You can say for example. I am the party. I am glad you are here. So you don't have to say that, but that's the kind of thing I'm thinking."

"Okay, well, I am the party. I am ready to have a good time. Come and join me. Have a drink."

"What would Christine answer?"

"Well, what would Christine answer?" She started laughing. "I'm not really comfortable with parties! I like people, but I am not really that comfortable about parties."

"But don't say how you feel. I mean talk to the party."

"Oh! I see what you mean! Well I'd say, 'I'm not that comfortable with you! I am not that comfortable with myself in front of you! That's because there are a lot of you. I am worried about who of you is going to come over and talk to me or not.

I'm worried about if any of you are judging me because of my weight, and I wonder if I look okay.'"

"Does the party answer or is that where it ends?"

"Well I think a party would say to come on in and have a good time. And don't worry about all that! Just come on in! Have a glass of wine. You'll relax and have an enjoyable time."

"Another polarity. Now, you say there is a girl there, and the painting. What do you think the girl would say?"

"What exactly am I doing here? Why am I here? She might be saying that to me, or she may just be saying that to herself."

"And what is the answer if she is saying that to you?"

"I think you are cleaning that painting. You are doing *something* to the painting! You are preparing it in some way. And it looks fine. It's so beautiful. It is so shiny, and whatever it is that you did, you did a good job. And you don't have to work on that painting anymore. You can go now."

"Anything else about the girl? Does she have anything else to say?"

"Well, she would say, 'I am a worker here. I am not somebody who is at the party or a part of it. I am someone who is doing work for the party. I am working to help make something look good, but I am not invited to the party.'"

"Do you have anything to say to her?"

Laughing, "I agree with you. I don't think you belong at the party. I think you are a worker."

"Okay. How about the painting? Speak as the painting."

"I am beautiful. I am shiny. I am big. I am so big that I am bigger than life. I am as big as all that mass of rock. I am big and colorful, and shiny. And I am deep! I have deep blues in me. I am a beautiful painting."

"And does Christine answer?"

"I also think you are a beautiful painting. I even think the sight of you is even a little bit awesome. You are so big. And there is such a shine, maybe from the water. I am not sure why you are shining like that, but I think it has something to do with the wet, or the water and the moon. And it is the night-time. There is a glistening, and a lot of depth. Deep blues. You look beautiful. You don't look like you need anybody to do anything more to you. You are beautiful the way you are."

"Can you relate that to anything in your life?"

"I think that is so nice, because I concern myself with the public. That my movie is going to come out in the fall, and it is going to mean they are going to book me on television shows. I will be out there and I worry about my weight. How I look. So now I've really got the pressure on. I'm always worried about how I look."

"That's wonderful to feel so confident that you look beautiful and big and wonderful just the way you are. It's like the rock. That it is beautiful just the way it is. What a wonderful message."

"Yes. And it's funny, because I do like myself so much and I really *do* think that I am a beautiful person. But I just really dislike how frustrating it is for me about the weight. It's too bad because I like so much else about myself."

"There is such vulnerability being out there. Like rocks. They are out there. For all to see. Even though they are beautiful and shiny, and glistening and all the wonderful things that you said about them, there is a vulnerability about being out there, exposed."

"And when you said exposed, you just reminded me that one of the things I feel sure about is that I don't think I was dressed, altogether when I was up on those rocks. I don't remember being naked, but I am sure that I was not completely dressed either. Right when you said vulnerable, I felt that ring."

"What about the ocean? Speak as the ocean. Speak to Christine."

"Well, I'm going to toss you around and you are not going to have any control whatsoever."

"Does Christine respond?"

"I don't have any control. This is too overwhelming. You are too overwhelming for me! And I am absolutely frightened of you. I am scared of you. I don't like being inside of you!"

"Does the ocean answer?"

Silence.

"It's okay. Don't force it. You don't have to answer. What significance is the concept of being frightened, being held inside? Of being controlled? Is there any significance to an event? A person, or something in your life? Is there anything that gives you those feelings?"

"There are a couple of things that have that element for me. My husband and I, we're a bad team when it comes to spending money. We're a team, and we are *not* a polarity. We are very similar. And we both spend money without having a good sense of control. So we never get ourselves to the point where we drown, but we're always on the edge. Recently we just took an increase on our mortgage. And so now . . . it's tight! We have to, like I described in the dream, this holding on. There is this feeling of being very out of control. I know the dream has something to do with this issue."

"Don't explain too much right now. Stay with our process."

"Okay, but the situation gives me that same sense I am holding on because I am going to get recognized. I know I am going to. And I know that I am going to be very successful. I know it. I just feel it in the deep of me. But I also know that I have to hold on and right now, I am frightened and feeling out of control. I don't like that feeling."

"So the ocean represents this notion of being pulled, being pulled under."

"Yes. But I jumped in! I jumped in, in the dream! And I

jumped in here too. Like with the house and the meals too. Every time we go out for expensive meals, that's me jumping in!"

"Good!"

"And I know I don't like that. Same as the ocean. I know I don't like that. And yet I do that. I can even say that about the food, about eating. But really, the feeling that I have in the dream is exactly like the feeling I have about the house."

"Scary."

"Right, scary. I jumped in with both my eyes open."

"And that's that panic."

"And I would not have had that panic, but we just increased the mortgage."

"Let's talk about the waves. Speak as the waves."

"I am going to toss you and pull you. I am very strong. I am going to pull you in the opposite direction of which you want to go. And no matter how hard you try, there is no way that I am going to let you get back to where you jumped in from."

"Good. Does Christine answer?"

"Well, if I can't go back to where I came from, then I am just going to reach underneath you and see if I can't protect myself in some way. Because I feel you are pushing me in the wrong direction. It's not where I want to go. I want to go back to where I jumped in. Can't you please let me go back?"

"Can you answer as the waves?"

"No. Because you already jumped in and this is the direction that I move in! There is no going back. This is the way my tide moves now."

"It's like you jump in and you just gotta go with the flow!"

"I just gotta go with the flow. But what I *can* do is reach underneath. And I think it is very nice of you not to swallow me up. Because you could and that would *really* put me in a panic. You could take me under. Your undertow is pulling me, but I want to thank you for not going over my head!"

"So you are thanking the waves because they are not responsible for you going under?"

"Yeah. You're not so big that you are taking me under. But there is a force happening here, and I feel like I am going to die. I am going to reach under and see if I can't find some ground. I am going to find some way to protect myself."

"Now the rocks. You said there are only three directions to go in, and that your fear is that you are going towards the rocks. While you are thanking the ocean for not taking you under, however, the direction the ocean is taking you . . . "

"Is to smack me. Smack me right into those rocks."

"You are the rocks. Speak as the rocks."

"I am massive. I am strong. You can climb up on me. You can hold on to me."

"Oh! So they're not scary, they're inviting. So you are afraid of the ocean, not the rocks."

"Well I thought if I was smashed into the rocks, it would have been the hit that would have killed me."

"Yes, but the rocks are saying, 'You can be safe.'"

"Yes. You can be safe here. You can climb out of the ocean. And you can use my edges . . . you can use my edge. There's a play on words! Isn't it funny? Use my edge! I have an edge you can climb on! I might feel a little bit slippery, but if you hold on tight, you can just wait here, because I am not going anywhere."

"And what do you answer?"

"I am so happy you are here! And that is just what I am going to do. I am just going to climb on you, and I am going to hold on to this stillness. I would rather, while I am feeling uncomfortable in this space that I am in, be on top of you. Even though I am up high, and might become dizzy, and at the same time I am feeling vulnerable and exposed, and I could slip! I would still rather be up here, because I have the power not to look down. I can look up towards those men and not look down and I would still rather be here, than be tossed around in the ocean. It is because on the rocks I have my ground. And I feel like I have more control here than I do in the ocean."

"Is there any mirror there, the concept of something to hold on to? Can you relate that to anything, or anyone? Can you relate that into your life?"

"I kind of relate that to me. It's myself I can hold on to. It's me who is going to get noticed. It's so close. I just have to reach up for these men to notice me. The sense I have about holding on and knowing that something is going to happen is exactly like that. Everything is going to be okay. It's a very solid feeling. And yet, I also have that element of vulnerability, of being exposed, because there is all of that too."

"And yet? Even with the vulnerability. You are already at the point of the Gestalt, if you will. Of your dream. I mean you are pulling it together."

"How? Can you connect this for me?"

"Well, let's just take it one step further. So this concept of clinging to this massive rock, and holding on. Why don't you speak as the two men who are in the front, who you describe as the pilot and co-pilot. What would they be saying to Christine?"

"They would not be saying anything to me! They'd say, 'I don't even see you. I don't even know that you are there. I have no idea that you even exist.' They do not acknowledge me."

"So they make you feel unseen."

"Yes."

"So let's go with that word. Can these two men who do not acknowledge you represent anything else? Something more abstract? You are in a panic. You are clinging for life, yet there is no acknowledgment."

"Well, I am going to give you a 'should.' It doesn't mean that I should feel that way, but if anyone in my family has a sense that I am clinging, or that anyone is clinging, there would not be any help available."

"What do you want to say to those two men?"

"Can't you please look my way? Why are you only looking there? If you would just look down a little bit you would see me. I am so close. I am so close to you seeing me. Why are you so focused somewhere else? Can't you notice anything a little bit below you?"

"Okay. And then we have the third man."

"If he was talking to me he would say, 'I think I see you. I think I see you struggling out there, and don't worry. I am looking after this. I see that you are out there, and I am going to make some phone calls to make sure that a helicopter is going to go out and get you.'"

"And what does Christine answer?"

"Thank you! Thank you for seeing me! HELP!"

"Okay. Take a look at all the different parts from the party to the girl to the painting to the ocean, the waves, the rocks themselves, the climbing, and the men in the tower. What does it all say?"

"Well, there is a pull about a panic and then a sense of control and then a panic and then a sense of control. It's got that rhythm to it."

"So there's the strength of the ocean versus the strength of the rock. But that's your conflict."

"I don't get it."

"Okay. From fighting in the ocean, from being tossed and pulled in the wrong direction towards the rock. It sounds like death and panic and the fury of the ocean. The fear of being thrown against the rock. You experienced the strength of the ocean, the loss of control, the massive rock and the panic that you are going to be smashed against them. And what happened?"

"I survived."

"Yes. Go on."

"I survived and while I was surviving I was still, even with the rock, vulnerable. But really, I needed to depend on somebody else to come and help me." (Laughing) "Right?"

"Well ultimately you are looking for assistance. But it seems that out of the clutches of going under, you kept looking for something to hold on to, something so that you *yourself* could manage to save yourself at that point."

"And I did!"

"And you did. What does this say about you in your current life situation?"

"It's optimistic."

"It sure is."

"What would you title this dream?"

"Stuck in between a rock and a hard place!"

"Can you superimpose that title onto your life recently?"

"I sort of feel that way. You know a mortgage doesn't go away tomorrow. And it is stuck in between a rock and a hard place. Although it is easier to pay a mortgage if you generate more income, but I think it's a big mortgage. And it's got that twenty-year feeling to it. It's not going away tomorrow."

"So there is a solidity to the mortgage. Being on the rock. But there is also a helpful kind of aspect to that rock."

"Right."

"It kind of saved you. Did the mortgage increase save you?"

"Well, yes, actually, it did. We wiped out our loans!"

"So then, as you move higher on the rock, you are striving to get where?"

"Well, I am trying to get noticed. I am moving up higher."

"Well yes, but even when you go higher, there are still some who will not notice."

"Right."

"But there will be those who will."

"Right."

"Can you accomplish these goals on your own in a vacuum? Can you do what you have to alone?"

"No."

"No. So, when you say that you relinquished it to somebody else to help you, is that reality?"

"Sure."

"So you are getting yourself as high . . . "

"Yes! As high as I can!"

"And then?"

"And then, I am going to need somebody to notice me!"

"Yeah, like your entire audience."

"The people who are going to see the movie. And there will be some directors who will see you and want you for another movie."

"And there will be others who won't."

"We could have done the helicopter, actually. You know. What is the significance of the helicopter? I mean in the dream it was a thought, but it's the ultimate. Be the helicopter."

"Actually, I would rather talk to the helicopter for a minute."

"Go ahead! It's your dream."

"You're going to make me feel *really* dizzy. And I would feel extremely vulnerable on you, because I like to be in a big solid plane. Where I am not getting any dizziness at all! So you're gonna make me dizzy, but you are also here to save me."

"Hold on. Go with that for a second, Christine. Besides dizzy, what else would you feel in that helicopter?"

"Nauseous!" (Laughing)

"Go on. Just stay there."

"I feel insecure. The front window is too big. The sides are all open! I don't feel secure, but I know that you are taking me *to the ground! Where I like to be.*"

"Good. What do you think that helicopter is a metaphor

for? Think. There's a big window, high exposure. You feel nausea, nervous, and vulnerable. Exposed. It's where you want to be Christine. Even though you feel all those things, it is where you want to be."

"Yes. In that helicopter, *is* where I want to be. I don't want to stay clinging on to that rock. And if that is not stuck between a rock and a hard place, I don't know what is!"

"And the point is, if you make it into that helicopter, Christine, you have arrived, where would that ultimate place be, in your striving to get high? Where would that be?"

"Literally?"

"Literally. In your life. What is your hope?"

"I want to be a major movie star!"

"Okay. But what did you tell me you would have to do?"

"I'm going to have to go on television and be interviewed. That is a very different experience than making a movie. I will be exposed. They will ask me questions about myself. It is not the same as *playing* somebody else! It is *me* they are going to want to talk to!"

"Now think about that. And think about that helicopter. Open. Exposed. Big Window. Vulnerable."

"It's very television-like. It even has the big screen!"

"And for all to see. So it's where you want to be, but it's the scariest place."

"The scariest place."

"But it's the ultimate place. It's going to take you where you want to be."

"You're right!"

"So the Gestalt of the whole dream comes together."

"The Gestalt is realizing the whole picture. One main story. Which seems to have everything to do with where I want to go. And it seems that I have to feel scared and vulnerable in order for it to get me back to the ground!"

"And even though along the way there are going to be pit-falls, like you're going to have these financial things to deal with, and there is going to be, you know; ocean stuff to deal with. But what does Christine do? She finds something to hold on to. And you climb out! And you strive to the top, hoping to get noticed. In order to go on to fame and fortune. Which will ultimately deal with your mortgage problem, if things go really well."

"That feels good. I feel like I get it now. The *whole* picture, though. So what about the disowned parts you talk about? I know I feel vulnerable, for example."

"But are you admitting to it? Do you try to hold down your fears? Do you try to ignore that you, Christine, have money worries? Do you try to hold back that you could be vulnerable, or feel exposed?"

"Yes. I do hold back some."

"Well that would be the disowned part, the part that you don't want anybody to know about. It is the part that you don't allow in yourself. The parts that you would be holding under the water with your rubber ball are the parts about you that you believe you are not supposed to be experiencing. If you don't allow in yourself to be needy, then you will probably not allow yourself to ask someone close to you for help. Maybe that is what you were taught. Were you taught that you are not sup-posed to need? I mean I am just throwing ideas out for you to think about. But those kinds of things could be your vulnera-bilities, the things that you need. The whole concept of the swirling water pulling you down. That might show you that you could be dealing with that sort of thing. But really, I see the Gestalt in this dream as being more about it representing metaphorically, which is what your whole dream is, beautifully metaphoric, that each of the metaphors in the dream is repre-sentative of something you are dealing with. It's a part of you.

I mean we made it very current, but it is all metaphors of you and your experience. I mean the ocean is the metaphor for the financial, the pulling you down, and your fears of going under. The rock, the metaphor for what is solid in your life. What you can cling to. And where you are going to climb. That is the part that will stay there. That's there for you."

"And it's so very accurate! It's so accurate about how I jump in."

"You jumped in, and you got yourself into a jackpot."

"Yes!"

"And you knew what you were jumping into even though it's a scary place to be. It's a place you don't want to be in, but you jump in anyway. The other metaphor that is quite lovely is the one that affected you at the beginning, is the painting. The way you saw the painting as a metaphor for you. The way you feel, but also that you are feeling very exposed. And that was sort of the precursor for everything else that came after in the dream about feeling exposed, and feeling, you know, out there. Like being at a party. Being judged. You putting yourself out there. But the audience! You are going to be judged. You are going to have a movie out there. People are going to see you on television. There is the opportunity for judgment, discomfort. It all started off at the party, Christine. The way you described what it means for you to be at a party. What it feels like for you to be judged and seen. And who's going to talk to you, and who's going to want to be with you. Really that, when I look at it now, set up the entire dream. It was all those feelings you experienced at the outset and you played them out metaphori- cally through the ocean and the rock, the control and the lack of control. The polarities in the dream are to illustrate to you that you have this part of yourself that is so insecure and vul- nerable, and yet you also have another part of you that is so strong."

"And the ambition and the moving forward."

"Exactly Christine. And that these polarities coexist inside the same person, you!"

"Well, that's what I needed. I was looking for the closure. And I even get the purpose of the polarities in this dream. I get it!"

A Footnote

After working, or better said, playing with this dream together with Christine, I was discussing the process and how it unfolded with one of the women who taught me Gestalt, Susan Saros. I will never cease to be amazed that each and every time you open a dream up to another perception, you catch another angle, another learning. Susan pointed out that the dreamer may have been saying she wants to have a rock in her life, rather than being the rock. The dream then would serve the purpose of letting her rehearse what she wants to express to her husband or another family member. Another important element Susan picked up on is that the dream can also be a person's attempt to come to closure on an issue. In fact this dream was unfinished. Through active imagination, I helped Christine set in motion her closure by asking her to bring the helicopter into the dream. But accepted at face value, it is true this dream ended before closure.

Accepting the dream as unfinished, for example, would be valuable too. It would help Christine accept where she is in her present situation. And her story *is* unfinished! Her movie has not yet been released and she has yet to be interviewed for it on television. I do not relate Susan Saros' observations to you in order to suggest that Christine's own discoveries are not valid or without so much learning, because as I am sure you have realized, they are. But if she so chooses at another time, Christine could try these other avenues into her dream and see if she agrees with them. Every new approach into her dream can hold new insights. It all depends on what feels right for her.

Top Dog and Under Dog

Another well-known and very effective Gestalt method of working through a dream comes from Perls' Top Dog and Under Dog. "Perls calls Top Dog and Under Dog the two clowns of the personality, constantly acting out their self-torture game beneath the level of conscious awareness. We have a Top Dog and Under Dog for each specific conflict, so whenever a conflict is sparked off by some present problem or event in life, the two clowns emerge and start their self-torture game. Both strive for control, and it is a battle to the death, dissipating all the energy which should be used for constructive and positive living."[2] Top Dog is the "authority figure" in your personality. He is condescending and controlling. He's the one who always knows what's best. He uses words like, "You should," and "You'd better." He's like the voice of your parents from the past, or sometimes the present. But the point is that Top Dog's voice is *your* voice! He's the part of you who comes down hard on yourself.

Now the person on the other end of all these "shoulds" is poor Under Dog. And while he protests against Top Dog's hammering, truth is, there's a part of him that kind of feels like he deserves the criticism. So he is generally defensive towards Top Dog. Sometimes he can be apologetic or whiny. He may even try to be manipulative, but the bottom line is, he has no power.

You want to find these two polarities and have them talk to each other. The technique of letting the dialogue flow reminds me of Freud's free association. With free association you also have no barriers, no rules for stopping the flow of thought. If anything the opposite is true. The only rule is not to judge any thought or memory that comes up. You pick something or someone from the dream and stay quiet for a minute, thinking. Soon, a thought or a memory pops into your head. You say it out loud, preferably. Then you stay resting quietly again and let the next thought or memory come up. In the same way, a Top Dog and Under Dog conversation can flow freely until something else is presented.

The characters who are conversing might change as the dialogue moves along. Just the same way you move or shift freely from one thought to the next with free association, here it is an improvisational script, a conversation that may also move from one Top Dog and Under Dog to the next Top Dog and Under Dog. Suppose the Top Dog in your dream starts out being a cow and the Under Dog is the path it's lying on. Well, after these two start a conversation, you may find yourself turning it into a conversation between you—the Under Dog—and your boss as Top Dog. And even though Top Dog and Under Dog usually fight with each other and disagree, you might eventually hear them agreeing with each other. Top Dog and Under Dog might even get to like each other! "If you get the right polarities, and you change, from fighting into listening to each other, then the integration will take place. It's always the question of fighting versus listening. This is rather difficult to understand because it's a difficult polarity. If you have ears, the road to integration is open. To understand means to listen."[3] Integration happens when the Top Dog and Under Dog in your own personality have come together, and you can begin to approach your life as a whole person.

Gerry and His Brother

A few years ago, a regular client of mine named Gerry felt upset with his older brother but never expressed his disappointment to him. That night, he dreamed he was arguing with his brother. One way of looking at this dream was as a kind of rehearsal, where he could see himself expressing his feelings to his brother. Gerry was practicing what it would be like to express himself to his brother. In this case the dream would move him closer to that goal.

Gerry has unresolved issues with this brother. Gerry also has a pattern of holding himself back from expressing his feelings, just as he was doing in this particular case. Ultimately these problems come down to Gerry's relationship between Top Dog and Under Dog where he thinks of his older brother as Top Dog, while Gerry himself plays the role of Under Dog. In Gerry's pattern Under Dog keeps his resentment to himself, until he ends up screaming it out at Top Dog. This fits with Gerry's life. When he has something upsetting to express to family members, he either screams it at them, or says nothing at all. He needed to begin to feel more comfortable expressing his disappointments, not yelling, and likewise not staying silent either. The dream afforded him a safe place to "practice" letting his feelings show.

Around the time he had his brother dream, Gerry was trying out a business idea to develop an Internet magazine. He hired and paid designers and writers who worked on the magazine for months. He tossed around several forms the business might take. For example, he made fliers that he distributed all over the city advertising the magazine, hoping to solicit advertisers. There were costs associated with designing, producing, and hiring people to distribute the fliers. Actually he had no responses to his fliers. But that didn't stop Gerry from continuing to forge ahead with his idea. The final step was soon approaching, and involved what he considered a sizable investment. That would be the cost of a firm to design and host the site for the magazine.

One time, his brother asked him if he had ever done a market study related to that idea. Gerry felt frustrated by his brother's suggestion because the cost of doing the market study was virtually the same price as it would have been to set up the site. He said to his brother, "Instead of wasting my money on a market study, I may as well just pay for the site, and that itself will *be* the market study!"

Gerry's brother responded, "I don't know. If I was going to put down six, seven, eight thousand dollars, I know I'd never do it without having some kind of study done first." Gerry felt upset at what he interpreted as his brother's criticism.

During one particular week, Gerry had successfully convinced a newspaper to write an article about his idea. While many of his friends were calling to congratulate him, or to say they saw his fliers around, to his disappointment Gerry's brother never telephoned him. In this instance he was clearly looking to his brother for approval or encouragement. This was regardless of the fact that Gerry had never told his brother about the fliers or the newspaper article. So his brother may not have ever seen the fliers, and since he travels frequently in his own business, may not have even been in town when the article appeared. It may have been a case of Gerry's needs overriding reality.

The Brother Dream

Gerry came to me with this dream in which he was arguing with his brother. We quickly connected it to the Internet idea and the fact that Gerry was upset with his brother for not calling him. Afterwards, I asked Gerry to speak as his brother. "Say what you think your brother would say."

Gerry began a conversation, playing both roles. He immediately fell into Top Dog and Under Dog. You can always tell a Top Dog and Under Dog conversation because Top Dog starts out sounding authoritative and scolding, while Under Dog sounds defensive and resentful. In this conversation, Under Dog says to his older brother what he really wants to say instead of holding himself back as he often might.

Under Dog: "Here I am trying to open a new business. I even went so far as to convince a reporter to write an article on me, and you can't even show me your support! All you can think of is a criticism! You're just looking for something I *haven't* done instead of all the things I *have* done!"

Top Dog: "Isn't this just like you to start trouble with me when you know I'm right and you should have done a market study before you even invested the money you have so far. Let alone the chunk you're about to lay down."

Under Dog: "Why do you have to be such a heavy on me? I am not such a terrible person, you know!"

Top Dog: "I'm not being a heavy on you! If you rush into this, like you have done so many times before, you will soon be back to me wailing and begging for help! You should be more careful!"

Under Dog: "And there you go ripping me again! Like I'm such a bother to you when I've had to ask for some help? Boy, you're not very charitable!"

Top Dog: "Now what kind of manipulative guilt shot is that? You know I care about you. Why would you want to put yourself in the position of possibly losing all that money before you have a solid indication the business idea will work? You'll just be out of money and feel so bad if your idea fails."

Under Dog: "Well, maybe you have a point, but you could be more protective of me you know."

Top Dog: "But I *am* being protective of you! Who else is going to advise you to do a market study, all those professionals who are sucking you dry of your investment? No! It'll be me who tries to protect you!"

Under Dog: "Maybe you have a point."

Top Dog: "Why are you arguing with me? You shouldn't argue the point with me. I only want what is best for you. I am your big brother, remember? I only want you to do good for yourself."

In the end, the Under Dog self concedes, admitting that Top Dog is probably right, although he dislikes his approach. When first beginning the exercise of this dream, Gerry was really struggling with his ideas and feelings. After some time he was able to imagine his brother having his interests at heart. His brother in the dream is simply concerned about the viability of the project. While he wants Gerry to succeed, since he himself has little interest in the subject of an Internet magazine, he feels pessimistic as to whether the general public will have an interest. As you saw, once Gerry *became* his brother he found himself standing where his brother was in the dream, wondering why he was being yelled at. When Gerry moved into the role of his older brother, only then did he begin to imagine the possibility that his brother needed to feel he is a good brother. It occurred to Gerry that he could have been misunderstanding his older brother's concern as a lack of support, and for the first time, Gerry imagined his brother feeling badly about this. When Gerry speaks as his brother in the dream he is eager to come to an understanding with Gerry. In this framework Gerry felt his anger and hostility dissipate, and came away with a better understanding of his brother's intentions.

His "older brother" self was arguing with his "younger brother" self. What was the pull? What was he weighing? Since this dream happened just around the time Gerry had to make a business decision involving a sizable investment, he needed to tap into his underinvested, judgmental side. Interestingly, Gerry describes himself as someone who feels disdain for people when he sees them making judgments of others. This is a good indication he is looking at a disowned part of himself. It is his Shadow. Yet, if Gerry were to employ this trait, he would be proceeding more cautiously before investing time and money into a new venture. He needed to *become* his older brother in this situation. This was especially true because the "younger brother" side of Gerry normally jumps into situations without carefully considering the disadvantages. His older brother, on the other hand, runs market studies and researches a subject very carefully before he puts an investment on the table.

So by engaging in a Top Dog and Under Dog conversation, Gerry realized that although his older brother does hold an authoritative position in the family, he isn't some kind of control freak. He really just has Gerry's best interests at heart. Gerry also realized he had to incorporate this cautious, "judgmental" aspect of his brother into his own approach. In talking so directly with this disowned part of his own personality, he became somehow more familiar with it, closer to it. Gerry became his *own* authority figure, instead of casting his older brother in that role. A wonderful advantage of the Gestalt dream work was how Gerry could finally get over his resentment towards his older brother and begin a new kind of relationship with him. Gerry achieved integration. This not only expanded his own flexibility in dealing with situations in his life, but also made him more understanding of the people he loves.

One sunny day, not long after Gerry had this dream, he walked by his brother's house to find him relaxing in the sun. The fact is that he had never shared with his brother the extent to which this business idea played a part in his hopes for the future. Actually, strangely or not, Gerry had never shared his interest about opening his own business with *any* of his family of origin. He took the opportunity to sit with his brother and share some of his dream of being his own boss. He also expressed his disappointment at his brother's seeming lack of interest in his business venture, and failure to congratulate him on the news article. Separate of the truth that the brother was not very enthusiastic about the idea of an Internet magazine, he actually *was* out of town on business the week the article came out. Gerry's role-playing approach led him to take his brother's cautious approach and do a market study. The results showed that that particular idea was a bad one. He could have lost money had he rushed to try it.

A Final Note

Before I close this subject, I want to discuss the resolution of feelings towards authority figures in general, whether with our parents or older siblings. In our relationship with authority we usually go from a submissive response to a "me, me, me" attitude, in order to get to the place where we can say "us." And that is what I want to explain here.

When we are children, we depend so greatly on getting support and approval from parents and older siblings, it feels as though we would die without it. Let me say that although it would be a valid reason for concern when we are five years old (you wouldn't want a parent to throw you out on the street with no food or place to live), the fantasy continues to adulthood, when it is no longer accurate. This is the same basic principle I was referring to earlier when I worried about "talking back" to my dad as a kid, and how I can slip back easily to that reaction if my husband speaks rudely to me today. There is a process we go through to get to the place where we realize we can support ourselves, and no longer have to feel stuck in reactions that aren't appropriate any more.

Frederick Perls described this process of maturation in terms of a baby who has to learn to breathe for itself. "The baby cannot breathe by itself. It doesn't get the oxygen supply through the placenta anymore. We can't say that the baby has a choice, because there is no deliberate attempt of thinking out what to do, but the baby either has to die or learn to breathe. There might be some environmental support forthcoming— being slapped, or oxygen might be supplied. . . .

"Now, the baby begins to grow up. It still has to be carried. After awhile it learns to give some kind of communication— first crying, then it learns to speak, learns to crawl, to walk. And so, step by step, it mobilizes more and more of its potential, its inner resources. He discovers—or learns—more and more to make use of his muscles, his senses, his wits, and so on. So, from this I make the definition that the process of maturation is the transformation from environmental support to self-support, and the aim of therapy is to make the patient *not* depend upon others, but to make the patient discover from the very first moment that he can do many things, *much* more than he thinks he can do."[4]

. I like what Perls proposes here because he gives you a pic- ture of how we grow. I think he is too extreme in what he said, though. I believe we can reach towards a place that is some- where in the middle of environmental support and self-support, but I do appreciate that it's hard to get there if we don't know what self-support feels like first. Because I think Perls has the basic idea I want to get across here, please allow me to describe some of his thoughts, but with my own interpretation attached.

The process of maturation happens like this. When we first want to have our own opinions about things and really *don't* want to feel like we need parental or authority approval, we find ourselves at what Perls called an *impasse*. That is exactly what happened with Gerry. On the one hand he wanted to barrel ahead with his own opinion, behaving as though he did not require his brother's approval. But it wasn't working for him. Emotionally, it was not working. Because try as he might to pro- ceed, the truth is Gerry was having great difficulty coping without his brother's approval and encouragement. The dream was spurred in the first place by his brother's lack of acknowl- edgment about the newspaper article.

As I'm sure you know from your own life, this emotional

ambivalence we experience towards our parents or siblings doesn't come from us alone. It is a byproduct of a whole family dynamic. All the people in the family play their roles, together. We hang together, the same as a mobile over a baby's crib. This mobile keeps its balance when each piece hangs the way it "should." So the people who play the authority roles, like the parents and eldest siblings, don't take kindly when members who have always played the subservient roles suddenly have a voice. It messes up the mobile. There is movement. People get dizzy and uncomfortable with the change. We all resist change. Taking responsibility for yourself is difficult enough, and the negative reaction you might get from the outside world creates more tension and makes the change even harder.

But let me get back to the person who is trying to move himself out of the place where he feels he can't survive without an authority's approval. Because he has a fear of the authority, he holds back, he *implodes*. He doesn't feel comfortable enough to say out loud, "I disagree with you!" so he says nothing. That is what implode means, to hold back, and kind of fill up. After a while of imploding, the person explodes. If you are so unaccustomed to expressing your disappointment, the first few times you do so, it may very well come out as yelling. You are finding your voice and in order to do so you may have to go over to the other extreme first.

After a bit though, it does settle down. Over time, and the brother incident is a good example, Gerry was able to re-evaluate his opinion about himself. He now attempts to work through the explosive layer with awareness. His greatest moment of awareness came when he realized he is his own authority figure. That voice exists inside him. Gerry stops himself from his conditioned reaction to situations, to reassess his choices. Is he slipping into the role he played in his family for so long, or can he trust his own authority? Does his opinion about a business idea and its value have to agree with his brother's? Does he need his brother's or his mother's approval to breathe, to survive? The answer is no. He doesn't.

So what happens when the baby learns to breathe for himself? Suppose you learn that you can support yourself, and don't depend for your life on the support of your parents or older siblings. Does this mean you have moved completely beyond them and have nothing to do with them or their opinions? No, it doesn't. Here is the biggest learning to keep in mind. If you are so far over at self-support, you are losing sight of the reality that we are not alone in this world. We can't just "self-support." We need people. From our earliest experience we are with mother. We come into this world primed to care about others, and primed to care about their opinion. Our experience, whether we acknowledge it or not, is a series of interdependent relationships. The biggest step towards your independence is your ability to acknowledge and accept that you are dependent! And while we know we can breathe and function without the support of those we love, the fact is that it makes us happy to have it. Once we believe in ourselves, we don't need to reject our authority figures or feel desperate to have their approval.

Gerry can afford to relax and be nice, because he believes in himself. His biggest accomplishment is the integration not only of the different parts existing in him, but also the integration that while he no longer needs an authority figure's approval, he can feel comfortable acknowledging he likes to have it. He has found the balance and wholeness inside himself.

There are some things to expect when using the exercises that you learned in this chapter. First of all, unless you are an acting student who is accustomed to doing improvisational scripts, don't expect to feel too at home doing this stuff in the beginning. I think it is really important to say this to you because I don't want you to throw away the incredible surprises you are going to get just because you feel a bit weird role-playing. What was it you tried as a kid that made you feel uncomfortable, scared, or silly but in the end turned out to be a blast? Was it dancing? Was it skiing? Was it public speaking?

The discoveries that Gerry and Christine made are not magic. The Gestalt approach to dreams has worked for me a hundred times. And by the way, no matter how familiar I am with doing a Gestalt exercise, I still feel funny anytime I try one, and I still, each time, discover a part of myself or an angle I hadn't thought of before in approaching a situation. I always come away learning something. If, like Gerry, your issue is with authority figures, you will find yourself establishing a new kind of relationship with the real authority figures in your life. Trying Gestalt exercises like talking as the different parts of the dream, and acting out Top Dog and Under Dog, can help you recognize not only the authority figures in yourself, but so many other parts of yourself. This experience is amazing because you realize and reown; you take back all the parts of yourself that you had when you were born. This is an opportunity to go forward living the rest of your life as a whole person with any number of options for any situation. This time, though, it is *you* who chooses how to behave, not anyone else!

I have saved the most powerful benefit of using a Gestalt approach to the very end. Gestalt gives you the practice of getting comfortable with change. And what is life anyway if not a series of changes? Yes, I know we are very uncomfortable about change and often resist it at all costs, but the sad or happy truth is life is a series of changes. And however you want to get away from them, you can't because they are regularly smacking you in the face. You lose your teeth at six or seven years old. Before that, you lost your bottle or mother's breast and had to adjust. When you are twelve or thirteen, you change schools. You can't avoid it. What if a parent dies? What if your parents split up?

What happens after your favorite grandparent dies? You have to adjust. What about when your best friend moves away? Should I go on? You change your jobs, your girlfriends and boyfriends, your stages, and your ages. So why not get comfortable with change? Why not even get good at it? I'm not saying that the process of change is going to disappear. I am saying the process will absolutely become easier, more manageable, because you will become less afraid and more adept at it. It is like anything else in life, the more you practice something the more familiar and less frightening it becomes. And a Gestalt approach, above all, makes you familiar with change inside yourself. It helps you embrace your own change. As Robert Bosnak says, "Dreamwork trains us in developing a sense of direction in the absolute unknown."[5]

LEVEL THREE:
Discovering Your Patterns

CHAPTER SIX

Looking Back in the Mirror

Peppermint Patty, sitting at her school desk. "Sorry, Ma'am. I was asleep . . . and I dreamed I was sleeping, but in the dream where I was sleeping, I dreamed I was awake. . . . Then in the dream where I was awake, I fell asleep, and in the dream where I was sleeping I heard your voice and woke up. Anyway, I think that's how it was. . . . Did you ask me a question? Please don't cry, Ma'am. . . ."

—Charles Schultz

When I use the term looking back in the mirror I am reminded of something I used to do as a child. I remember standing behind the door of my bathroom and arranging the mirror that hung in such a way that it would reflect into the mirror hanging on the wall behind the door. That way I was able to see myself in a mirror that reflected another mirror, inside another mirror inside another mirror, and so on, far away into an unknown distance. It fascinated me and actually, you may not be surprised to hear, still does today. This reflection of the same image has a kind of tunneling effect. In the same way, the issues we face in our current lives reflect familiar attitudes and feelings from our past.

There are a few advantages in discovering how your dream mirrors feelings and events from your past. First, it gives you the opportunity to see if your reaction in the present is an appropriate and accurate one. In the Overview, I gave you an example of how at forty, you might feel disgusted and curse yourself when you spill papers all over the floor. It might turn out that your mother treated you as though you were an incompetent fool when you were four years old for spilling milk. Your dreams afford you the wonderful opportunity of linking a reaction you are having in a current situation to other familiar incidents from your past, or sometimes to memories of the place where your reaction originated. And then you can reassess whether you still feel the same way. For example, you may realize you have a different opinion than your mother had! You might decide to change your opinion. After you understand where your judgments are coming from, you start to catch yourself when you react the way you did as a child.

Another advantage to tracing the origin of your current reaction is that you get to make sure your feelings really *do* belong to your current situation. For example, Henry is overcome with jealousy because he sees his second wife laughing with a business associate of his at a party. His second wife is very devoted to Henry, and he knows that. Yet the scene he is looking at sparked a memory of what he felt fifteen years earlier when he discovered his first wife in an affair. Henry's emotional memory has kicked in. His reaction doesn't fit with his current situation. When you analyze your dream at this level you can tap into where your reaction comes from, and then evaluate if it is appropriate to what is going on now. Henry won't be screaming at his second wife for laughing with his associate after realizing where his reaction is coming from. He is more likely to share his experiences with her, and work together on a more appropriate reaction in their current relationship. In this scenario, his wife can be available to support and understand Henry. That is surely a healthier and more intimate experience for him than yelling at her would have been.

When you link reactions you are experiencing in your current life to familiar situations from your childhood, you have the opportunity not only to reassess the situation, but also to *forgive* the situation. I hope you can always keep this in mind as you look back in the mirror. When you look back in the mirror now, you are looking back as an adult. You can revisit instances from your childhood and discover new emotions which might very soon reside comfortably right next to the ones you felt back then. And your reassessment or opinion may not disagree with your parents. It doesn't always turn out as the spilled milk story did. In a number of instances you may find yourself more understanding of your parents' reactions when you look at them now. Many times, old wounds can become instead a new understanding and along with it forgiveness. Anger is a very hard thing to hold on to. If you can find some understanding and forgiveness through looking deeper into your dream, you can lift some of the weight and feel lighter.

Free Association

So then, how can we go about the business of looking back? In the process of psychoanalysis, Dr. Sigmund Freud invented what he called "free association" to uncover the basic meaning of dreams. He considered this his greatest contribution to science. I agree.

Free association is particularly useful for making links to your past because it helps you tap into that bottomless filing cabinet we each have tucked away in our unconscious mind. Every memory, experience, and feeling you ever had is all recorded in this amazing database called your unconscious. So actually, each time you experience something in your current life, your mind opens the filing cabinet and goes right to the section where you have had similar experiences in the past.

Imagine that the files are filled with CDs and tapes. The recording of your memory plays back and that is where you get your *initial reaction*. I am calling it your *initial reaction* because hopefully, this book will help you decide if in fact you want your initial reaction to remain your *only* reaction.

Free association lets you open the filing cabinet consciously and actively. A good way to start is by looking at your dream map and asking, "Do any of my associations here seem familiar?" or "Does anyone in the dream spark a memory of someone from my past?" Or how about looking to find the major themes in your dream, and asking yourself if they remind you of anything in your life. Or you can try some of the following questions: "When have I felt this way before in my life?" or maybe, "Have I had this reaction somewhere else in my life?" or "Does this behavior feel familiar to me?"

After you ask yourself these questions, or others you come up with, let the answer pop into your head. Go with the first thought that occurs to you. It might seem funny or bizarre, but don't worry about that. Just trust the process. Let your thoughts take you where they want to go.

We saw a beautiful example of a familiar behavior from the past unfolding in Annie's dream, which I discussed earlier. As you'll remember, Annie dreamed she had to inform her siblings of her father's death. We were able to arrive at a memory from her past by looking at what *action* Annie had to take in the dream story. Where else in her life did Annie feel like she had to take responsibility for her siblings? When she asked herself this question, she immediately remembered caring for them as a child while her parents were out, even though she was still so young herself. That memory led her to another, more poignant one in which she worried about having to be the caregiver of her parents in their old age. Annie was able to link those memories and her feelings about them to her current situation, where she felt responsible for everyone else's good time in Montreal. In making this connection and realizing her behavior was the same now as it was then, Annie could step back and re-evaluate her position. Now her reaction to her current problem became a fresh and adult decision.

Here is how Freud himself described free association: "The patient should take up a restful position and close his eyes; he must be explicitly instructed to renounce all criticism of thought-formations which he may perceive. He must also be told that the success of the psychoanalysis depends upon his noting and communicating everything that passes through his mind, and that he must not allow himself to suppress one idea because it seems to him unimportant or irrelevant to the subject, or another because it seems nonsensical. He must preserve an absolute impartiality in respect to his ideas; for if he is unsuccessful in finding the desired solution of the dream, the obsessive idea, or the like, it will be because he permits himself to be critical of them."[1]

So, once you are relaxed with your eyes closed, you can choose a part of the dream you want to free associate with. When you want to work at this deeper level, here's something else you can do. Pick a symbol or an image from your dream. Say the symbol to yourself, or you can write it. For example, if there was a door in your dream, say the word door. Maybe you want to just say it aloud to someone. Then, let the next thought just naturally pop into your head. See what that is. Just continue listening to each thought as it leads to the next. Thoughts do not necessarily come to your mind quickly. If there is a pause in the thought process, don't worry. Just hang in there quietly. I promise, a next thought or image will come.

Jung's direct association, you remember, is spontaneous but needs to constantly come back to the dream. Freud's free association, by contrast, can go far away from the dream, so far away that it no longer seems to have any association with the dream at all. Wait and see though how, even though you think an association has nothing to do with the dream, afterwards you will be able to connect the dots with astonishing results.

Here's an example that came to me from Michael, a recovering cocaine addict, who after his initial understanding of his dream decided to try some free association. Once he connected the feelings from his dream to an incident from his past, he had a better understanding of his reaction to his current and past situations. Before we look at his steps to use free association, here is Michael's dream. He had this dream after his first six weeks of abstaining from drug use. Michael was just beginning his recovery by joining a twelve-step program. I have quickly addressed the initial connections Michael made and how those connections related to his current situation, so you can see how his associations to his past mirrored his current dilemma.

Michael's Dream

He described, "I was walking along a lake with some people. I realized my late father-in-law was there. I told him I miss him, and how happy I was to see him. He was pointing to the other side of the lake, saying how one day they are going to discover five genies buried over there. There was a sense in the way he said it that people didn't believe him yet, but that one day they would.

"Suddenly, I was in a factory or warehouse. I know it was a warehouse because it was made of cinderblock. There was a window to look through to the warehouse. When I looked through the window, there was no machinery though. I realized I was late for an appointment with my old therapist. The appointment time was three o'clock. I looked at my watch and it was five thirty. I went to the phone to call my wife, but when I got to the phone, I dialed my mother's house. I banged down and called again. I could not get in touch with my wife. Suddenly, Jerry (a person from my past) was standing beside me. I said to myself, 'Something is not right here.' Then two people came up on either side of me, each holding me by my arm and said, 'It is time to go now.' I turned my back on Jerry and the warehouse, and we walked through a wall. I knew I had died."

The Interpretation

The following are a series of links that Michael made in order to connect his dream to current events in his life, especially his recent recovery from drug addiction. He is *walking along a lake with some people* because he is "reflecting," just as a lake reflects. Michael was re-assessing events from the past month or so of his life. After years of abusing drugs, he had finally taken steps to help himself, but like any change we go through, the beginning was difficult for him. Change can move many into what I call blackness. It is a depressed place, like a hole, a frustration. It is the place many of us dip into before we can rise up to the task of change. You know that expression, "Things might have to get worse before they get better"? It's like that.

Often you can use your dreams to gauge your feelings or growth as you move along through a crisis. Michael's dream showed him that he was coming out of the "black" and into the reflecting stage. And he is not alone in his reflection. He is walking with other people. They are different parts of him reflecting on his situation and his decision to help himself, not only by abstaining from drug use, but by joining a program to help ensure his success. He still feels ambivalent, but he is moving forward.

Michael brings his *late father-in-law* into the dream for several purposes. One is that his father-in-law is dead and so in one way represents his past. So does his drug use. His active using is dead and buried, like his father-in-law. When Michael said to

his father-in-law in the dream, *"I miss you,"* he made the connection by telling me, "I miss my past, my drug." While
Michael had made a decision to help himself, the addicted part
of him was missing his drug use and feeling unsure about
moving forward to do the best for himself. He is fighting
recovery. He is holding onto his habit of using. It would stand
to reason that a man who had been in active addiction for over
twenty years would be experiencing some ambivalence about
refraining from drug use.

Michael also said of his father-in-law, "I feel happy to see him
because I respected him. He represents someone who was accomplished. The man was very independent." Looking at his dream
from this perspective, Michael's father-in-law is the part of him
who is going to help the addict in him attain a successful recovery.
He represents Michael's sense of self-respect, or his Higher Power.
Notice how the father-in-law, by representing both the "dead" user
side of Michael and his strong, "moving-forward" part, embodies
the pull Michael was feeling between using and quitting.

At the time he had this dream, Michael had just "crossed over"
to a new way of life, a new behavior, just like *the other side of the lake.*
The buried genies, like his father-in-law, represent Michael's active
addiction. They, too, are dead and buried. But when the father-in-
law said that *people didn't believe him yet, but one day they would,* this
goes back again to Michael's ambivalent feelings towards his
recovery. Michael was having difficulty accepting that he had
really stopped using drugs. "I guess when I say that 'one day they
will find the genies,' I'm kind of telling myself that one day I'll be
able to use again. Genies come up in a 'puff of smoke,' don't they?
It's like I still hope I'll be able to find the 'smoke' one day."

And yet, like his father-in-law, genies are strong. I asked
Michael, "Can you see how finding the genies can be a strength
for you?" He was quick to answer, "Genies grant wishes, don't
they? They are powerful." The dreamer reminds himself of his

strength again, as he did with his father-in-law. The genies also represent his Higher Self. They (these parts of Michael) can work miracles. They may be stuck in a bottle now, like the dreamer stuck in his addiction, but when they are freed they will grant Michael's wish.

The more Michael looked at this dream, the more he saw signs of a pull that had been inside him for many years, ever since his childhood. About the warehouse, Michael said, "All those twenty or so years ago, when I started smoking dope, were the same days that I used to work in a *warehouse*." And *"Jerry, a person from my past,"* he explained, was someone from his teenage years whom he used to get stoned with. So Jerry too represents the past. He is another symbol of youth. Jerry represents a way that Michael used to behave, in his past (since he is no longer using). Michael added, "At forty-five, he still lives at home with his parents. He is still stoned and still working in a warehouse."

I offered, "So he is 'still,' unable to move, like the genies in the bottle."

"Yes!" he agreed. "And Jerry is also the antithesis of my father-in-law. He is an example of an insecure, unaccomplished, overdependent person who has a very low self-esteem. He has no control, and I feel disdain for him." Here we have Michael's disowned part, his Shadow. It is the side of himself he disdains.

When he *went to the phone to call his wife, but dialed his mother's house*, Michael explained his wife had been hounding him to stop using. She was behaving like his mother. "I *could not get in touch* with my wife," he said, "because she refuses to be my 'partner in crime' any longer. And she is immovable on the subject. Even though I was swearing to her I would cut down on my using, I simply could not get in touch with her, literally. She doesn't hear me anymore. I feel very separate from her." Michael realized that on the deeper level, he was having trouble getting in touch with the part of himself he loves. It is another ambivalence in the dream.

When he says, *"Something is not right here,"* it is simple. Even Freud said, "Sometimes a cigar is just a cigar!" The dreamer knows something is not right. And he feels nervous. There's a sense of fear here because change and recovery are a scary business. On the other hand, when *two people came up on either side of him, holding him by the arm,* Michael gives himself the solution to his dilemma. In bringing those people into his dream, he displays his ability to support himself the very minute he becomes fearful. Also, the two people on either side of him are Michael's way of telling himself to reach out for support. In fact, at the time of the dream, he had only just joined a recovery program. The program he is in closes their meetings in a circle. They say, "With an addict on my left and an addict on my right, God behind me, and my program in front of me, I have nothing to fear." He seems to have created that same imagery in the dream.

Michael says that in the dream he *knew he had died.* Actually, Michael called to have his dream interpreted precisely because he woke palpitating and frightened silly that the dream meant he was going to die. The death in this story is not a premonition. It is a re-evaluation. This dream is a perfect example of how an apparently negative message is in reality a metaphor for a very positive decision. Michael decided to say "good-bye" to the using side of himself. That part of him had died. But this is not a death. It is a birth. He wakes frightened and palpitating because what he has decided to do in his re-evaluation is go forward and recover. And that is scary.

Getting There

Michael was able to get back to the place where his drug addiction started by using free association with the feelings in his dream. When I first asked Michael to choose a part of his dream to free associate with, he had some difficulty trying to connect. So, I asked him to see what comes to his mind when he thinks about his father-in-law, about what it feels like to look up to someone, to believe in what they say is going to happen even when others may not. I asked, "Where do you think you have felt that before in your life?" He just couldn't do it. All he could come up with was that he respects and looks up to his boss.

When you find yourself blocked while trying to free associate, give it up. Just move on. Pick some other piece of the dream. He did, suggesting we go to the end of the dream. I asked Michael, "You say you said to yourself, 'Something is not right here,' and next thing you knew you were dead. What did that feel like?"

"It felt like there was no turning back. These men were serious when they said 'It's time to go now.' I felt that sinking feeling. The inevitable, no escape."

"Just relax, and breathe. Think about where you may have felt that feeling before."

"That's easy. I felt that way when my father died!" he said sounding a bit frustrated. Then he added with some skepticism, "I mean, there are any number of a million subjects a person can choose where in their life they had a sinking feeling!"

"Well, yes," I agreed, "but just go with me on this one for a minute. When someone dies, unless you murdered them, it's not like they died because of anything *you* did. When you attach this dream to your current issue, it has more of a sense that the inevitable conclusion is based on some responsibility on your part too. That's different than the example of your dad dying, although I can relate to that sinking feeling there. Is there any other situation where you had that sinking feeling you can connect to where you played a part in the inevitable result?"

His answer was swift. "Yeah. My functions exam, grade ten."

"What happened?"

"I failed my exam. I had to go to summer school. It screwed up my whole summer. I never understood functions the whole way through high school. I had no idea where to use logarithms. I just didn't know what to do with them."

The reason I want you to become familiar with using free association is not so that you should go so far away from the dream that you never get back to it. I am introducing free association to enable you to link your reaction in today's situation to the place where it originated, for the purpose of giving you insight. It can help you re-evaluate the situation then and decide if the one today is the same. Do you want to choose the same reaction? Did it work then? Do you think it will work now? It is your choice. That is the point. I believe with insight comes choice and with choice comes power.

Remembering that Michael tried to telephone his wife in the dream but ended up telephoning his mother's house instead, I inquired, "What happened with your mum when you failed functions? Was she angry with you? Did she support you?"

"It wasn't her problem! It was my problem. Her attitude was very simple. You got yourself into this, now you have to get yourself out."

"Did you feel upset with her?"

"No. I agree with her."

"You can agree with the bottom line, but you could have still felt that you needed her support, though."

"No," Michael disagreed with me. "It would have been different if I would have come to her at the beginning of the year and said, 'I'm having trouble with functions.' She would have supported me and hired a tutor. But I didn't. I just let things get out of hand and now I had to deal with it. I would feel the same way if it were my own kid."

Remember Gerry and his Brother Dream? Part of the reason Gerry brought his brother into his dream was because his brother represented the authority figure that lives inside Gerry. And that is what we often do. We'll bring a parent or older sibling into the dream in order to tap into that Top Dog aspect of ourselves. We see this here in how Michael brought his mother into his dream. Her presence is his unconscious way of reminding himself of his own responsibility for letting his drug use get out of hand before asking for help. She's his Top Dog.

I asked Michael, "Where is the learning in the dream? Does your associating so quickly with summer school have any learning or connection to your current issue about being in a recovery program, and feeling angry with your wife in what you feel is a lack of support on her part?"

"Okay," he admitted. "I see the connection. My wife can't do this for me. I have to do it myself. I let things get way out of hand just like I did with functions. I guess I have trouble asking for help or acknowledging there is something going on until it is too late."

"And does that seem familiar to you from your past? Can you connect that to anything that comes to mind?"

Michael thought for a minute, seeming somehow more open now to the process. He smiled. "When my father died, I was young. So was he. The house and people in it were in turmoil for a long period of time. I learned it was better to just lay low and stay in the background. I imagine that is where I learned not to ask for help. I didn't want to disturb things that were already so upsetting."

"Beautiful," I said. "You came full circle. By the way, did you pass your functions course in the end?"

"Yeah. But I passed it because I cheated on the exam."

"Well, it seems to me you are making a more honest attempt in getting yourself out of your mess this time as the adult. After all, you have joined a recovery program and have been able to ask for help."

Finally, what is the learning? Next time Michael feels himself holding back from asking for help, he can link his level of discomfort to the situation it belonged to then, his father's death. But now he can ask himself, "Is this the same? Will I be completely disrupting a household if I express my needs in my current situation?" And he can base his decision on the answer to that question. He will have separated his emotional memory from his current situation.

In closing, Michael's ability to link his dream to his past taught him three main things. One, that when re-evaluating his anger towards what he perceived as his wife's lack of support, he instead became focused on his own responsibility for joining a recovery program. And in this case, he found that he, the adult, agreed with his parents' message when applied to his current situation. But feeling more comfortable about asking for help, he decided that the old message doesn't fit for his situation now. And so he, the adult, can decide today to get more comfortable in a recovery program where the main focus is your ability to admit to your powerlessness and ask for help. Chances are Michael is on the road to change, and hopefully will be getting more and more relaxed about asking for help long before he finds he's in too deep.

Here we are again. We have arrived at another truth sprinkled with ambivalence. In admitting your powerlessness, you gather your strength. And the sure sign of a truly independent person, is someone who is comfortable acknowledging his dependency on others.

While Michael's starting point for free association was that sinking feeling of the inevitable, another dreamer might use the *events* and how they unfold in the dream as her starting point to free associate because those events remind her of some past event. You know, while I appreciate the learning available for us when we access that cabinet in our unconscious, it doesn't always have to be so serious. Here's an amusing example of an event in the dream that triggered the memory of an event from the dreamer's past.

As you'll read in the next chapter, I went back to some of the dreamers whose stories I describe in this book, in order to discover if they have experienced any changes in their approach to situations since analyzing their dreams. I took a walk with Annie and was so happy to learn that in just the last few days, she had woken with a puzzling dream and had decided to use some free association in order to see where it might lead her. Since she was alone while doing the exercise, she wrote her associations down without stopping to think about what she was writing. That is a great tool to use, especially when you're alone. And the rules are the same—don't judge, just write anything that comes up. So Annie dreamed she was at a yoga class, which is something she really likes to do. She went into the washroom before the class and was shocked and disgusted to find excrement all over the place! She decided it was not her job to clean it up, just took her towel and went to begin the class. There she was lying on her towel during the class, and she realized there was some of this stuff on the back of her towel! She just continued on with the class. The scene changed and she found herself in the hallway of the house she knows was her late aunt's. Annie said that while she felt uncomfortable that her aunt was somewhere there, she knew and felt safe that here was the place where she could get cleaned up.

Here she was with her writing pad thinking . . . "Now where did this poop come from? Where in my life have I experienced poop? What does it make me think of?" The answer was not long coming. When Annie was a young child, she and her two little sisters were sent off to their aunt's house for a few weeks over the summer vacation. Annie was the eldest sister, and so felt responsible for watching after her younger siblings. One

night the three little girls were in the bath together, and the lit-
tlest one pooped right in the tub! Annie remembers feeling mor-
tified. She recalls questioning her little sister emphatically,
"Why? Why did you do that in the tub? You know better than
that! We'll never get invited back here!" Poor Annie certainly
couldn't clean up that mess herself and they called out to their
aunt for help.

At this point Annie stopped, thinking, waiting for the next
thought to come. There it was. The same trip. The same sister,
who must have been around three years old, was given a sandwich by her aunt. That was a time when Annie wasn't around.
It was during that lunch that a horse came by. A horse coming
by was considered a big event and Annie was sorry that she
missed it, sorrier still when she heard that her little sister had
taken the sandwich her aunt made for her and thrown it in the
horse's dung! Aha! Annie thought, more poop.

I hope Annie's experience has shown you that you can have
fun with free association. There is no one standing there telling
you what you have to discover or when. Your unconscious
mind knows exactly how and when to take care of you and
move you along this road to awareness. It's like they say about
when to tell your kid about sex. I believe the rule of thumb is,
don't give out any unasked-for information, but when your
child poses a question it is because he is ready for the answer.
The same is true here. Your unconscious is not going to give
you anything you can't handle. And while I'm in this area of
discussion, you don't have to bother pushing yourself to make
some miraculous overnight change of reaction to any given
subject. The key word is change, some change, and small
change. The second key word is process. You know you're not
going anywhere, are you? You've been this certain way for how
many years? Give yourself a break and have fun with it. Use
whatever discoveries you make as an opportunity to pat your-

self on the back for your cleverness, and for the sheer thrill of the investigation!

Figure 4: Sarah's Uncle Dream

When Sarah wanted to look deeper into her dream, I asked her to think about the main themes (see page 22 for the dream map).

"What are the salient issues in your dream?"

Sarah thought about the notion of commitment. Then relaxing and letting one theme lead her to another theme or to the next thought, she spoke out loud.

"The main theme that runs through both mirrors of my dream is commitment. What is my commitment to myself? Am I willing to make a commitment to myself to succeed in my work? Am I committed enough to myself to speak up for what I feel *I deserve* in my relationship? Committed enough to speak up for what I want?"

"So your theme is more than a commitment, but it is also about how much commitment you feel you deserve?"

"Yes. That is what I think I must weigh. What do I think I deserve? And it is the answer to that question that will determine what action I will take in either of my situations."

I repeated back to her, "Deserving or not. Do you deserve what you get? Think about that for a minute. Take your time. Don't push anything away that comes up. Just wait. Does that feeling seem familiar to you? Do you remember ever weighing what you think you deserve or not?" She was thinking, drifting. I added, "Why don't you add to that a sense of feeling uncomfortable and weird, maybe even angry or frustrated about the weighing. I'm saying that because there is an element of your feeling uncomfortable in both mirrors too."

"Well I know exactly when I felt weird, uncomfortable, frustrated, and angry! And it is exactly when I was questioning whether I got what I deserved or not! When my father died!"

Sarah had found the link to her past. She had lost her father when she was a preteen. Sarah remembered asking herself the question, "Why me? Why did I lose my dad? What did I do to deserve this terrible thing that has happened to me? Why am I being punished?"

Issues about our level of confidence and what we feel we deserve can manifest themselves in times of crisis. These feelings can present themselves when we try to answer that "Why me?" question. How can we feel deserving of good things at the same time as feeling we have been punished? In some ways Sarah may have felt undeserving of great success because her unconscious remembers the assumptions she made long ago as a preteen. Sarah said she felt punished for losing her dad at such a young age.

Once more, the use of an uncle from her father's side of the family had many purposes. He brought to mind the question of how much success she felt was coming or not coming to her. By re-examining feelings and assumptions from long ago, Sarah took the opportunity to re-evaluate those assumptions from a different perspective, her adult view of the situation. When she was thirteen years old, Sarah understandably felt punished on an emotional level. As the adult, she knows rationally that life takes some weird and difficult turns for each of us in different ways.

On an intellectual level Sarah believes that her father's death was not a punishment to her, and yet she understands there is a part of her that will always remember having felt that way at the time. I am not suggesting that this added perspective erased the feelings of the thirteen-year-old girl who still lives inside Sarah. I am focusing on the benefits of obtaining an alternative perspective. In this regard, I believe you can achieve great success in changing the way you feel about yourself. Faraday calls dream work the place that can lead us "to a reappraisal of our whole mode of being."[2] And so it did in this instance.

Age or Time Frame

Allow me to introduce the method of focusing on the age of someone in your dream, or the time of life that the dream brings you back to. This is what I call "age or time frame." We can use this element as a point of entry in a few different ways. Before I discuss how age or time frame can help you discover important deeper aspects of your dream, let us look first at how it can often help you solve the puzzle of the dream by linking you to the current issue in your life.

Say, for example, there is a person in the dream who is twelve years old. This information would come out during the interview and mapping stage, if in describing a person you mention his or her age. And it wouldn't be an accident that you give this information. When a dreamer says a person's age, pay attention! It is there to point you to a relevant association that has taken place. When using an age number as a point of entry, you can ask questions like, "Did anything happen twelve days ago? Is anything coming up in the next twelve days? Does any memory click about something that may have happened to you twelve years ago? Are you twelve years away from turning forty, fifty, or sixty? Was there anything major that happened to you when you were twelve?"

You saw me use this method in Chapter 3 when my daughter Chelsea dreamed she had *three weeks* to live. We discovered the dream's meaning by realizing that her exams were beginning in *three weeks*.

Time frame or age frame can come into a dream as a place, too. A certain place can make you think of a time when you used to behave in a certain way, and it is there because you are reacting to a current situation in the same way as you used to react then. I remember feeling totally unable to cope when I first sent Lisa and Chelsea to overnight camp years ago. I would lie around missing them all day, every day. I had such a difficult time letting go and getting on with my days. I felt as though they were never coming home again.

In one dream of mine, I was preparing dinner in the town house where I used to live during the year I gave birth to Tina. In the dream, I even went upstairs to the room I had prepared for her when she was born. When someone pointed out to me that perhaps I was associating Lisa and Chelsea's leaving to how I felt when I placed Tina in an institution, it clicked. I found my "child leaving home" file in the filing cabinet, and it turned out that the most important recording came from the day we placed Tina in an institution.

Once I brought this discovery out to my conscious mind, I was able to separate the two situations and create a new memory based on Lisa and Chelsea, who would only be gone for seven weeks. I am not going to suggest that the minute I understood the dream, I was also immediately able to separate the emotions as different. But the truth is, it actually didn't take that long before I was appreciating the free time their stay at overnight camp gave me. Pretty soon I was feeling an emotion much more appropriate to the circumstance I was facing.

Here's another cool link about time frame and the way we can associate people in our dream with a certain time in our lives. It is precisely around the time her father died that Sarah may have had feelings of being more closely connected or *married* to her uncle. That shift of relying on an uncle or aunt after your mother or father has passed away is very typical and actually helpful, especially when you lose your parent at a young age. And the transfer of dependence to that relative might even seem *weird,* which is how Sarah described she felt in her dream. Sarah's shift to feeling figuratively married to her uncle would have happened around the same time that she got the notion or belief that she had been punished, back to the time when she first felt undeserving in some way. These are the core issues of Sarah's dream and, of course, another reason why she chose the symbol of her uncle. Besides all the other reasons we have discovered for his appearance in the dream, her uncle is there to link Sarah to that time in her life when all those emotions became Sarah's way of operating.

More Mapping for Fun

Sometimes after I have an understanding of a dream, I like to look back to the map. I'll tell you why. It is not only because I am a puzzle maniac, it is also because I continue to be positively astounded by our level of precision when choosing symbols and metaphors. And you can more easily see these linking metaphors after you have discovered what the dream was addressing in the first place. Once I have cracked the initial code and attached the dream to a current issue, and to a particular person the issue is with, I go back to the map. It's so exciting to find all the links. Sometimes I discover one symbol that carries with it multiple meanings. And sometimes I can see how a message was repeated with different images.

So, this is what you do. You are breaking the symbols down into categories, or parts. Stay open to thinking like this. The number twenty-seven is not only the number twenty-seven. It is also nine times three. It is also eighteen plus nine, and twenty plus seven. A house on the street where your brother lives might be there to remind you of your sister. They are both your siblings. Similarly, sometimes you'll see someone in the dream who has a feature that looks like the person you are trying to say something to yourself about. Freud called this phenomenon displacement, when you dream of one person in order to remind yourself of another. Remember the example I gave you whereby if I want to say, "I am scared" to myself, it can appear with three different pictures in a few or the same dream. This happens because in my personal, emotional dictionary, "I'm scared" can come across as a ghost, the abyss of a cliff, or equally by seeing my grade five teacher in my dream. And the dream repeats the message to make sure I am getting it. Earlier I referred to this function of dreams as rote.

This dimension of rote operates in Sarah's dream. We saw it when looking at the dream Sarah had just before the Uncle Dream. In the first dream, there was another male from her past, just as her uncle is from her past. The man in the first dream was someone Sarah thought she could trust, same as she thought she could trust her uncle. Do you see what I mean? Sarah has said "a male I know from my past, who I think I can trust" to herself twice, each time using two different people. We now know that the person she was having a problem with at the time of the dream was her boyfriend, and he is a male, who she thinks she can trust, that she knows from her past. There are two more ways she pointed to the issue being about her boyfriend. One was how her friend who appeared in her first dream used to be her boyfriend. So here she was saying "boyfriend" to herself. The second is in how the ex-boyfriend in her dream behaved out of character when he suddenly pushed her into the closet. The metaphor is repeated in the Uncle Dream when he too behaves out of character by proposing to her. Look at all these repeats. Sarah is saying "a person from my past, who I thought I could trust, but who is behaving out of character." More specifically, Sarah is saying, "My boyfriend, who I met years ago, is behaving out of character."

You'll just be amazed at the way your own mind makes connections in your dreams. When you are trying to say, "I know this person from the past" to yourself, the image in your dream might also come in the form of a house you used to live in during the same time frame as you met that person. Maybe it will be a room or even a street you lived on in your past. When you dream about a certain person from your family, your current issue may not be with that particular family member at all! You may be just attempting to say "family member" to yourself. Ellen recently dreamed about a home that is on the street where her brother lives. A little free association with the house in her dream pointed her to a problem she was working out that actually had to do with her sister. This is exactly how our personal dictionary and associations appear in our dreams. We are really just talking to ourselves in the language that only we understand! And when you think about it, it really isn't so strange that we do this. When you are talking to *yourself*, why would you really need anyone else to understand but yourself?

Figure Five: The Emma-Jo Dream
Part One: A Woman's Place

To connect the meaning in the Emma-Jo Dream (see pages 26–27 for the dream map), to something deeper, something inside my belief system that originated from my childhood and continues to operate today, I looked at the main feelings running throughout my dream, fear and excitement. There is adventure, into the unknown. And there is danger and panic. Where did I feel these emotions before? Where have I acted this way in my life?

When attempting to focus on where and when in my past I could have taken an adventure into the unknown, and felt fear and excitement, I must be honest that I was more quickly able to connect to the many times *I missed* having those feelings and experiences! My father was a European from the "old country."

He had a strict set of rules. A very loving parent, he had a ridiculous sense of humor, and a beautiful singing voice. My father was a tenacious businessman, one of the most tenacious people I have yet to meet. He had a very strong personality and had the power to make me shake in my boots if I didn't follow his way of doing things. He was the boss in our house, the authority figure in my head.

I grew up in the sixties. While many of my friends went to Woodstock, that was an adventure I never even would have *thought* to ask my parents if I could go to. I remember being in a city choir when I was around thirteen years old, and having the opportunity to travel to Europe with them to perform. My father forbade my going. Several of my friends traveled to Europe backpacking when I was around seventeen. Like the Woodstock concert, it wasn't necessarily a matter of my parents refusing me, I never even asked. As far as moving out of the house was concerned, that was something a woman would do only when she was getting married. Going against my father's word was something that would surely have given me that sense of danger and excitement, but that was something I did not venture out to do.

I am not suggesting that I was a model child or something. I wasn't. I by no means paid attention to everything my parents said, and many times I "opened a big mouth" as they put it, to my mother, but about matters like travelling or moving out, I followed what was considered appropriate in my parents' view. It is fair to say I was not encouraged to become independent. If anything, the opposite is true. When I was growing up, I understood a message. A woman had her place. Her place was at home raising the family. More than once when I worried about a grade on an exam, my dad assured me, "Don't worry! It'll be okay. You'll get married!" Now there's a message for you. You don't need to succeed. Someone else is going to look after you.

Interestingly, by the time I was in my early thirties, my father had moved away from his original message. It was my father who backed me in the kiddie ride business after my divorce from Murray, and taught me everything I know about business altogether. He was a very patient and encouraging teacher. I followed what he taught me to a tee. If there have been times in my life when I have blamed my parents for the messages they sent me, dream work has helped me realize there is no blame. I am a parent. I am human. I do not believe any parent wakes up some morning and says to him or herself, "Today I am going to teach this child not to strive for her highest potential. I am going to screw this kid's confidence up!" All parents do the best they know how to do. And they do it with *what they have*, with what they *know*. Yet this "less than" message was transmitted to me, and I accepted it.

I chose to move ahead full steam with doing dream analysis publicly partly in response to my midlife crisis. In the second half of my life I desire to give something of myself to helping people, while at the same time taking the opportunity to engage in a career that I love. As Oprah Winfrey would say, I have discovered my passion, I have found my spirit. But at this new stage in my life, I am still grappling with the original messages I picked up when I was young. In going public with my dream work, I was questioning my potential, my worth. What were my chances of success? I found myself like the boy in *The Alchemist*, "He had to choose between something he had become accustomed to and something he wanted to have." However difficult change is, even in the face of tremendous fear, once I have an idea in my heart, it becomes harder and harder to ignore it. In the story of *The Alchemist*, The Sun advised the boy, "Even if you pretend not to have heard what it [your heart] tells you, it will always be there inside you, repeating to you what you're thinking about life and about the world. . . . People are afraid to pursue their most important dreams, because they feel that they don't deserve them, or that they'll be unable to achieve them."[3]

Let us get back to the questions that continue to surface from my personal emotional memory. Is it a woman's place to be out in the world, working and achieving success? Is it appropriate? Am I comfortable with success? And similar to Sarah with her Uncle Dream, do I feel deserving? *Each* of you too has your *own* issues that you face in your life. You will all have the challenge, and the opportunity, to rise above your habitual way of operating. Your filing cabinet is going to push open and play that same CD every time you venture out to try something that contradicts what your initial messages were. The Emma-Jo Dream pointed me to mine. And if I succeed in my new business venture, I *am* in some strange way rebelling against the status quo. In running out of the car, Emma-Jo also symbolizes *me,* breaking away from what I imagined were my parents' ideas of my capabilities. I am individuating. No wonder I felt the fear of danger! It was a move far away from where I had been taught a woman should venture. I was rebelling against my father's messages of my youth and he wasn't even here anymore to witness it. But my fear of danger and excitement were *alive.* "Under optimal circumstances, a metamorphosis has occurred as we emerge from midlife. We have been able to grieve our lost youth, free ourselves of the inner constraints of our parents, master the emotional blocks lingering from childhood, discover new identities, and define ourself in new ways."[4]

Part Two: Numbers in Dreams

So now what? Now that we have "grieved our lost youth, freed ourselves of the inner constraints of our parents, mastered the emotional blocks lingering from childhood, discovered new identities, and defined ourselves in new ways," does this mean we're out of the woods? Can you somehow miraculously make all your conflicts and insecurities go away? Well if I can, then how come I actually feel panicked and screaming in the dream? Before I address the answer to that question, here is another piece I discovered while investigating my Emma-Jo Dream. And I want you to notice how, by discovering a different aspect of my dream, I was in the end able to put them together to help me come to a resolution that really satisfied me. I am asking you to notice this benefit because it is one of my main points in writing this book, to illustrate to you that less is good, but more is better.

Remember I discussed the value of working in a group setting? You get the advantage of having such a broad perspective when you work with a group. There are that many more people's life experiences and perceptions to widen your understanding of your dream.

In the group that discussed my Emma-Jo Dream, we were talking about how I was having trouble "getting a hold of" that little girl. A woman in the group asked me if anything ever happened to me when *I* was four. I almost fell off my chair. You see I almost died when I was close to four. I had the croup. Though my family doctor thought it might wait until morning, my mother followed her intuition that evening. Not that long after he left the house, she and my dad rushed me to the hospital. The hospital staff saw that I was having trouble breathing. They apparently threw me on the operating table with my clothes on and gave me a tracheotomy. I have but a vague recollection of that experience. I mean, I know it happened to me. I have a scar on my neck, like Elizabeth Taylor's, to remind me. I just have never really thought about it and certainly was not prepared for what suddenly occurred to me at that moment. Another reason I had brought four-year old Emma-Jo into the dream was to remind myself about looking after my "internal" young child.

And furthermore, as far as I am concerned, it is no accident that the image of this little girl appeared in my dream to remind me of my close encounter with death at a time in my life when I had my *own* four-year-old. You see, Emma-Jo was blaming herself for having caught the chicken pox during that week and was very worried that she may have "swallowed a pox by mistake," as she put it to me. I had to assure her over the phone that she was not responsible for contracting her illness.

Thinking back to this conversation I had with little Emma-Jo, I came to imagine how frightened *I* must have been when I was four. To make matters worse, when I woke from the operation I was unable to speak, and had the trache in my neck. I know my parents were very frightened by the experience. Worried that I might catch something else, my Mum, I understand, refused to send me back to school for a long time. In her account, she describes the doctor as trying to calm her down, to alleviate *her* fears enough to send me back to school, so that our family could return to a normal life. Forty-some years ago parents and professionals were probably not as sensitized to the importance of the *child's* reactions to traumatic incidents. They were not likely as concerned about the fears I must have been experiencing as they would be today.

Since understanding this level of interpretation of the Emma-Jo Dream, I have changed the dream in two ways. Having worked with the Gestalt framework that I discussed in Chapter 4, I was so tapped into the different parts of the dream being parts of myself that I sometimes take the part of the little girl in the dream. Using active imagination, when I picture it now, I see *myself* with the blonde curly hair I had as a child, walking into the field instead of little Emma-Jo. (Her hair is light brown.) This helps me connect to that little girl who was surely so frightened by her childhood trauma of a near-death experience, and waking in a hospital in pain, unable to speak.

The second way I use active imagination is for the benefit of bringing forward my motherly characteristics, so they can take care of this little girl inside me. I imagine my adult self, as I am in the dream, but now using the calm I take from my male side, to get out of the car and find Emma-Jo. I walk into the field with her. I experience a kind of dual picture. The child is myself, and she is Emma-Jo too. Here and now, in the present, it is not too late for me to console the part of myself who was so frightened back then. Especially since I have the good fortune to live with a child that age and can actually see how she feels responsible and worries about matters that are not, in fact, her fault. When I hug Emma-Jo, I can use those moments to visualize me hugging myself as a little girl. This method is very effective. Here is another reason why I believe it was no accident that I chose to have that particular dream at that exact time in my life. I believe that the act of visualizing myself hugging a little girl of four years old was easy for me to do, because I had one. And what better time for me to practice taking care of my own inner child than when I am caring for my actual child.

Footnote: A Move Toward Maturity: Individuation

Letting go of an internalized way of operating is no easy feat. It is common for people to procrastinate about the changes that need take place in order to separate from their parents in a healthy way. Holding on to the past is a great excuse for not moving forward. It is a way of avoiding risk—the risk associated with failure and the risk associated with success.

Let's look at this. On the one hand, I am suggesting that for me to succeed is in some way going against the expectations of my parents. For if I were following the messages I understood as a child, I would stay home with the kids, and leave it up to my husband and my inheritance from my father to look after me. And you already know that I have taken the opposite decision by going ahead with my business idea. As you learned from reading Chapter 4, the way I have accomplished this is by attempting to push down that female side of myself in order to let my male side drive the car.

Yet just now, only a few short paragraphs ago, here I was discussing how I can use my motherly, female side to nurture the little girl inside me. Don't you want to say, "Hey! Make up your mind!" Well okay. Go ahead and say it, because we seem to have arrived at the same ambivalence that we looked at in Chapter 4. So when I tell you that letting go of our internalized way of operating is no easy feat, I mean it. We are never out of the woods. Our initial reactions will always be there. That is because you never *do* entirely let your internalized way of operating go.

But that doesn't mean you have to let it hold you back. I am coming full circle here. It's true, you can't entirely let your old reactions go because of that darn filing cabinet we talked about. They will always be filed there under your *initial reaction*. And I think that's fine, as long as you have that awareness. When the drawer flies open, you might say, "Oh hi there! Here you are again, my old familiar friend!" But don't say it in an angry way like, "Oh no! I am reacting like this again!" Accept this part of yourself. Welcome her. She's part of you. This is not about cursing yourself, it is about knowing and accepting yourself. And by the way, when you open the cabinet, don't forget the bonus of adding new data to the database.

So I say again, these polarities, these ambivalent parts can and do coexist inside you. And I am so happy they do, because in my case I don't want to disown my female, motherly side. I need her to nurture that little girl in me who almost died! And I can access her to be kind enough to myself to accept her presence in myself. I mean, she is there for my girls, why can't she be there for me too? I don't have to ignore that side of myself the second I am thinking business. I want to point out to you that no matter which framework you might use to think about your dreams, the salient issues you feel ambivalent about are bound to resurface. The thing is that any of the frameworks you choose presents a different angle. One will click with you better than another. Or maybe you are like me and want to investigate all the angles. What do they say? "Whatever works, use it."

Finally, I want to address one last point about successfully breaking away from our parents. We never *do* stop having a mother or father image around. If we try to stamp out that part of ourselves, we will only be ruthlessly holding down a part of our personality. And if we think it's *bad* to have that image, then we will be ashamed of that part of ourselves. Anyway, maybe it's easier to reach real forgiveness if we can accept that we will always have a parent-child relationship with our parents. It is what I was talking about in Chapter 5. We are interdependent, and considering that is our human nature, we may as well accept that part of ourselves.

So the purpose of looking to this level of a dream is only in the first place to understand the origin of your reactions to events in your current life. Secondly, it is at this level that we can re-evaluate those reactions and decide if they fit for us today. But you reap the most benefit when looking to this layer so you can better understand your parents' good intentions. That is something I think we can only accomplish from looking back as an adult. And what a bonus when you can go back to where you come from and conclude with the ability to forgive your parents for simply being who they are. Surely that helps you forgive and accept *yourself* for simply being who *you* are!

Resolving the Pattern

"And to think I could have been a simple brain surgeon!"
—Sigmund Freud,
as imagined by Ralph Steadman

Once a dream has helped us identify our patterns, how then do we go about resolving those patterns we have formed? In this chapter, let's examine how the original solutions to the dreamer's current problem can be applied to other issues in her life. One place to begin is by asking, "How can I apply the *specific solution* to the specific problem identified in this dream, to the *patterned responses* I have just discovered?" We saw this happen with Annie when she became aware of her patterned reaction to responsibility. After using the dream to identify her behavioral patterns and build on her strengths, she was able to superimpose the dream solution from her current problem with her siblings to a later situation concerning her husband and stepdaughter.

The dream work gives you the opportunity to re-evaluate how you see yourself. You can then decide to change what you see. When you see yourself differently, you automatically *treat* yourself differently too. As I pointed out earlier, when you spilled milk on the floor and your mother looked at you as if you were a clumsy incompetent, you may have just accepted and adopted that as a truth simply because it appeared as your mother's truth. (She may not even have felt that way, but instead was expressing her frustration and you perceived her frustration as a comment about your incompetence.) Either way, once you have identified your pattern of coming down too hard on yourself every time an accident occurs, you won't have to feel stuck in your reaction anymore! There is an almost immediate shift in your perception, the moment you have the awareness.

I am not suggesting that you would immediately stop cursing yourself for spilling papers off your desk and onto the floor. It may continue to be your initial reaction for some time. But the truth is, it won't take long before you catch yourself each time you slip into that old pattern. Then you can replace it with your new, reassessed opinion of yourself. And as you learned in Chapter 4, once you have learned to exercise the different aspects of your character, you are no longer stuck in that "I always react that way!" phrase.

Although we often resist change for fear of embarking on new territory, take this opportunity to see your potential as an *adventure*. Besides, you'll never be bored with yourself. Nor will those around you. They'll never know for sure what to expect from you! I like to think that I spent the first half of my life in a certain mode of behavior, so I may as well try something new during the second half.

I wanted to subtitle this chapter "Playing a different game on the back nine." I'll tell you why. That really describes exactly what the general theme of this book is turning out to be. Our dreams have led us to a general discussion about the process of separating from our parents and maturing into the unique person each of us is. And hopefully, this does take place as we go through our lives. There are those who never really develop the interest of looking in. I am not judging that. I do believe though, that life becomes more interesting if we look to play the back nine differently than we did the front. There's no one over you like there was when we were kids to tell you what to do. You are free. The world is at your fingertips and you can exercise it all.

And just to model a change for you, here you will find the Emma-Jo Dream. Now, had you gotten used to seeing her towards the *end* of each chapter with some general learning to close off? Well, adjust your rhythm, for here to begin the chapter is the Emma-Jo Dream, with some general human tendencies you can familiarize yourself with right at the beginning. Just wanted to make sure you're awake! I'm doing it differently for the back nine in the book too.

Figure 5: The Emma-Jo Dream

After analyzing my dream through the layers so far (see pages 26–27), I came up with two separate elements. One as you remember, is for me to acknowledge the side of myself who feels frightened in the face of my other entrepreneurial, risk-taking side. It will help if I smile and say hello to this fearful part of me when she appears, rather than pushing her down like that big beach ball. She will just keep popping up. So I may as well expect her, maybe even embrace her. The second element has to do with my family and my past. Looking back in the mirror, what have I discovered? I discovered that my male side has manifested itself in the way that it has because of my father's modeling as I was growing up. It is the behavior I adopted from his influence that pushes forward whenever I find myself in a scary or difficult position in life. He showed by example how confidence, hard work, and luck always led him to success.

My dad was self-taught. He was the most persistent person I ever met. If he took an interest in astronomy, he set to reading every book he could get on the subject. He spoke eight languages. It was only in his early sixties that he decided to learn Spanish. After a short while, he became fluent. He knew numbers, business, philosophy, and religion upside down. That never-give-up attitude I got from him continues to drive me through any major issue I have experienced in my life. Whatever else my father may have done that I feel disappointed about, for this incredible drive he showed me, I am thankful to him.

When I tap into this part of myself in the Emma-Jo Dream, it is almost as if I must completely ignore the panicked part of me in order to turn the car around. I literally have to look the other way. It is this same fearless mechanism I adopted from my father that helped me ignore the panic and focus on my determined, optimistic side when I decided to become pregnant with Lisa so soon after having Tina. Another example was when I went public with dream analysis and opened The Dream Interpretation Center, forging ahead despite the panic lurking in the background which inspired the Emma-Jo Dream in the first place.

I see this push and pull in every important decision I have made in my life. It is what Alfred Adler would have called my *lifestyle*. You have your own "lifestyle" too. You can see it in the way you approach all your major decisions. It's your general style related to your actions and reactions. It is the way you live your life. For instance, some people are laid-back people and others are go-get-it people. You'd probably say I am a go-get-it person. I agree, but at the same time I feel afraid and try to ignore my worries.

The most current example of my lifestyle is happening right now, on this very page. As I learned more clearly through the process of understanding my Emma-Jo Dream, I am able to reveal some of my deepest inner conflicts in this book while at the same time feeling fearful that you will judge me. Frankly, I know I will be judged for some of the things I'm saying here. Some of you will use my example as an opportunity for you to focus on what parts you play in your life, while others may be judging what parts I play in mine. But my fear of what readers might think of me does not stop me from writing this book the way I think it needs to be written. I put my fear to some place peripheral, and set to the task of completing the work and saying what I believe needs to be said.

Right around now you may be noticing something funny going on here. I can picture you saying, "Wait a minute, Layne. How can we reconcile these two different ideas you're putting forth, what Adler called our *lifestyle* and what *you* call playing a different game on the back nine?" Well, you're right. They do seem inconsistent, or at least they form a difficult polarity. Can we alter our lifestyle? Is it even possible to play a different game on the back nine?

Emotional Reactions and Emotional Habits

In light of the fact that the title and point of this chapter is to help you resolve your patterns, I want to talk here about the different ways your patterns manifest themselves in your life. What *I* refer to as your habitual *emotional reactions* has a lot to do with Adler's *lifestyle*. This is partly a question of inborn personality and natural emotional reactions, and it is also where you find your filing cabinet. It gives you your initial emotional response, and your first impulse as to what action you want to take in any situation. And while we've been working on stretching our emotional reactions and responses through dream work, as you know, your *initial* responses may change very slowly or not at all.

However, I want to make the distinction here between your habitual *emotional reactions,* and what I call your *emotional habits.* Your patterns reveal themselves, not only in how you react to situations, but also in whom you choose to be with in your life.

And that's what I want to investigate here, because I think our emotional *habits* may hold the key to playing it different on the back nine. Here too, I want you to be aware that my discussion in this book involves two principles, equally. One is the process of decoding and understanding the dreams you have while sleeping. The second comes from understanding the part of you that is sleeping while you are awake! This is what I consider real lucidity in waking life. Here's an example for you.

Earlier I shared how my dad had a temper. When I was growing up, I became accustomed to hearing him raise his voice at me when I didn't behave in a way he considered respectful. Afterwards, he would feel sorry and make up with me. But first came the yelling. After many years of being conditioned to this dynamic, it is not that I necessarily felt I deserved to be yelled at, as much as it was *being* the way *I knew*. In my adult relationship with my husband before I had this awareness, this is what often happened. See if you can relate to some of these dynamics in your own relationships. If I felt unhappy about a situation, I would (unconsciously) be indirect with Andy or sarcastic in my approach. This would almost guarantee raising his frustration level and increased the chance that he would raise his voice at me. I sometimes would yell out at him, and that was *sure* to get Andy yelling back even louder at me. In this way I unconsciously helped perpetuate a role I was accustomed to, all the while wondering how this situation had even happened, as though in a sleep or dream where I had no control.

I am *not* suggesting here that I am responsible for anyone else's reaction to me or that his impatience and yelling were my *fault*. What I *am* saying is, becoming aware of the part I play in events is my idea of being lucid while awake. And while you may think that in any given situation you have not played a part, you have. *Everyone* plays a part. Things don't just happen to you. And it's almost like we can smell the people out there who will fit into our role. We become attracted to them. It's like radar. You'll just attract and be attracted to those people who will help you repeat the role you are comfortable playing.

Now don't go throwing out your wife yet because you've just connected to how like your mother she is! One reason we attract these people is because we resist change. We simply like to continue in the roles we have become accustomed to. It's what we seem to think is the easy way. Another reason and a much more uplifting one, is that in attracting the people who help us perpetuate our past behaviors, I believe we have the chance to learn something new on the back nine. Who better to help you resolve your emotional habits and reactions than someone who is just like Mom or Dad?

While my personal belief is that most of our emotional habits come from our primary relationship with our parents, I also think the relationship with our siblings and the collusion that takes place among all family members and the roles they play are important factors in our psychological development. And then add to that the influence of our friends or peers, and our relationship to the authority figures we established in early childhood. Our partners are our best teachers, that is, if we choose to learn from the experience.

Freud had a term for this phenomenon, where we attract situations and individuals into our lives that will help us perpetuate the roles we have grown accustomed to playing. He called it "the repetition compulsion." This exotic term sounds psychotic, like a person who has repetition compulsion is deeply sick. I use the term *emotional habits* because I don't think you need to be sick to have it, just human. I think we all repeat scenarios in our lives (unconsciously). It is somehow understandable on some level that we do this, even though often the repetitions are painful ones and may make us a little neurotic. But then, who among us is not a little neurotic? The point is, we *do* set up situations and attractions, and we don't even realize that we do. I've heard the Buddhists say you choose your Karma so that you will end up with certain people in your life, because they help you learn the lessons you are here to learn. There is Deepak Chopra who says you can open yourself to receiving something different for yourself. What you feel you deserve, the universe will send you. In the song "Brown Shoes Don't Make It," Frank Zappa said, "Do you love it? Do you hate it? Here it is the way you made it." They are all in essence saying the same thing. My assertion is that if you become aware you are doing something, that in itself can be a help. I personally don't want to look back when I'm eighty and think I coasted through this whole experience. How boring that would be. And just in case the spiritual stuff is true, I'd rather come back next time to a new and different show, than experience a rerun of this life because I had no growth.

The parts we play in waking life are the same parts that appear in our dreams. For example, let's look back for a minute at the scene I just set up, where I have unconsciously hit the button that will set Andy off to yelling at me just like my dad would have done. First of all, this gets his attention. It may not be positive attention, but it still affords me the repetition of creating the same scene I had as a child. Now watch how the cast of characters I describe here in the waking-life situation may seem familiar to you. I push Andy's buttons and yell at him just like a bratty four-year-old girl. And then the minute after I've opened up my mouth, and I see what is coming back at me, the child in me stands still for fear he will stop loving me. And that screaming, hysterical woman who wasn't in control in the Emma-Jo Dream is coming out in my waking life. Because now *he's* mad, and I am no longer in control. Now Andy's holding on to something, and I can't control how long he's going to hold on to it. And he knows he's in control now, and that I'm upset.

Thankfully, the last part of this scenario plays itself out just like it did in my childhood, because Andy, like my father, doesn't hold on to things for more than a few hours. After the yelling is done and it is time for making up, here comes Andy so affectionate and I am the baby who gets the snuggling and comfort. A few years ago though, I began to have the awareness of what this familiar scene was bringing up inside me. I would catch myself and realize I was in the role of "little girl" during practically the whole scene. Either a bratty little girl who was testing her limits, or a scared little girl who wants to be taken care of! I would figuratively "wake myself up" and use the opportunity to access the underdeveloped part of me that can express myself! Now I was developing a new cast member, Layne, the adult woman, who realizes I have the right to speak. I don't have to stand there shaking in my boots. I have several options for growth. I can change my reaction by saying, "If you are going to continue yelling at me, I am going to leave the room." And I can, in fact, leave the room. I can leave the house. I can let him know during a calm and peaceful time that I will be leaving the room or the house whenever I feel the yelling is too much for me.

Did I hear you say, "Layne, what about *your* part in the play? Didn't you just say you were responsible for this?" Okay, so let us not forget my part. I can stay awake to catching myself when I push those buttons in Andy. I can become aware about being direct when I have something to express to him. I can approach him myself in a more calm way, instead of those times I yell out. I can ask Andy (which I did) to remind me when he thinks I am being indirect. He can help me out by expressing what is going on for him before he blows his cool. My lucidity might help me become more in touch with those times when I need comfort. You can see how you don't have to go through all the steps I just described in order to arrive at the snuggle. You can just ask for the snuggle, which for some of us, I appreciate, is difficult.

And what about our joint responsibility in this play? Well we made a decision, a contract. In honor and acceptance of our humanness, for those times we don't catch it, either one of us can say, "Time out!" When either person says, "Time out," the action stops, right away. Today if we have a screaming argument once a year it is a lot, and then we get in only a few screams before one of us puts a stop to it. We go to another room. We give ourselves the respect, the space. I have the confidence he's still going to love me. I no longer have to get it all out and now! I wait. Things calm down. A few hours later, we talk. And it's all okay. Change has actually taken place.

I believe the balance of polarities that I discussed directly in the context of the Emma-Jo Dream is the same balance that allowed me to resolve my "emotional habit" with Andy. Well, at least the awareness of those polarities and my attempt to achieve a balance helped me recognize the emotional habit and work to move beyond it. I caught myself reacting like the "little girl" as opposed to "the adult woman." I even created a situation that encouraged me to act like the "little girl." In my case it was also that father-little girl dynamic. But what I had to do was grow closer to Andy both as the child and as the adult woman in me.

This is what happened for me. It may be something entirely different for you. I assure you though, if you look, you will find what it is. And if you practice this kind of lucidity for a while, you will find that the polarities and underinvested aspects of our character that we battle with in waking life are the same themes we find in our sleep dreams. The same Shadows bubble up, asleep or awake. My personal objective is to narrow the gap between knowing what I am thinking about in the day or in the night. I search for a greater fluidity between my conscious and my unconscious.

I don't expect myself to be perfect. I don't even want to try to be. I've said it so many times before, that little girl is here to stay. It is better to accept that I have my certain slants and my Shadows and emotional habits. I just want to know them, to recognize them. If I am more lucid in my wakefulness, I will be more inclined to have less fear and take more risks.

A Final Thought about Our Partners

In 1999, I attended a lecture and workshop given by Dr. James Hollis from Houston, Texas. While looking back through my notes I thought you would be interested to hear some of his ideas, because they are related to this question of emotional habits in our relationships. Dr. Hollis believes we are forever caught in some moment from our past. He says, "We are projecting our experience onto the other. We are always with another time, another place in *this* moment. And then we are disappointed once we realize the other is different and separate from us. It is impossible to meet and see another person as a totally separate individual." Our unconscious mind, he says, is always seeking to repeat our first, early relationships. We are seeking to repeat an experience, compensate an experience, or heal an experience.

I know what many people will think of this idea. "Are you kidding? The last thing I want is to be married to my mother (or father, or sister, or brother)!" But whether you agree with Dr. Hollis' specific ideas or not, I'm sure you will recognize there *are* many times when you project some other experience into your current relationships, and this makes you lose touch with the current relationship *as it really is*. Do you read things into what your "significant other" is saying? Do you feel disappointed when he doesn't respond automatically in a certain way? Do you compare him unfavorably to someone you used to know or someone from your past? Are you measuring him against a fantasy or a memory?

Think about this for a minute. If what I am saying is true and we are in fact caught up in an unconscious fantasy of repetition, it would stand to reason that we would quite regularly be feeling disappointed in our relationships. If you know, and *I mean know* and accept your partner as truly individual and separate from any fantasy or idea you have, you would then have to *ask* for what you want and need! You wouldn't be expecting the other to just naturally *know* what it is you want. The door to mind reading will begin to shut, and a new beginning is on your horizon. You can begin the path towards *real love*. And *real love* then, is allowing you to be who you are even though you are not feeding my agenda. The greatest gift the other gives you is his "otherness." It is exactly that which forces you out of yourself. Take these thoughts to heart and have a new adventure inside your old relationship!

A Look Forward from Some Dreamers

I attempted to contact some of the people whose dreams appear in this book to see if my theory about changing your patterns through dream work holds water in their experience too. Here are some stories about their current situations and how the issues from their earlier dreams have resurfaced in their lives. How have the lessons of their dreams helped these people discover solutions to other similar problems in their life?

Annie

As you read in Chapter 6, I had the occasion to take a walk with Annie almost a year after her dream in which her father died. You'll recall her more recent dream, where she attended a yoga class and discovered excrement in the bathroom. When Annie found the mirror to this dream, she saw it had to do with a birthday party she was in the process of organizing for her mother-in-law. As so often happened, she had taken all the work on herself. Watching Annie do this, the girlfriend of one family member wondered out loud, "Gee. If I marry into the family, will I too be expected to help organize family get-togethers like this?" Actually, this woman made the comment because she had noticed that Annie was doing this job alone, with very little if any help from her husband's own sisters.

Annie responded immediately, "Well, I do the job, because I like doing it." But as soon as it was out of her mouth, Annie wondered to herself, "Now why did I say that? I don't love taking the whole responsibility here!" This exchange is what in fact spurred the dream.

Remember in her current dream, Annie finds herself in the hallway of her late aunt's house feeling uncomfortable. Annie said that while she felt uncomfortable because her aunt's spirit was somewhere around, she also felt safe that here was the place where she could get cleaned up.

Using free association, Annie linked herself to the time she spent with her little sisters at that same aunt's house. This is where the "poop" stories come from that we discussed in Chapter 6! But then Annie had another memory, from that same period at her aunt's house all those years ago. During that trip, she had made fast friends with a neighbor girl her own age. The two wanted to go into the forest to play one day, and oh, how Annie loved the forest. Even though her two sisters protested, and Annie herself wanted to be alone with her friend, she insisted her sisters come along with them. She realized that having her sisters with her was the better of the options, because if she left them behind at her aunt's house Annie realized she'd be unable to really relax and enjoy her day.

I think Annie came to a very important learning from linking her dream to this memory. She said, "You know, I took them along with me because I knew if I didn't, I just wouldn't have been able to relax and really enjoy myself in the woods.

And that was what I wanted to do! I'd have been wondering at the back of my mind what kind of *shit* they were getting into. So while it is true I had to give up being totally comfortable with my friend alone, I was better off bringing them. My small discomfort led me to have a good time." Then she connected the mirror for me. "That is what happened in the dream too. I am relaxing in a yoga class, but I feel a certain discomfort behind me, niggling. It is some excrement stuck to the back of the towel that I am lying on. And then, in the second scene, while I have this period of general discomfort in the hallway, I do have the sense that I am in the right place where I can get showered, cleaned up, feel good. And there is the learning."

She continued, "I have a sense of this side of me who feels a responsibility to make things happen and be sure of everyone's good time. Yet I also am in touch with the smaller side of myself who wants to relax and do the things I enjoy. In this particular case, my "responsibility" side opens the door to the relaxing part! Family get-togethers are so fun and relaxing for me. If I gave it up to my sisters-in-law, the fact is the job wouldn't get done the way I want it done. So in taking it over, I go through this hallway, or waiting period, with this kind of uncomfortable niggling, yet knowing that I am going to get the relaxation and fun I want, *in the way that I want* at the end of it."

I inquired, "I am remembering how your dream last year helped you feel less responsible for your siblings' good time. Some time later, you mentioned that you were also less inclined to feel responsible about helping to ensure a good relationship between your husband and his daughter. Do you still feel that way?"

"Yes. Actually I do still feel that my husband's relationship with his daughter is his affair. In the case of my siblings, while I would surely be interested in showing them a good time, I think that today I would also feel less inclined to take so much responsibility as I did last summer."

There is a very significant learning here that I want to call your attention to. Annie is no longer stuck. Yes, her initial reaction will likely always lean towards feeling responsible, and surely in situations where her enjoyment and relaxation are weighed against it. But you see Annie is aware of that polarity inside her. And her awareness puts her in the wonderful position of being able to assess each individual scenario. In the case of her husband, her free association (her filing cabinet) brought her back to a memory in which she was given responsibilities she did not want. This conclusion led Annie to realize that she does not want to feel responsible for her husband's relationship with his daughter, and so she mixes out and frees herself. In the case of organizing a family party, she takes on the responsibility because she has made a conscious decision that she wants to. And her decision was solidified because of the memory she arrived at through free association. Again, it was a memory from her filing cabinet, but this time where she *wanted* the responsibility. You get to the memory from your past, and then you reassess what your feelings were. What stuff was put on you, what stuff did you want, and in which situation? The memories you tap into are not random choices. Your filing cabinet opens to the story that gives you the answer to what you want to do in your current situation. Trust yourself.

Now let's just wrap this around to Annie's emotional habits. What part might she be playing in these scenarios? Does she naturally attract people who are more laid-back so she can perpetuate her role as chief organizer? You know how when you see a group of people meeting for the first time, there are some who jump to the task of doing something together? They are the natural organizers. Or maybe the other people in Annie's life wouldn't be so laid-back, except that she doesn't leave them anything to do!

Annie might try staying very quiet next time something

comes up, just for the sheer adventure and curiosity of playing it another way. What will happen to the other players if Annie is quiet and non-volunteering? Will the job get done? And if she feels unable to stretch herself that far, or just doesn't want to, how about delegating? What really would happen if some time Annie took the lead but delegated too. Just the act of asking for help might be an adventure in itself. Here's the thing. Life is easier when you are making conscious decisions instead of emotional ones. You feel more in control, more powerful, and more in touch with yourself.

Sarah

Sarah had made the connection to feeling punished when her dad died. But what was her specific solution to the problems she faced in her current waking life? In the case of her term paper, Sarah needed to practice being more like her aunt, and make a commitment to succeed. With her boyfriend, Sarah again tapped into how her aunt would behave if she found herself in a situation where she felt she was being treated poorly. Sarah needed to speak up about her disappointment to her boyfriend, and in doing so set the stage for the kindness and respect she feels she deserves in her relationship.

Today, in her thirties, Sarah still keeps in contact with me. One day I asked her if there has been any situation in her current life where she felt herself slipping into the part that feels undeserving. Has anything happened where she found herself wanting to react like the underachieving "uncle" side of herself? I wondered if she found herself using the lessons from her Uncle Dream to tap into the confident, deserving, aunt side of herself.

It didn't take long for Sarah to think of an example. Right after graduating, a friend of hers approached Sarah to work together in a start-up company designing Web pages. Her friend lives in another city and her idea was to join together and thereby gather clients in both cities. While her friend is a graphic artist, and was willing to teach Sarah how to use the programs, Sarah at first declined to join. Even though she feels at home on the computer and is very artistic, Sarah just didn't have the confidence. She didn't think she would ever be able to accomplish the task, and more importantly, do it successfully.

After finding herself caught in that now familiar pull between balancing her capabilities with what she feels she deserves, Sarah decided to try. She told me, "That's certainly something my aunt would do. She'd try." And so she did. Today, Sarah runs a very successful partnership. Besides catching on quickly to designing Web sites herself, she later discovered it was the administrative side of business that she most enjoyed. She oversees several employees in a thriving and growing business.

Johnathan

You won't be surprised to hear that the first question I asked Johnathan after not speaking with him for some four years was, "So? Are you married?" I must have sounded like one of those aunts we all have!

"Well," he answered, "we have had a few stalls, but now we seem to be right on that track. I feel some pressure but not at all the same as I did before."

Johnathan told me about some changes in his life since we last spoke. Not too long after we met to discuss his dream, he decided to go back to school. He was accepted to a university out of town. His girlfriend moved on as well and has done things professionally and personally that have really helped her grow. Johnathan added, "One of the reasons I just didn't feel ready then was because I felt there were things I needed to attend to on my own first, like going back to school. While we have had spaces inside these past few years when we were in fact together, we were physically separated for around two years over a three-year period. Now, we are both back in the same city again, and have been living together for the last six months, stronger than before. The time we took to do things for ourselves was time well spent. Our relationship survived. We are both more stable. You might be interested to know that we have just bought two basset hound puppies! A brother and a sister, numbers five and seven out of nine."

I reminded Johnathan a little about the dream he had then, and what he thought it meant. I got to the part of reminding him how that smiling bulldog well represented his position on getting married. I added how he said about dogs (and marriage) that they were something he aspired to, but like the bungalow in the dream, couldn't accommodate at that time. Then I remarked, "Well, you seem to have found room to accommodate dogs in your life now. That surely must be a movement toward a commitment to a marriage!"

"Funny that you mention that bulldog. You know a basset is difficult to bring up. They are stubborn like a bulldog."

At this point, I thought we could try a little free association to see if Johnathan connected to a memory that reminded him of the feelings he was experiencing. I asked, "Is there some place you can think of where there was some pressure, maybe associated with some kind of commitment or having to care for someone?" I explained to Johnathan that I added the feeling of caring for someone because I was looking at the map of his dream while we spoke, and noticed he had associated dogs with neediness. I heard the sound of his breath making a connection. "Is there something that came to your mind?"

"Well, it doesn't really have directly to do with me and yet it did."

"That's okay," I told him. "Don't judge the memory. Just try it."

"Okay. I thought of how around that same period of time I

watched the breakdown of my sister's marriage. It was so intense and really affected the whole family. Then there was my brother. His marriage broke up too. It was not as gruesome as my sister's but it was pretty messy too. She moved back to town with her children from another city. She needed a lot of care and support. Her husband gave her a really rough time. I respect the institution of marriage, but at the same time it is something that requires great thought. When it came to my girlfriend and me, I wanted to slow the ship down but not stop it."

"That's a good connection," I said. "And it is interesting that you picked that one. It helps me better understand where you were coming from when you had your Labrador Dream. You had watched some suffering. It makes sense to me that you would have wanted to proceed slowly. Do you want to try another association? What does that association make you think of? Is there some memory from your childhood where you felt that certain way? Actually, you did that inside the dream already in how you brought forward the labs and the bulldog. They were associations from your past."

"Labs and bulldogs are really different. And then basset hounds are more like the bulldogs. We used to have bassets too. A lab, like most other dogs would run through fire to get to you, to obey your command. The charming thing about bassets . . . well, you may not agree it is charming, is that they think before they go to you. They consider before they respond to a command." He was thinking. "I guess I am reminded of my parents. I was one of the only kids in high school whose parents stayed together! And they didn't stay together because they were happy. They stayed together because of us. I felt guilty because I felt responsible for their collective misery."

"But you know somewhere inside you that it wasn't your fault what went on between your parents."

"I know that my mother believed that good Catholic girls

don't get divorced. And my dad kept the marriage together more for business appearances. We did the country house thing, and everyone thought we were the Cleavers, but really I knew they were miserable."

"It's interesting. Four years after your Labrador Dream. It is kind of cool how looking back at the dream and the memories you choose now, that in all you were more of an observer than a participant. I mean you were affected by your parents' marriage, and too by your sister's and brother's divorce, but it wasn't your marriage or your divorce. It was more something you were observing even though you were greatly impacted by the experience. And in the lab dream you were also an observer. What about how you describe bassets? You say that they really consider before they respond to a command. It's very connected that you and your girlfriend chose to have two bassets. After all, you also really stop to consider before you run to a command."

"It's true," Johnathan giggled at the connection.

After giving Johnathan a mini explanation about our filing cabinet, he, being an avid computer user, renamed my filing cabinet the "motherboard." I learned something from him too, because he said the motherboard holds all the original data in the memory. To that you can add new files, he explained, but you would always need the information stored in the motherboard. He suddenly wondered if it is not an accident that the piece was named mother.

"Excellent!" I said. "What you want to do here is add the new file."

Johnathan was making the connections. "The lessons learned," he offered. "I experienced my parents' relationship. Then fast forward to my sister, who I am so close to, that I must help pick up the pieces of her life. I fast forwarded to my brother and his divorce. When I have to make a heavy decision, I go to my database and what do I have? That's what happened when I thought about marriage four years ago. I had to assess. I felt that we were moving too quickly. I felt like the relationship was not there. Then I asked myself, 'Why is it not there?' The answer was that I wanted to go back to school. She did not appreciate what I felt I had to do. In the past, professionals didn't have to augment their skills like they do today. I went out of the workforce completely to do what I knew I needed to do. I tested the situation. I knew I was better to do it alone. Some people thought she would leave me; that the relationship would end. I took a calculated risk. There was more in the win column in taking the risk. I had the confidence she would stay around, and she had stuff to go through too. If we went through the type of things each of us had to alone, it was better that we did so without the encumbrance of a marriage. I believe that I was able to ask the right questions of myself because of my past."

Many children of divorced parents, or parents who had a rocky relationship, approach marriage with this cautious attitude. In Johnathan's case he really didn't want to take any chances, because he had just seen what happened with his siblings. But have you noticed how he kept coming back to dogs in our conversation? The bassets and the bulldogs and the labs. These dogs were actually a great way for him to keep tabs on the different parts of himself. The bulldog or basset hound part, which was stubborn and weighed every decision carefully, was obviously uppermost on this issue. (You could almost call it the "top dog"!) This was also the part that was more of an *observer* and less of a *participant*. On the other hand the labrador part, which had a much more spontaneous way of loving, had been pushed under.

I offered, "Now that you realize this, and you know you can add new data to your files, you might try and greet this methodical, basset-type self of yours next time the subject of marriage comes up. That would be the learning now. This part of yourself who is connected to thinking things through to such an extent loses the spontaneity that a lab might have. That's the part of yourself that might be sleeping, the part you might want to wake up. I don't even golf, but in the book, I call it playing a different game on the back nine. What do you think?"

"I like that back nine, and I think you have a point. Now that I feel so much more comfortable inside my relationship and it is *time to get serious*, I might try being more spontaneous."

"Well, actually," I offered, "you spent the first half being serious, now it's *time to have fun!*"

Deborah

While putting this chapter together, I telephoned Deborah curious if she still *holds all her bricks together* when she falls over. She laughed when she heard me ask that question. While speaking with both Johnathan and Deborah, I couldn't really pose my queries in the same way as I could with others like Sarah, Annie, or Michael, who are familiar with my current method. Working with Johnathan or Deborah four years ago when they first told me their dreams, we didn't specifically discuss the notion of polarities coexisting inside us, disowned parts of ourselves, or the process of accepting and balancing our different parts. My approach at that time did not have the same precision of method I have since developed.

Nevertheless, I relay our conversations because they show how we are always learning and growing, even without the benefit of a step-by-step approach like the one you're getting here. As our recurring emotional patterns continue to resurface again and again, I believe we are progressing on issues even without the interpretation of dreams. I do think we can grow faster with even a minimal understanding of them, though. And of course we get the biggest advantage when we have a certain approach that we can grab on to and utilize to its greatest potential.

Deborah is soon to be married, and was so delightfully eager to look back at her dream from four years ago and compare her reaction then to her situation today. I said to her, "What a great opportunity for us to look at your reaction and see if there has been a change. When you had your leaning dream it was associated with your feelings about the transition you faced when moving to Toronto, and here you are in the face of another transition. Are you giving yourself permission to have excited and nervous feelings? Do you notice a change in your reaction to change?"

"It is interesting that you telephoned this week," she answered. "Actually, I had what I call a wedding dream just two weeks ago. I feel concerned that people won't come to my wedding since so many live in other cities. It's why there were so few guests at the wedding in the dream!"

The Wedding Dream

"It was my wedding day. I could not believe it came so soon. I looked out from behind the curtain, and was so disappointed to see that there were only ten people there! I was wearing Shakespearean-style underclothes. White garments. I was frantically looking for a dress. Nothing fit! I found one that was dirty and old. It didn't look like what I thought it would. I remember not wanting to go through with it. Nothing was like what I expected it to be. I had to put something on. I was going down that aisle. I found a bustier and a crinoline and put it on. I woke feeling so relieved it was a dream."

Deborah connected her dream at the first level to the fact that she had just moved again. She also informed me that it was, believe it or not, the third time she had moved in these last four years. The apartment she and her fiancée had just moved out of was so beautiful, she explained. "It didn't turn out to be like what I thought it would. Nothing was like what I expected it to be. It was a dirty mess that had so many other problems that we had to decide to break our lease and move." I expect you are noticing the exactness of Deborah's expressions related to the apartment, and how they mirror her experience in her dream. She said of the move, "I remember not wanting to go through with it. We found another place, but I have lost my confidence sure that my moving is never going to end. Now I worry about what else might go wrong."

At this point in our conversation, I was attempting to fit Deborah's current experience into the requirements I had in my mind for this chapter of the book. So I asked her, as I would have in Chapter 6, to try some free association and tell me what comes to her mind when she thinks about the feeling that she has to go through with something she really doesn't feel prepared for. She said after a minute, "When I finished school I was set to go to live in Israel for a year. My parents have an apartment there. Not that long afterwards, my dad sold his business and the house, and my whole family came to join me in Israel. I felt uprooted. I had lost my home base. It was a family business and I had emotions around that change too. My parents expected me to now stay in Israel. I was so unprepared to go to my father and tell him the truth. My plan was to stay the year that I was supposed to. I wasn't going to stay any longer than that. I planned to return to Canada. However frightened and worried I felt about approaching my father, I had to step forward and tell him. I not only went through with that, I also went through moving back to Canada on my own."

I have to be honest with you. And it is not only for the purpose of relaying our conversation in the way it unfolded. I have to be honest with you because while most of the time the dream work method fits, there was a problem in this case. If you are like me, you might find yourself having to be careful not to turn your dream interpretations into a Procrustean bed, where you have to chop off more and more of the person's limbs to get him to fit! Truth is, that is exactly what I caught myself doing while I was speaking with Deborah. The experience gave me a headache. Things do not and will not always fit exactly the way you want them to. Most often they do, but don't wrack your head over trying to make all the pieces fit. Go for the learning instead. You are guaranteed to find one if you are looking.

Deborah said, "I'm not being much help here, am I?"

That was what hooked it for me. I admitted, "Isn't this ridiculous? We are both struggling to fit you and your experience right face inside this chapter. Guess what? Let's blow off the whole idea and talk about something much more important. You really move a lot, don't you?"

"Yes," she said. "And I hate it! I wish I could just settle down in one place. You know what? It's not over yet either. My fiancée is going to graduate and we'll be moving again to another city for him to do his master's degree!"

"And you are getting married. There is another transition. And how are you faring with all these changes? Do you notice any difference in how you approach your changes now from four years ago?"

"Yes, I do. I used to keep the whole anxiety locked up inside myself. Now I don't anymore. I do express how I am feeling to the people I am close to. I find some comfort even though I am sure it must take its toll on them too."

"Why do you think it takes a toll?"

"Because I worry about any number of things going wrong. I hate that part of myself. It is hard for those who care about me to listen to my focusing on what else might happen." She admitted, "That is what I do when I am anxious about a change."

"Soon you will be with your husband, and you won't be alone anymore for the moves that take place going forward."

"Yes. That is so nice, and he is so nice. I will have some stability in my life. But that craziness in me still does come forward whenever change is taking place. Interestingly," she noted, "it is only around the anticipation about a move or change that I become so upset. Once I am moved and set up, I feel fine."

"I remember around your leaning dream that we used the expression, 'When all of this is over, I am going to sit down and have a nervous breakdown.' That was in how you push down that part of yourself who you say gets crazy around change. And you did that in order to focus on the tasks associated with the move. Are you very quick and organized about your moves so that at least you get that settled feeling fast?"

"Are you kidding? I am unpacked and totally organized right away. Then I feel relaxed. It is my nervousness that helps me get through things."

"And that is why, Deborah, when that nervous part of you shows up in the face of change around you, maybe next time you might try greeting her, like an old familiar friend. She is the part who helps you get through things. You just said it yourself. You don't have to push her down. Bring her up! Know she's there. She is the one who inspires that organized, calm, take-care-of things girl."

And so we didn't manage to fit Deborah's current life story into the mold of this chapter. What we did do, though, was decide to drop the things that weren't working, and instead move with the flow of what *was* happening. Pay attention to what is going on with the dreamer. The dreamer is paramount. Now Deborah has the awareness of that part of herself that will always want to push her in a certain direction. An awareness of your path, your past, and your process is what it is about. You continue to be on it. It is a part of your life.

Deborah promised to get back to me closer to the wedding. We are both optimistic that our conversation and her discoveries will help her through her next transition. She's even invited her nervous wreck side to the wedding and is expecting her to show!

I asked Deborah if she thinks she unconsciously might attract situations that will involve moving. "Do you think there is something to all this moving you do? You might want to think about how it keeps coming your way, or have some awareness here of repetition." Deborah assured me that her moves have been more a case of circumstance and some bad luck. I admit I am suspicious if some unconscious emotional habit is not at work here. Time will tell. That's the thing about our emotional habits. They are unconscious, so it's hard to pinpoint them except by first mentioning them and later developing a greater awareness. In Deborah's case, if there really is something going on with her moves, I doubt she'd be able to completely forget about our conversation. If she were to keep moving in the same way she has been, she might begin to feel suspicious enough to investigate if she is not herself playing some part in her destiny.

It works the same way with a woman who keeps ending up in relationships with losers. She blames it on "bad luck." She has no awareness of what it is she might be putting out that helps create the situation. Here's another example of an emotional habit. Marsha grew up the youngest of five sisters who were all significantly older than she was. Her sisters had a certain rapport with their mother that would have been impossible for Marsha to have, given the age difference. Marsha would often find any one or a few of her siblings engaged in conversations that would stop as soon as she entered the room. Sometimes she'd find the sisters whispering among themselves. When the discussion was about boyfriends and she was only six or seven years old, even though Marsha might try to join the conversation, she naturally didn't feel included. When the women were in the kitchen cooking, Marsha would ask to help, but again was out of her realm and most often given what she considered to be baby jobs. So Marsha spent much of her childhood striving to feel included in the bunch, but to no avail.

As a result of these circumstances, she grew up with the feeling of being excluded. Then as an adult she would find herself over and over again in situations where she was always the initiator and the other, whether that other was a girlfriend or boyfriend or even her husband, was not a reciprocator. The experience became extremely frustrating, and Marsha's frustration and hurt formed a regular theme in her dreams.

Marsha and I discussed some of her dreams together and made these connections. Once Marsha had realized she might be playing an unconscious part in her situations, she started consciously and actively taking note of her patterns, and made some decisions about how she might incorporate changes to facilitate different results for herself. There were two main things she discovered about her behavior. When meeting new people one on one, Marsha found that she was always the one who gave out her telephone number, took the other's phone number and then she would be the person who initiated the next meeting. After a second meeting, if the new person didn't contact her within a few weeks, Marsha would make another approach. This dynamic would leave Marsha feeling that although the new person seemed to enjoy her company, this other person obviously didn't enjoy it enough to initiate a get-together.

You know, many of us do that dance. When someone is moving towards you, it is only natural for you to move backwards, and when he is moving backwards, you might take a step forwards. This dynamic can't happen if you are always the one moving forward! So Marsha consciously created a balance. She held back the side of herself who so naturally initiates first. She waited for the other to initiate the second get-together. If it didn't happen, Marsha had to make some choices. Did she want to continue in relationships where there was no reciprocation, or was she really deciding she deserved another style of people in her life? In fact Marsha stopped initiating, and slowly the sort of people who like to dance both ways came to play a bigger role in her life.

The second behavior Marsha discovered about herself would take place in a larger group of people. In this situation she noticed herself laying low, not initiating conversation with anyone at all! This was exactly the opposite of her behavior in a one-on-one situation. So in a group Marsha would soon find herself feeling terribly uncomfortable because no one was approaching her. She would move closer and closer to the corner and the more she did so, the more she would perpetuate this feeling of exclusion. When she became aware of the pattern, Marsha decided to make a conscious and nervous effort to step forward in a party situation and say hello to people. She helped herself feel included, and she was so pleasantly surprised to find that strangers were happy to engage in conversations with her.

We have come back to the gym, you and I, haven't we? No, I am not suggesting these changes are easy ones to make. They are not. And you might and probably will feel strained and uncomfortable trying them. Your new behavior will hurt same as your muscles do when you use new ones. Believe me, it was not easy for Marsha to sit there and wait for a new friend to reciprocate with a phone call, requesting a second get-together. Sometimes she felt like she had to sit on her hands to stop herself from making the call herself.

As Johnathan would say, here are the lessons learned (I hope) in this chapter. There is no box with neat little ribbons tied on it. That's not life. This reminds me of something Andy and I do. We both love doing puzzles, big ones. Whenever we have finished a five hundred or thousand-piece puzzle, just before we glue it onto a board for framing, we always take out a piece or two. When people see the puzzles on the wall they ask us, "Why is this piece missing?" We answer, "Nothing is perfect. The pieces don't all fit. Often all the pieces aren't even there!" Welcome to life.

Change is slow but change is possible. Johnathan, Deborah, Annie, and Sarah don't show some miraculous, one-to-one correspondence between understanding their dreams and solving all the problems in their lives. But there has been movement in these dreamers. If you *want* change in yourself, change will come. And I still maintain that if you are making a conscious effort to record and understand your dreams, and are taking the lessons they offer you, your growth and movement will be accelerated, to a significant degree.

Change is possible. Dreams do come true. You can actually become more and more comfortable playing a different role. Your dreams are there to help you identify the new roles you want to play, and then rehearse them. It is not any different from an actor learning and becoming a role. It does come more naturally after a while. Respect your initial reactions and get to know your emotional habits. A whole new possibility awaits you.

CHAPTER EIGHT

Recurring Dreams and Dream Series

"The insight that emerges when we study a series of dreams is that dream figures are in a constant state of development. Like any living organism, they come into being and decay."

—Robert Boznak

In this chapter I am going to discuss recurring dreams and dream series. Let's start with recurring dreams. It's pretty easy to know when you've had one; you just remember having the same dream over and over. Maybe it's exactly the same dream, or maybe it's almost the same but with slight variations. Sometimes you think it's the same dream, but when you write down the details you find some small differences from dream to dream. Either way, a recurring dream probably signals a situation, feeling, or action that you're stuck in. The same situation keeps happening again and again—or you keep *doing* the same thing again and again—but you know on some level you need to change.

A dream series is a little different. This is a collection of dreams, often over a short period of time, where there are recurring metaphors, symbols, or themes. In some cases the symbol repeats itself so you can assess where you are, how you are *progressing* on a certain subject. Say that for a few weeks or months you notice a very similar dream happening again and again. If you take the time and write the dreams down, you will find the differences in each of the dreams. And then the differences you find can help you discover solutions to the issue you are working on, or at least allow you to track and view your progress. You can learn some very surprising things from following a dream series.

The important distinction I want to make in this chapter has to do with the difference between progressive dreams and repetitive dreams.[1] Repetitive dreams show no change, no progress, no movement on a subject. For me it is not only because the same actual scene is repeating. You may remember I mentioned earlier that I had a series of dreams in which I was walking around on my knees. The dreams were different, but in each one I was on my knees. They had not only the quality of a recurring image, but *there was no resolve, no progress.* I awoke feeling the same way during the whole series until I looked at the dreams to discover *why* I was kneeling.

Progressive dreams, on the other hand, show movement. Look carefully at the differences between one dream and another to see if there's a change in the way you are using the symbols and images in the dream. Are your feelings in the dream different? Is an image scary in one dream, and reassuring in the next? You might also consider how you feel when you wake up. You might go to sleep in a horrible mood and wake the next morning feeling relaxed and refreshed. That is an indication that you have had a progressive dream cycle. Conversely, repetitive dreams might find you waking in the morning feeling exhausted.

Let's look at some dreams that have a recurring quality. Probably you will be able to quickly spot whether these dreams are repetitive or progressive. The trick is to realize this with your *own* dreams. Sometimes it's harder to see where *you* are stuck than where someone else is. That's why it helps to write your dreams down, and do the exercises in this book to understand what they mean.

Patricia's Dream

Patricia came to me with a recurring dream. Because all she could remember was the same fragment each time, we set to work with what material we had. Besides, a fragment of a dream is so telling! In the dream, she kept finding a spot of dirt on the wall in her apartment. She wiped away the dirt with a cloth, but the spot reappeared on the wall. She wiped it away again, but the spot continued to reappear, time after time. Patricia had become increasingly concerned about the dream because it kept recurring.

I asked her, "How do you feel in the dream?"

"Frustrated," she replied.

I inquired, "Tell me what comes to your mind when you think of dirt."

She thought for a moment, and said, "There is one thing about dirt. No matter how many times you clean it, it will always come back, and you'll always have to clean again."

I asked, "Is there any issue in your life in the last few days or weeks that might make you feel that no matter what you do to remedy a situation, the remedy is short-lived and the issue keeps coming back?" Patricia was already smiling. Having worked with her dreams in the past, she knew what it feels like to make the connection. I continued, "Is the feeling of frustration you experience in the dream similar to any feeling you have had in the last few days or weeks?"

Patricia had found the mirror. Most days when she came home to her apartment from work, she would find her two sisters making themselves at home in her place. She loves her sisters, she explained, but she is a person who needs her privacy too. Patricia felt this was a sensitive issue, because they live in the same building. She would entertain them without addressing the issue, hoping they would leave satisfied with the time spent together. But the next day, they reappeared! Now we had solved the mystery of the dream.

Don't you find it appropriate that Patricia would conjure up a *recurring* dream for her problem? Her dilemma was a *recurring* situation that she wasn't doing anything about! In fact there's a kind of double echo here, because the recurring dream itself is highly repetitive—the same thing happens over and over again, even within a single dream!

What is the strength in this dream? The strength is in how Patricia is actively trying to solve the problem in the dream. She does not give up. She keeps wiping the dirt away. These traits are in the dreamer. Patricia's unconscious is asking her consciousness to get in touch with her ability to act. It is not as if she is sitting still in the dream watching dirt pile up and not doing anything about it. Here, we see a person "practicing" the answer to her problem. And what is the answer she gives herself in that dream? In the dream she makes a physical move to eliminate the problem. Now, if she chooses to, she can apply the behavior she has been practicing in the dreams, to waking life. She can take action, and speak up!

Speaking up is difficult for Patricia. We can see that by the fact that she did not express herself to her sisters even though she had wanted the situation to change for some time. So I asked her to take a small step. She might ask for *some* privacy *one day*, because she feels tired and wants to spend some time alone. The process of expressing herself honestly to her sisters will only become easier for Patricia once she has attempted it and then realized that she survived. Just doing something even once changes your perspective about your abilities, *and* possibilities. Bringing conscious awareness to a problem helps us deal with it more directly.

Stacey's Dreams

Remember Stacey from Chapter 2, with her four dreams about getting and giving attention? Back in that chapter we discussed how Stacey had four dreams from the same night with the same theme. I'd like to go back to these dreams now and look at their repetitive patterns more closely, but before I do, let me just refresh your memory.

In the first dream, Stacey was trying to *track* some people down and she said, "get their attention," but they said they would *get back to her later.* She added that in waking life she had been trying to track her newspaper delivery boy down to give him a tip, and he was *not getting back to her.*

In the second dream, there were bad guys, she said, "paying attention" to her. She did not want their attention.

In the third dream, she was trying to get someone's attention, but he did not even notice her. He was in a hurry. She said, "He thinks I am an insignificant person."

Finally, in the last dream, she said she was a man in the mid to late 1800s. His wife was recuperating from an illness. The wife took a sudden turn for the worse and he (Stacey) found himself hoping he would be able to have sex (get some attention) soon.

These dreams form a connected series because they revolve around the main theme of giving or getting attention. Once we talked about the dreams I asked Stacey to think about other questions, like who is the attention coming from? Is it needed attention? One thing was for sure. Stacey was not getting the attention she wanted, not in any of the dreams.

Once she clicked on the meaning, Stacey told me that these dreams are about her relationships with men and how she has in the past gone into relationships where she was not getting the kind of attention she needed. Stacey was working out her problems on the subject in these dreams. Most recently, she was thinking about starting a relationship with someone she had been good friends with for a long time. Over the years, he would share his dating experiences with her, often admitting that he cheated on whomever he was in a relationship with at the time.

Because their friendship was so much fun, at a certain point, she privately tossed around the idea of making it more than just a friendship. Stacey told me she considered his unfaithfulness a "sickness," which she hoped he would recover from with time. See how her words repeat themselves? That is the story of the fourth dream! In that dream she finds herself hoping that she'll be able to have sex, or to get some attention soon.

Here is the mirror. She is talking to herself about how she hopes her friend will change and stop cheating when he's in a relationship with her. That's because Stacey realizes she wants to become more than his friend. She wants to *turn things around*. Get it? That's how it is that in the fourth dream, she's the man, and her friend is the wife! Their roles have been turned around.

But in the dream, the wife *does not* recuperate. Can you find the answer to this dream? While at the beginning of the fourth dream Stacey describes that the wife is recuperating from an illness, in fact, she takes a turn for the worse in the end. You know, even though we might be able to lie to ourselves in waking life because we're wishing for something to happen, we never lie to ourselves in our sleep. When we sleep it is our unconscious doing the talking. And your unconscious never lies to you. The wife in the dream doesn't get better, and takes a turn for the worse, because Stacey is trying to let herself know not to get her hopes up about her friend's cheating. I guess she knows deep inside, after being friends with him for so many years, that he's not going to change. In fact, she knows her friend doesn't even *want* to change. Stacey's final dream tells her that she should put a stop to the thought of a romantic relationship with her friend *before* the doomed possibility is even set in motion. It is another example of how your unconscious mind is problem-solving and looking after you, even before you get yourself into a situation which you know on some level will bring you pain. The answer in the dreams is for Stacey to start looking somewhere safer to find that special attention she wants.

By now you may remember how we described these dreams in terms of rote repetition, back in Chapter 2. According to the idea of rote, Stacey is using different images to repeat to herself how she isn't getting the attention she wants. Well, you are right. It is rote. But Stacey's dreams were also repetitive in a dif- ferent way from rote, because there was no resolve, no progress, and she woke feeling exhausted in the morning. Sometimes the exhaustion comes to us because we feel like we worked so hard to get somewhere but went nowhere.

Recurring dreams may not only signal urgent problems in the present, but probably also emphasize recurring situations and patterns of behavior. Recurring dreams may be a sign that the dreamer needs to place a special urgency in dealing with patterned responses. I like to think of a recurring dream in the same way as I do a nightmare (which they often are). The dream is there because your unconscious is screaming at you in order to get your attention. A recurring dream is just another great way to grab your attention. It is a case once again, of your unconscious taking care of you.

In Stacey's case, we see dreams with a recurring *theme,* which signals both an urgent problem (in the present), and a recurring pattern of behavior from the past. It's a great idea to take note whenever you see repetition or repeating patterns in your dreams, whether it's literally the same dream or not. It could be a sign that you have to look for that element of repe- tition in your life or in your responses to life. Perhaps what is more important to emphasize here is that the repeating pat- terns and situations you have in your life might not only come to your attention through a literally recurring dream like Patricia's, where she keeps wiping the dirt off the wall. Your repeating patterns can also often come to your attention by having a series of dreams that are *repetitive* as opposed to *progressive.* Here's what I mean.

When you are problem solving, your filing cabinet flings open. If there is no successful data available to you from your archives, you might sit in a holding pattern and keep a repeat going, like a record skipping that can't move forward.[2] If, on the other hand, your archives contain files with similar issues from your past, which have been resolved successfully, then you will have material to work with and so can have a progressive dream, or a progressive dream sequence.

As I pointed out earlier, a recurring theme in your dreams can point to some rut you are stuck in. Often, if you understand it, it can be a powerful motivator to help you get unstuck. If you see the same story repeating itself over and over, pay attention! The same goes for actions, emotions, and events in the dream. If the same thing is happening over and over in your dream, maybe this means the same thing is happening over and over in your *life.* Or it's *not* happening over and over. Either way, your unconscious is hammering you over the head for you to get the message.

My Editor's Violin Dreams

Deborah, my editor, plays the violin. She has had a recurring dream over the years in which she is playing her violin. Each dream is different, but in each one she is playing. She told me about one she remembers especially well. "I am taking lessons. I think I'm a music student, maybe at the Yale School of Music. In my dream I'm taking lessons and practicing. Months go by. I'm getting better. I can hear and feel myself getting better. I know I'm moving closer to the goal. I know that in a reasonable period of time, maybe a year or two, I'll be good enough to be a professional musician."

Deborah understands her repeating dream theme. "They are inspirational dreams and I always have them when I haven't played for a while. The dream will inspire me to take my violin out. The thing about a violin is if you don't play for even a week it shows." Sometimes her violin dreams have more of a feeling of anxiety, as if her unconscious is prodding her with an element of fear to make her do what she knows she really wants to do. But this particular dream gave her a vivid taste for the goal. When she woke up, her first feeling was one of disappointment that it was just a dream! Deborah told me, "The dreams keep me in mind not to be lazy and stick with it. And this dream gave me hope, and made me think I am not that far off."

I like to refer sometimes to the differences between Freud, Jung, and Adler as visual. I tell people how where Freud was looking backward towards the past, Adler was looking forward towards the goal, and Jung was looking outward towards the circle of universal meaning. Alfred Adler believed our dreams give rise to an emotion, and the emotion gives us the impetus to move forward towards the goal. Deborah's violin dreams are a good example. She admits, "The truth is, my violin dreams really are an effective prod!"

Adam's Tornado Dreams

Adam, a financial advisor, telephoned me one day, curious as to why he kept dreaming about tornadoes. He said, "It is the most curious thing. And I guess it caught my attention because I had a dream with a tornado in it about five months ago, and this morning I awoke with another. What's with tornadoes?"

Adam described the first dream. He was in the ballroom of a big hotel that was surrounded by mountains. Suddenly, there was a tornado. "The wind was out of control. I stopped to take as many jewels as I could. I was stuffing them into my pockets, trying to get past the guard and out of the ballroom. The tornado came and scooped me up. It was throwing me around. I had no idea what was going to happen. I had no control. I felt frightened."

I said to him, "I realize that you had the dream five months ago so it may be more difficult to connect to what may have been going on at the time. Do you have any idea what it could have been that was frightening you and made you feel so out of control?"

"I know exactly what it was about. The woman I have been in a three-year relationship with decided to end it and I moved back into my place. I have always kept my place, even though I really spent most of my time at hers. She wants to get married and I just don't have the strong feelings that I imagine I should have towards her for marriage. I was always honest about that. She met someone else and decided to pursue that relationship. I can't even blame her. Still, it was a shock, suddenly being asked to leave and instantly no longer with her and her son. I admit I was accustomed to spending the time with them. That would have been my chance to profess my love but honestly, I just couldn't. That was the tornado then for sure. I felt so, so weird. We have kept a friendly relationship you know. We have tried to cherry pick and keep the best parts of the relationship. There was so much good friendship and we're connected on a business level too. We are trying to hold on to that and we keep in touch. Keep the business part, and drop the emotional part. Believe it or not, she is engaged to that guy."

"Could your stuffing jewels into your pockets and getting past the guard have been your attempts to keep the friendship and business aspect alive between the two of you?"

"Yes! What imagery!" He continued, "Now, what do you think the appearance of a tornado in this morning's dream was about? In today's dream, I was gently picked up by a tornado and it took me on a tour of a lake. It was a gentle tornado, this time kind of circling. I was wondering where it was going to put me down."

"Do you feel in control in this tornado?"

"No, but it is so gentle. There is no stress related to it, only curiosity. Curiosity about where I am going to land."

"Have you started dating yet?"

"Yes, actually, I have a third date with a woman coming up tomorrow night. I'm not sure where we'll end up, but she seems nice . . . That's the tour. I know it. I'm dating and not sure but curious who I am going to end up with. Who am I going to have a relationship with next?"

Adam's dreams are a perfect example of a *progressive* dream series. There is a recurring image that points to the same real-life issue, and it gives him the opportunity to see his movement on the issue, literally. The tornado in his first dream was associated with being "tossed out and about." He chose this metaphor to describe his feelings about the relationship. When his unconscious is making a comparison or reevaluating where he is now, in his current relationship, it uses the same point of reference. Makes sense, doesn't it?

This time when the tornado appears, Adam describes it as a gentle one. He realizes he still feels somewhat out of control as to where he might land. While he is allowing for the mystery of his destiny, his trip inside the tornado assures him that he is feeling much calmer about his situation now than he was five months ago, when the tornado first struck.

Josie's Control Dreams

Here are Josie's dreams. I call her dreams a series too, because while they don't have a recurring image, there is inside them a repetitive theme, one about control, how much and how little control Josie has been feeling over the past few months. Like Adam's Tornado Dreams, they are progressive in their nature. And the same as you saw with Adam's recurring tornadoes, the repeating theme is there so that Josie, upon analyzing them, was able to track her movement. Maybe these types of dreams exist for the dreamer to assess what her next move should be. It helps her to go over the events again by using the same theme or symbol as a point of reference. Her mind forms a picture, and in the end, at a moment of growth the theme yields to a new feeling. It is important to figure out the meaning of a recurring dream theme, because the mere fact that it repeats is the indication that your unconscious is trying to call your attention to solving the problem.

So here is Josie's dream series, illustrating her running theme about control. Notice the degrees of Josie's loss of control in each dream. And take notice too of the movement in her feelings about her loss of control.

In the first dream, she was absolutely unable to get a piece of chewing gum out of her mouth. Josie told me that she felt like she was unable to get the situation under control. Together we decided it was safe to say the dream was describing that she couldn't get rid of something (the gum).

In the second dream, Josie searched endlessly for a washroom. Some had no doors; some were very dirty. She said there were many women around. In a spa or gym setting, she couldn't find a toilet that worked, so she just urinated out in the open. Josie's main concern here leading up to her loss of control was wondering why she couldn't find a toilet that worked. She said, "You would expect to find at least one toilet to work. Even in the messiest of bathrooms, you can usually find one!"

I repeated back, "So something you really would have expected to work, didn't."

Josie added, "And I feel the frustration that it doesn't!"

In this dream her loss of control had a sense of relief attached to it, even though it included some embarrassment or exposed feelings.

In the third dream, Josie watched an airplane blowing up in the sky from a distance. I commented that in this situation she was an observer; I also pointed out to her that in this dream story she really does lack the ability to control the situation.

In the last dream, Josie found herself in an elevator that went out of control and she described that it "didn't stop at the appropriate floors." In this dream, she said she was advising the people in the elevator to hold on. Although they did not listen to her, she braced herself and didn't even get hurt! Josie felt so proud that she had looked after herself. See how in this situation she was able to maintain herself while something else went out of control?

With some insight into Josie's life story, we can see the progression in her thought. Here's what Josie revealed about her situation in waking life. Let's see how her dreams mirror what was really going on for her.

After being with the same boyfriend for years, Josie had recently realized she was in the wrong relationship. She had come to decide that she wanted to end it. But Josie felt concerned, because not only did her boyfriend consider himself her fiancé, but her whole family and his too were, as she put it, "expecting" them to marry. Everyone thought they were the perfect couple.

The gum represents the fact that she felt *stuck*. Like the relationship, the toilets that she expected to work were not working. She couldn't find a place to urinate in private because the family would of course find out that she wanted to break off the relationship! Yet, Josie decided to use the bathroom anyway in the dream. This mirrors the fact that she had decided to relieve herself of the weight, in other words, to tell the family.

She imagined her family's reaction would be, in her words, "explosive." This explains the dream of a plane blowing up. And see how in that dream things were completely out of Josie's control, and she was only observing the action? Well, that is exactly as she imagined it would turn out in her waking life. She thought she'd announce her decision, and her parents would blow up at her. Do you see how helpful Josie's dream was? She was reminding herself that there is really nothing she can do about her parents' reaction except observe it. Josie, like the rest of us, has about as much control over how someone else is going to react to a situation as we do while standing on the ground watching a plane blow up. What was she supposed to do, marry her boyfriend just so her parents wouldn't blow up? Josie realized that she would have to take the plunge and witness their reaction. She wasn't going to marry somebody just for the picture, or just to satisfy her family.

From these dreams Josie did go forward and tell her parents how she felt. You can see her progression by her final dream. In the last dream Josie has found out how to brace herself and survive, even though events around her are out of control. We can see how she has shown movement about her fears also by the fact that she is an active participant in the final dream, not an observer. Josie is in that elevator advising people to brace themselves, not just standing and watching like she was in the dream when the plane blew up. Sometimes the movement of an elevator between floors in a dream can represent a transition. This dream shows how, besides bracing herself for a transitional time in her life, maybe Josie, in expressing how she really feels, has ultimately taken control of her transition.

So as you can see, looking at a series of dreams with a main theme can teach you to notice how you're moving along on a certain subject. Josie went from feeling completely out of control, having that big wad of gum stuck in her mouth, to knowing how to take control of her destiny, by actively bracing herself (like she did in the elevator) and telling her parents she was breaking off with her boyfriend. Her understanding of her dream series gave her the impetus to brace herself and make the move.

LEVEL FOUR:
Tapping Your Spiritual Strength

CHAPTER NINE

Finding Your Archetypes

*"The most unfair thing about life is the way it ends. I
mean, life is tough. It takes up a lot of your time. What do
you get at the end of it? A death. What's that, a bonus? I
think the life cycle is all backwards.*

*You should die first, get it out of the way. Then you live
in an old age home. You get kicked out when you're too
young, you get a gold watch, you go to work. You work forty
years until you're young enough to enjoy retirement. You
drink alcohol, you party, and you get ready for high school.
You go to grade school, you become a kid, you play, you
have no responsibilities, you become a little baby, you go
back into the womb, you spend your last nine months
floating . . . then you finish off as an orgasm! Amen."*

—Perspective on life according
to George Costanza (*Seinfeld*)

This chapter is about finding the universal dimensions in
your dream. And if you look, you will surely find them.
We human beings all have and have always had many
things in common. We share fears, wishes, desires, and needs;
they are part of our common human destiny. We all pass
through transitions, different stages of life. We each understand
different rites of passage, teen years, our rebellion against
authority, marriage, mating, maturation, separation, sadness,

loss, joy, love, excitement, and happiness.

But why would you want to focus on those elements inside you that are a part of your common humanity? For one thing, many people find value in realizing they are not alone in their experience. Dreams with a universal quality typically come during transitions, or at times of great stress, or uncertainty about moving forward towards individuation. And it is during these stressful times that you might get to feeling you're alone, and no one can understand how you feel. Does that seem familiar to you? Have you ever found yourself thinking that no one else has gone through what you are going through, or at least not in quite the same way? Knowing others have gone through what you are going through helps sometimes, especially when you are feeling alone.

The things we have in common, it stands to reason, have appeared in stories since the beginning of humanity. And the images and themes from familiar stories show up in our dreams, the same way as they have in plays, movies, poems, and fables throughout time. There can be tremendous value in bringing these images and motifs to the forefront, and seeing how they appear in your dreams. In this chapter you'll be honing your ability to connect to something familiar to *you*, because when you recognize the story or element *you* chose you are bound to discover a lesson. Your current experience can be enriched by looking at someone you can think of who went through a similar experience before you. How did that person respond to the situation?

When you identify with a powerful character or image in your dream, this can help you recognize a source of great wisdom or strength in yourself. Or you might even find your dream reminds you of a story that ultimately prods you to *rethink* your position, because you *don't* want to get caught like the person in the story! Remember how you can put yourself in

a more powerful position by reassessing from an adult perspective the things you learned as a child? As you discovered, often
we change the opinions our parents had and then make new,
adult decisions for ourselves. You may find yourself doing the
same in this chapter, for here you will learn that our dreams
bring shades of old stories and decisions that you can try to
emulate, or change, as you like. Once you connect personally to
the similarity between your story and the theme that you feel
has appeared in your dream, you can assess if you want to
gather strength from the characters in the story by behaving
just as they did, or gather strength because you are making the
decision *not* to go it the same way they did!

One person who took a lot of interest in our universal
common nature was Dr. Carl Gustaf Jung, a student of Sigmund
Freud. Actually, Jung was the first thinker to really focus on how
our dreams reflect our universal humanity and, in a sense, bring
us all together. Carl Jung's whole philosophy and goal was
towards wholeness. Jung wanted to make the understanding of
our dreams bigger and wider, as opposed to smaller. I hope I do
some of the same in this book.

Jung would look for the whole picture. He wanted to understand how the dreamer was affected by the dream, and also by
problem-solving his current issue. He would seek out the
dreamer's reactions into the past for a clearer understanding of
where the dreamer was coming from. But then Jung would take
his understanding of the dream to a wider spectrum. He took it
outward. Jung decided to look at those aspects of our dreams
that seem similar to other people's dreams, or even to stories
and images from around the world.

Jung wanted us to take the dream, see it, and learn from it *all*
that it could give us. That meant he didn't stop at the psychological learning, but instead continued into the spiritual realm.
Carl Jung felt it was unavoidable to arrive at the spiritual aspects

of dreams, because he knew that however we try to rationalize and deny the existence of fantasy, superstition, illusions, religion, and mysticism in our psyche, we cannot escape this aspect of our "humanness." The imagery still appears in our dreams. We are a combination of the rational and the mystical. That is what makes the "whole" of each of us. And our modern world has come to deny the very aspect we need to acknowledge and integrate.

So, in the same way as Perls wanted us to reown the sleeping parts of our personality, I believe Jung wanted us to reown the mystical, spiritual aspect of ourselves by seeking out the collective themes, stories, and characters in our dreams. Jung called this process of finding collective images *amplification,* because he thought of it as *amplifying* the details of your individual dream out to a universal framework. I like the word *amplification* because it brings an image to my mind. I think it's the old NBC Radio logo from my childhood. There was a gigantic transmitter. The transmitter has circles coming off the top, and those circular rings get larger and larger as they transmit out. They amplify, and that is exactly what Jung was doing. Robert Bosnak describes, "Amplification makes an image reverberate with *similar* images and stories from our collective consciousness: our fairy tales, myths, anthropological reports, TV programs, movies, literature, cartoons, poetry, gossip, art, news, and religion. This reverberation amplifies, as it were, the signal contained within the image so that it becomes audible to the conscious mind. Amplification pumps significance into an image until it spontaneously bursts into awareness."[1]

Jung believed these universal characters and images form the *collective unconscious.* He wrote, "I call it 'collective' because, unlike the personal unconscious, it is not made up of individual and more or less unique contents but of those which are universal and of regular occurrence."[2] In what Jung referred to as the collective unconscious, we find the archetypes. The archetypes are ideas he proposed we are born knowing because they are universal to human existence. The images rise up spontaneously from our unconscious. They are the collective thought patterns of the human race. We cannot prove there is an instinct for these universal feelings and ideas, but we can put a picture on it. That is what the archetypes do. Jung wrote: "We do not assume that each new-born animal creates its own instincts as an individual acquisition, and we must not suppose that human individuals invent their specific human ways with every new birth. Like the instincts, the collective thought patterns of the human mind are innate and inherited. They function, when the occasion arises, in more or less the same way in all of us."[3]

This idea reminds me of King Solomon's verse from Ecclesiastics. The passage was such a favorite of my late father that he requested the inscription be written on his headstone, which it is. "That which has been is the same as that which will be. And that which has been done is the same as that which will be done. And there is nothing new under the sun." I like that thought. It has helped me make something that feels so big into something smaller and more manageable. The thought connects me to the rest of humankind. It helps me realize I am not alone in my suffering, when I am suffering. I am not alone when I expect my mother to be nurturing, when I see an old man as knowing and wise, when I view the Lord as powerful, when I look up to a hero, when I see a newborn baby as a symbol of innocence, or when I feel uncomfortable about certain parts of myself and refuse to acknowledge them. I find I am not as hard on myself when I can connect to stories and myths that have similar themes to my current experience.

My Kneeling Dream

Let me give you a quick example of the kind of reassurance and help you can get from hooking into the universal element in your dreams. I'll just provide a brief description of the dream and its first levels of interpretation, so you can see how I worked down and then back up. I think I've mentioned my kneeling dreams, a dream series in which I was trying to make my way around on my knees. In one dream, I was clumping around a lower campus of what seemed like a familiar university (maybe Asheville, North Carolina). I seemed to be getting around okay, until I had to make it up a hill. There was snow on the ground. It was impossible to maneuver myself. I could not stand up in order to climb the hill. I started to click on the meaning of kneeling only when I shared the dream with my husband one morning. When he heard me say to him, "I couldn't stand up," he asked me who was I having trouble standing up to.

A few days later, I dreamed I was on my knees again, this time in the office of a man named Neil. The pun struck me almost immediately—I was kneeling in Neil's office! When I used free association with Neil, my brother immediately came to my mind. Neil is my brother's age, and has worked with him from time to time. While I wouldn't say he is his close friend, Neil is certainly someone my brother is friendly with. This led me to conclude the dreams were about my difficulty in *standing up* to my brother. Of course I arrived easily at this conclusion, because I *was* in fact having difficulty approaching my brother about a certain subject.

As it turned out, the Perls Gestalt technique you learned about in Chapter 5 revealed that *the dream-character Neil was actually the solution to my problem.* When I pretended to *be* Neil and spoke in his voice, when I had a conversation with him and imagined his response, I realized I had to approach my brother exactly the way Neil would. Because besides being friendly with my brother, Neil is a businessman. He represents the part of my personality with the ability to approach my brother in a non-emotional, businesslike way in order to get my point across. Neil brought out to my conscious mind, once again, the emotional/businesslike polarity we've already seen in the Emma-Jo Dream. Since I know that the best way to turn my brother off about an issue is to approach him while being too emotional, this dream reminded me I had to practice "being" Neil in this situation. I had to grab onto the "Neil" (or "Andy," in the Emma-Jo Dream) side of the polarity. (I even planned to borrow a tie from Andy, and put it on with a vest and jacket of mine when I went to approach my brother!) And I decided to speak with my brother in his office, rather than his home. I made that choice from the fact that my dream took place in an office. I also knew this would really help me maintain my businesslike, unemotional stance when speaking with him.

But there was a deeper level to this dream. I thought to myself, "Why am I on my knees, afraid? Why am I having trouble 'standing up' to my brother?" Moving back through the layers in this dream, I wanted to understand whether it revealed a pattern in my life. I asked myself where in my past this response originated. The answer came back that *I used to behave this way with my father,* who as you already know was the authority figure in my childhood. So I was transferring my fear of authority from my father (where it rightly belongs, or so I think) to my brother. Now, I felt as though I had redirected the misplaced fear to the right person.

As we've seen with Annie and other dreamers in this book, a good understanding of my dream could help me in all kinds of situations, not just the immediate situation with my brother. I had discovered a pattern in my behavior: my habitual response to authority is too emotional. It is both ineffective and inappropriate. Now I was beginning to see that a more "Neil-like" response would be more effective with *all* kinds of authority. I was ready to start replacing my old patterns of behavior with this new, businesslike approach. My dream revealed a whole new aspect of my self, stronger and more confident.

You might think I was ready to close the book on this dream and start practicing my newfound personality traits by calling my brother right away. But here's where the universal elements in this dream come out into the open. As soon as I started thinking about it, I realized that *my* issues with authority are actually universal human issues. I asked myself—am I unique in having a fear of authority? Am I the first or only person who has had these feelings? And now we can see that I wasn't alone in my feelings at all. People have *always* feared authority. So I asked myself, "Who is the ultimate authority figure, anyway?"

I was spontaneously released from my self-judgments as the answer occurred to me—God! God is the ultimate authority. And how many humans through the ages have stood in fear of God? I immediately connected that people have not *stood* in fear of God; they have *knelt* before Him! Kneeling before God is an archetypal image. You find it in culture after culture, through thousands of years. I realized that greater than my fear of authority as represented by my father, is the fear of God.

This helps me place my father and my fear of his authority in its more reasonable place. After all, he was only human. He was not God. In realizing and accepting this, I not only feel less afraid of my father, I am also less angry with him and more forgiving. True, my father made mistakes. He yelled at me sometimes, spanked me when I was little, and grounded me as a teenager. This made me angry, but now I know *that's all right*. When I can feel my anger without worrying about eternal condemnation, I can finally forgive him for his mistakes. Once I understand that I responded to my father as if he were a *divine* authority, I can redirect my fear to God and enter into a fully human relationship with my dad, despite the fact that he is departed.

I still sensed another dimension here though. What exactly am I afraid of? Suddenly I realize—the fear of authority for me is directly linked to a fear of rejection. If God rejects me, He could take away my life, my soul. God might close the Gates of Heaven to me. If my father rejected me, on the other hand, he might have never spoken to me again. These are some of the worst things I can possibly imagine. I have good reason to be afraid.

Let's go back to the dream, though. In the dream I am kneeling, like someone kneeling before God. Maybe I can find some comfort, some strength in my fear by returning again to the universal, archetypal level. So I asked myself who was the first person to kneel before God. And the answer came to me right away: Adam and Eve. They were the first couple to worship God. I realized something else, too. Adam and Eve were the first people to be *rejected* by God. In His wrath God sent His only children out of the Garden of Eden. Probably the worst thing they could imagine actually came to pass. But here's the strength in the dream—even after kicking them out of the house, God forgave His children. He loved them. We might not live in Paradise, but we're still around and God still takes care of us. That is what it was like for my dad and me—maybe he yelled at me, or maybe I felt sometimes like he was kicking me out, but I know he always loved me. Even though he's gone now, I still feel the strength of my father's love.

So now I know that my fear of my father ultimately comes from my thinking of him as if he were God. When I remind myself of his humanity, my fear diminishes and so does my resentment. I also remember that there is no danger of rejection, that God will always love me. This makes my fear much less. You know what was the biggest comfort I took from this archetypal image of kneeling? Somewhere inside me, I stopped thinking of myself as such a chicken! When I connected to how every human stands or kneels in fear of someone at some point in his or her life, it kind of brought me together with the rest of the whole world and moved me away from judging myself so harshly. By acknowledging my fear and then accepting myself, I really did strengthen my ability to approach my brother.

In fact, after interpreting my dream I found I was much more comfortable about the whole situation with my brother. This happened because once I looked into my dream from a universal level, I moved far away from feeling stuck in my fear about his reactions. My whole perspective widened. I had more confidence because now I understood that my fear was not actually related to my brother. It didn't *belong* to him, but to God. Now, my fear was in its right place.

There was something else that had changed. My fear of my brother was really a fear of rejection. But now I understand that people can argue, disagree, even yell, without actually rejecting you. What's the worst that can happen in this situation with my brother? He could disagree with me, or maybe think I'm acting silly. But if God could banish Adam and Eve from Eden and still love them, if my father could ground me for a week and still love me, surely my brother can disagree with me about an issue without rejecting me. This perspective gave me a much more rational view of the situation, and greatly helped me maintain a "Neil-like" approach.

Of course, like any new perspective on your behavior or your relationships, the wisdom you get from an archetypal understanding of your dreams doesn't soak in all at once. You have to practice. I can tell you though, today I find myself more able to move through my fears in the face of *any* authority figure, and through any fear of rejection I experience.

Here is one example. There is a woman friend of mine who somehow always had the upper hand in our relationship. After all these years, the dynamics of our friendship seemed set in stone. I would often sit, allowing her to dominate conversations. There were countless times I made myself available to nurture her needs at the expense of my own. Very soon after the kneeling dreams, I took a decision to express to her what was missing in the relationship for me. I was more honest than I had ever been. Somehow, I had reached a point in my life when I no longer felt ready to accept certain behaviors from others, even in the face of authority or my fear of possible rejection. And let us take that worst-case scenario—what if I *did* get rejected? My kneeling dreams gave me the strength to follow through. For one thing, I realized that disagreement doesn't equal rejection. I also had more faith in my own worth, which would make people want to stay with me even if we disagreed. And finally, I knew I could always rely on the inner strength I felt from God's love, no matter what else happened in my life.

My friend has actually changed in her behavior towards me. When we are together, she no longer dominates the discussion. She no longer interrupts me. She asks what is going on in my life, and listens while I answer. She has obviously decided that our relationship is important enough to her to change her behavior, and the result is a more enriching friendship for both of us.

So as you can see, while each layer of interpretation of my kneeling dream stands on its own (excuse the pun), there is great benefit to looking at the universal images in this dream. They have given me the strength to make permanent changes in the way I live my life. I think it is interesting how this dream series shows that as we enter deeper into our own souls, we come closer to the universal human soul. You have seen that the deepest source of my strength in standing up to my brother ultimately arises from the power and faith I feel, just like the Israelites and like *many* ancient religions, in kneeling before God.

More about Jung

Early in his career, Jung had a dream where he saw skulls in the basement of a house he was walking through. He went to his mentor and friend, Sigmund Freud, to ask him for help in discovering the meaning of the dream. When Freud, his elder, suggested the dream hid a murderous wish, Jung lied because he did not want to face Freud's possible rejection.[4] Later, Jung concluded the dream was in fact a dream with collective imagery. A house can be a universal image representing the Self. In Jung's house dream, he was descending deeper and deeper floor by floor. This symbolized the fact that he was looking deeper and deeper into his unconscious mind.

Before we look at other people's dreams from a collective or archetypal viewpoint, I'd like to point out some things in Jung's dream you might want to watch out for. First of all, notice how easily it can happen that a dreamer moves to the analyst's tune. Jung went along with Freud's interpretation, even though it didn't feel right to him. Watch out for that. The trouble with trying to follow someone else's perception is that in doing so, you are no longer in touch with your own intuition. I say that also in the case of reading about Jung's archetypes. Don't try to fit things into his definitions too rigidly. Trust yourself and your own instincts.

You know, he said that himself. Archetypes become meaningful only when we ask what the feelings are. How does this particular archetypal or universal image make *you* feel?[5] We are developing our individual conscious identity through archetypal images. Jung learned from his own experience, and often reminded his pupils, "Learn as much as you can about symbolism; then forget it all when you are analyzing a dream."[6] I ask you to keep the same in mind while reading my section on the archetypes. They are for your general awareness, and applied with some flexibility can help you find great insight to your dream's meaning.

I admit, some of Jung's archetypes don't resonate with me. That's one area of trouble I have had with my experience in attempting to connect with Jung and his ideas, or maybe better said about some of the lectures I have attended given by Jungian therapists!

Funny, in preparing for this chapter, I took out all my notebooks from the different lectures and workshops I have attended. Between the lines, or not so, are little notes that the person beside me and I have sometimes written to each other. I share them with you because I hope that you might learn from my experience. Here are two examples.

One lecture was about how more and more people are no longer feeling obliged to maintain membership in religious organizations. There has been a decline in people attending services since the 1950s and a deeper decline since the 1970s. Other than the use of religious institutions for major events, like baptisms, bar mitzvahs, and funerals, it seems we as a society are no longer identifying with religious values. The lecturer went on to discuss how this religious vacuum has been filled by other practices such as Eastern spiritual techniques, astrology, and tarot. We have experienced a change in the God image, the male patriarchal God, and now look at a conception of divinity that encompasses all of us. Our culture is working towards a deeper consciousness through self-realization.

While the topic of discussion was an interesting one, I found myself wondering how this connects to me in a concrete way. I am aware that is how I learn something new, by connecting to it, by seeing what I can do about it, even if only in a small way, or by seeing how a matter affects me personally. Yet, it appeared to me that most of the people in the audience felt very connected to the discussion. I mean, one woman even brought up the planets and how the lecturer's point related to the "Big Bang"! A friend sitting beside me wrote, "These people seem so intellectual it makes me feel like, a) either I am a complete moron, or b) I don't belong in this environment." I wrote back, "The discussion is too heady. I really prefer when it is brought down to the individual experience."

Here is another example. In what I considered a very enlightening workshop about Shadows, suddenly the lecturer opened a discussion on how the feminine is about process and the art of becoming. Feminine represents matter. The feminine is embodied in the present. She said the feminine is the "I am." The masculine, on the other hand, is about product. Our masculine quality is future oriented. When we would say for example, "Tomorrow, I will lose five pounds." Or, "The stock market is soon going to take a turn." Understanding these yin and yang dynamics, the Jungian analyst can then better attach meaning to what is going on for the dreamer.

Again I ask you, is it just me? Am I the only one who feels confused and alienated during these abstract discussions? Somehow, I often come away from a Jungian lecture feeling like everyone else knows so much more than I do. This also happens because I get the impression, which I am sure is valid, that the more *au courant* or knowledgeable you are with Greek mythology, Indian mythology, Early North American, Aboriginal Indian culture, native African, and Far Eastern culture and lore, the better equipped you shall be in connecting your dream images to archetypal images! I mean, I have attended lectures that focus on the hunters and farmers among us and how throughout the ages, we can be divided into these two categories. With hunters the authority is inner. *The meaning of the group comes from the individual (the leader).* Farmer-types have outer authority. *The meaning of the individual comes from the group.* Hunters are about freedom, while farmers are about bondage, containing.

Now, please don't get the impression that I do not find these metaphors interesting, but I walk away wondering how can this be applied on an individual basis. Having some knowledge of personality types can help you understand yourself and others, too, but I ask myself, "Where is the learning I can grab on to here? There must be so much studying to do!" I think to myself, "Is it all worth it? It will take a *lifetime* to read all the Greek myths, history, plays, ancient stories, and origins of religions, to get to where I can recognize all these archetypes and their meanings!"

You know what? Forget it! The beautiful thing about Jung and what I believe he really meant for us to do, is that you can find a story or theme that you really *do* know about and see if you can't find some strength in that. If you recognize a story or archetype in your dream, will this help you feel more powerful? That is the focus and task of this chapter.

And here is my final thought about archetypes. Realize always that they each have in them strengths and weaknesses, just like we do. There is a positive and negative side to each. After all, when we are adolescents we want to be in a hunter mode because it is as a hunter that we will move forward to discover the world around us. In that circumstance, we would not want to be in a farming way. Now, when we are in the life stage of marriage and family, we are hopefully cultivating and feeling bonded, and so we are in a farmer mode. In this stage of life, we wouldn't want to be on the hunt, now would we? So you see, each archetype, story, and ideology has its place, both positive and negative. When you find an archetype, the trick will be to grasp the positive side of what is appropriate for your current experience, and how you can use it.

Here is what to take. The Jungians are focused on polarities too. The goal is to move those opposites that we are, closer together. By holding what is foreign to us close enough and long enough, that after a time it no longer seems so foreign. And they get there by amplifying the themes out to images we all know, without a master's degree in theology! The goal remains the same, a striving to bring more of our unconscious forward to our conscious mind. In so doing, we create more wholeness, and increase our ability to tap into a vast reservoir of resources as we travel through life.

How Do We Get There from Here?

One way I get myself there is by asking, "What are the problems, situations, or solutions in my dream that all humans share?" But let's take a step back for a minute. This is what you do. Break the dream down, the same way we did when attempting to decode the dream with a dream map. But instead of, for example, isolating a symbol in order to determine its meaning, let's isolate a picture, an action, or a motif. Jung worked with *images* and *events*. Hold that thought for a minute and let's start from there, using Karen's dream as an example of connecting yourself to a universal theme.

Karen, a woman in her forties, telephoned me with a recurring dream after making our initial connection over the Internet. She is from England. She first understood the dream to mean that she was symbolically trying to see her grandmother again, which she was unable to do since her grandmother had died a few months before.

Karen's Dream

Karen explained, "I was in the cockpit of a two-seater airplane. I was sitting in the co-pilot's seat, but I had no controls in front of me. The pilot had all the controls. It could have been a large commercial plane, because he had many stripes on his arm, but it was not, because I could tell by the controls it was a small plane. Each time we flew up to a certain altitude, the sun was there shining in our faces. Though we put both visors down, mine did not block out the sun's brilliance. Also each time we rose to a certain altitude, the plane would have engine trouble, go putt, putt, putt, and we would have to go back down, and get another plane. It was not as though it was ever an emergency, panic, or scary situation. It was only engine trouble. I never saw more than the pilot's arm. It was the most frustrating situation!"

After more discussion, Karen informed me that in fact her dad was a pilot, and a military man too. "Oh!" I exclaimed. "Is the pilot in the dream your dad? Is he the person you would depend on to help you?"

She explained, "Well, if any person could get me there, it would be him, but even he could not!"

Believing dreams at the first level pertain to a current issue, I inquired as to whether she was experiencing other frustrations in her life at the time. As I would have guessed, she was. At this time in her life Karen was also going through tremendous frustration with a messy divorce in court. Her ex-husband had not paid any child support on the false grounds that he was unable to afford the costs. After years in court, when Karen had finally proven his fraud and won the case, he skipped the country. And in yet another frustration, in the few months since her grandmother's death Karen had been having conflict with her mother.

So, although Karen hoped in the dream that the pilot would fly successfully (or her father would be able to help her), she was left with tremendous frustration. Her father was unable to save her from any of the situations facing her at that time in her life. Looking for a wider view of the past, I inquired, "Was your father an authority figure in your childhood?"

"No," she responded emphatically. "My mother was the authority figure in our house, and my father had absolutely no control over her." So Karen's anticipation and hope of her father's authority, which came out in the dream, was, she explained, a recurring theme dating back to her childhood. I like the imagery of her sitting right beside him in the cockpit.

It illustrates the closeness she said she felt towards him. Karen used the many stripes on his jacket arm to symbolize her high hopes for his ability, yet at the same time the small size of the plane illustrates the reality of the situation. She was not feeling big and powerful at that point in her life.

Now, let's go back to the thought I asked you to hold. Look for an image or an event in this dream. Here's the one I want to pick. The fact is that they are going up in the air and each time they get to a certain altitude, the plane can't make it and they have to come back down. The event keeps repeating itself again and again. It was that continuous up and down movement that hooked me into the story. I saw these two people, going up and down and up and down, and never going forward.

Once you have isolated the event or image, ask yourself, "Is there any story that I have ever heard that has a similar ring to it? Where else have I heard this?" The process I am talking about is the same as comparing Shakespeare's *Romeo and Juliet* to *West Side Story*. There you are looking at two separate stories written so many years apart from each other, and yet the main action is the same. In the up and down frustration of Karen's dream, I saw the story of Sisyphus. Sisyphus, a Greek mortal, was punished by the gods who made him roll a huge rock up a hill for eternity: whenever he reached the top, the rock would roll back down, and he would have to start all over again. Now don't you agree that is just like what happened to Karen in her dream? By the way, please feel free to disagree with me as we go through some of these hypotheses (which after all, is all they are). I invite you to see what story you might think of, and discover what learning is waiting there inside it. But for now, let's examine what Karen might take from the story of Sisyphus.

There are two aspects of the story that I can see learning or gathering strength from. The first, which requires no work on Karen's part, is also the most obvious. This story reminds Karen that her frustration is universal. It is part of the human condition. All humans experience the frustration of realizing we cannot see someone who has died, in this waking life again, anyway. Amplifying the emotion of frustration from myths like the story of Sisyphus can help you come to terms with your frustration. If your frustration is, like Karen's, about wanting to see a relative or friend who is departed, the story points to realizing that it is pointless to push against the way of God, the way of life. Karen, like the rest of us, has as little chance of escaping the realities of loss as Sisyphus did in going against the gods. And so I imagine that is how Karen can take this story in order to apply it to the loss of her grandmother. At least she is not alone in her suffering. And maybe her surrender is the first step to acceptance.

The second, less obvious lesson from this story comes from asking, "How is this character behaving in the story I have thought of? Do I have something to learn from his behavior? Can I find some strength in reacting like he does? Do I want to act like him in my current situation, or is the story there to show how I *don't* want to react?" Look at Sisyphus. Let's be honest. He's as doomed as Romeo and Juliet were. He has no control over his situation. He is doomed for eternity, powerless over his fate. What about Karen? Does she want to be like this guy? Would you want to be like this guy?

I mean, I realize Karen *feels* like Sisyphus. I even understand how that imagery, as Jung would have said, *spontaneously* rose up from her unconscious because in fact she is behaving as if she has no choice or power to change her situation. But is she really powerless? No actually, she isn't! While her chance of success in winning control over her ex-husband and mother's behavior is doomed for eternity, she can choose *not* to be like Sisyphus! How? By realizing there are elements of her life that Karen *does* have the power and control to change, herself. Karen can change her own attitude.

The myth of Sisyphus illustrates the positive and negative aspects to the archetypes. In the conclusion to *Man and His Symbols*, M.-L. von Franz wrote, "we can see that the archetypes can act as creative or destructive forces in our mind: creative when they inspire new ideas, destructive when these same ideas stiffen into conscious prejudices that inhibit further discoveries."[7] Karen was stiffening and inhibited, stuck in her "I am powerless" mode, just like Sisyphus. Yet, if you find an image like that in your dream, you can use it to assess and possibly search out ways to take your power back! Taking our power back, and rising up with great strength in the face of adversity and great frustration is also a universal, timeless, human characteristic. This is the positive potential that comes from that same image of Sisyphus.

We can't control the behavior of someone else. Karen felt great disappointment and frustration while growing up from her father's inability to stand up to her mother. But Karen's decision going forward, learned from the example of Sisyphus, might begin for her the process of accepting and respecting her father's experience as separate from her, in his relationship with her mother. This might even encourage her to accept her situation with her ex-husband, and move on.

As you have already learned in this book, we have the ability to change our imagery, to change our minds. Actually, it was Jung who introduced the concept of using active imagination in order to change the ideas put forth in the dream. I explained to Karen, "The solution to this dream is for you to move over to the pilot's seat! Take control! Although there are issues in life (like death), which we do not have control over, there are so many events which *are* in our control. This dream is about getting in touch with the aspects of your life you *can* take control of. It is about letting go of depending on someone else to *lift you up!*" Unlike Sisyphus, Karen did have ways to escape from her pattern. She needed to find a job in order to care for her children, something her ex-husband was very obviously not prepared to do. And what about her situation with her mother? Karen need not be doomed for all eternity waiting for her father to resolve her situation with her mother! It is up to Karen to do that herself. She has the power and ability to approach her mother on her own.

So let's look again at how Karen and I were able to connect the themes or pictures in her dream to a universal human dimension. In Karen's dream it was the theme that caught my attention. Or you could almost call it a movement. That motion of going all the way up, getting nothing for the effort, and having to come down again, over and over. This, along with the feeling of frustration, got me thinking of Sisyphus. But the point is how first we saw a theme or a movement, and then we looked for another similar theme from another story. So her dream had to do with stories, stories about doing the same thing again and again but getting nowhere. Then, once we found another story we looked for the lesson in it.

I think it is really important to mention here that we were cheating, if you will, because I was the person, not Karen, who connected to the story of Sisyphus. It is optimal if the dreamer herself makes the connection. In this case it worked out okay, but only because Karen was able to connect with him too. If she couldn't, the amplification would have simply been of no use to her. That's what I have against these arbitrary, heady, abstract approaches that many Jungians take. Keep it to something the dreamer knows about. You don't have to have a degree in theology and Greek mythology to understand and benefit from amplification.

Another Karen

Here's another Karen, my sister-in-law. She too amplified her dream out to a universal, collective image, but instead of a story she used a single picture, simple but deep. The dream I am describing here came when Karen already knew that her father had cancer and also knew, somewhere inside her, that he probably didn't have long to live. This is how Karen herself relayed the story to me. Watch how she amplified the image in her dream right out to a universal image without any questions from me.

"The kids, your brother, and I went for a Christmas vacation to Barbados. Two nights before we were to return to Montreal, I had a dream. The time of year was early spring, when the leaves were still their tiny, tender green. It was a sunny day and my father was wearing a black-and-white-checked bathrobe and his black slippers. His face was extremely pale. He began to walk in a circle around the tree on our front lawn. As I watched him walk, I noticed that his feet were not touching the ground. When I awoke, I told your brother the dream and expressed my fear that my father was gravely ill and that we had to go home. Seeing that our returning flight was the following day, I decided to wait the twenty-four hours to return. It's funny that I didn't call home. I knew he was sick, and I didn't want to know the answer to my question. Besides, my family did have my coordinates.

"We arrived in Montreal at midnight. From the airport, I immediately telephoned my sister. I woke her out of a deep sleep and asked her, 'What's wrong with Daddy?' My sister replied, 'Nothing, Karen. He's fine.' I said, 'Where is Daddy now?' She replied, 'He's at home!' I persisted in my questioning, insisting, 'Where is Daddy?' My sister asked, 'Karen. Have you had one of your dreams?' I replied, 'Yes.' My sister asked that question because I have had intuitive dreams more than once. I was extremely disturbed. I went home with this terribly uncomfortable sensation. I was so certain that something was wrong, and I couldn't relax my body. At four o'clock in the morning the phone rang. It was my mother, who was crying, 'Come quickly. Something's wrong with Daddy!' When I arrived at my parents' house, the paramedics were already there. My father had suffered a massive stroke, which had robbed him of his speech and paralyzed all of his limbs. After six weeks in the hospital, he died."

I stopped to cry. I mean me, Layne.

Karen said, "And you know, it's totally symbolic."

I said, "What do you mean, symbolic?"

She answered, "The tree. Rebirth. The spring. His walking in circles around it. The circle is a symbol of eternity. There is no beginning and no end. The tree was rebirth. My father's feet off the ground, was death. And in the end in fact, his death was a gift to him. It wasn't an old tree. It was a young tree. The color of the tree was that fresh green. I mean, why would I have someone walking around a tree in a circle? And his whiteness. It is such juxtaposition, having a pale old man walking around the young freshly budded tree. And you know that fresh smell at that time of year? Spring is birth! Winter is the great death and spring is the birth," she said, "especially when you live in this climate!"

As you can see, Karen took great comfort in amplifying the scene in her dream out to a universal level. Jung would have proposed that the image sprang to her spontaneously from the collective unconscious. It was the image she needed to see at that particular time in her life. It is the answer, if you will, to the issue she was facing at the time, the loss of her father. And the comfort the image brings is the knowledge of the never-ending circle of life. A circle is not finite but infinite, continuous, so Karen came away with a sense of hope rather than one of an abrupt ending.

What did she do to get there exactly? It's not like we get to step into Karen's head to know what thought led to the next, but you can kind of guess how it went, can't you? She saw the tree, and asked herself what that tree reminded her of. She even spoke as she was remembering, and noticed the fresh green color, the new leaves, and conjured up the smell of spring in her mind. Soon after, she understood the contrast of her father walking in the circle, the old around the new. But the most important piece to see here is that Karen was using her own interpretation from her own understanding of the world. And the information resonates so precisely because it all came from her. That's what will make the experience of looking at your dreams from a universal layer meaningful. It happens when you bring it home to your level.

Now, while it is optimal for the associations to come from you, that doesn't mean to say they have to. That's why I love dream work in a group. As you have already learned by reading about my experience with the Emma-Jo Dream, a group brings with it a wealth of ideas to tap into. Just make sure that you feel a strong connection with any suggestions that come from outside. That is the most important part.

This happened with Karen (the airplane Karen) when I suggested the story of Sisyphus. She immediately connected to my idea. Maybe we each connected so firmly to this thought because the motif of frustration as seen in Sisyphus, going up and down but getting nowhere, rose up spontaneously from Karen's unconscious at a time when she needed to see it. Jung proposed these ideas are ones we already know, deep inside us. We all have a collection of images and characters that we don't need to learn, but are born knowing. So, in light of the fact that I am admittedly not a Jungian expert, I'd like to present just a few archetypes, ones I feel are easy to connect to, so you can better understand your dreams. Just keep in mind as you read, to visualize these images in your own personal terms. Then I promise they will become meaningful. And remember you don't need to limit yourself to the archetypes I mention here. Any image or action in your dream that reminds you of a bigger story can have a special archetypal meaning for *you*.

Some Familiar Archetypes
The Hero

One archetypal symbol is that of a hero. *Hero* images have appeared in stories and myths all through time. A hero symbol might come forward in a dream when the dreamer's instinct is telling her that she needs to step forward and be strong "like a hero." Hero images can arise in a dream during times of transition, when you need the courage to look deeper inside yourself for some answers. And while that idea might be frightening, it is the hero in you who will forge ahead despite any fear you may be facing. A dreamer might bring anyone from Jerry Seinfeld, to Marilyn Monroe, to the Pope into his or her nighttime experience. The appearance of a hero image in a dream might be saying, "I need strength," or "I am tapping into my strength." We just saw Karen bring the image of her father, someone she looks up to, into her dream at a time when she needed to tap into her own inner strength.

I was on *The Laurie and Olga Radio Show* in June 1998. It was their final late night broadcast, because the two radio personalities were beginning a new Saturday afternoon show. Actually that Saturday they worked both shifts to begin and end each show. In between shifts, Laurie went home and napped. When I came on that night she said on the air how she had dreamed that very afternoon that the star of *Another World*, Tom Eplin (her heart throb and Hero), walked right into the studio to be interviewed. The fact that she was starting a new show and finishing another was making her feel pretty emotional. On the one hand, she felt sad at the idea of saying good-bye to the nightspot where she felt secure and comfortable with regular listeners who called in. Yet, while the new show meant excitement it also brought feelings of anxiety. An afternoon slot means a greatly increased listening audience. Would the new show succeed? Her instinct told her she needed some strength to face the new challenge.

Archetypes are images and emotion at the same time. They come to life as you attempt to discover why and in what way they are meaningful to you.[8] Bringing Tom Eplin into her dream not only served the function of tapping Laurie into the strength and courage she needed, he also conjured up the excitement she was feeling. He is her Hero.

I spoke once with a fellow whose wife had recently left him for another man. He dreamed Jerry Seinfeld and George Costanza (both of whom he loves watching) were standing outside his house. They said, "Montreal is sophisticated yet laid back." In describing Montreal, they were describing the dreamer's qualities. The simple act of their appearing outside his home gave the dreamer a sense of his own importance. At a time when this dreamer needed some inner strength and a positive sense of self, he brought his Hero figures forward.

The Shadow

As you know, Carl Jung called the disowned or unlived aspect of your character your Shadow. It is another example of an archetype. The Shadow is a little different from the Hero, because while everyone sees heroes more or less in the same way, a Shadow will be different from person to person. On the other hand, the Shadow is universal because we *all* have parts of ourselves that we feel uncomfortable about and need to develop. You can surely recognize a Shadow figure in your dream by the fact that it will be someone or something that makes you feel uneasy.

The most productive way of dealing with one's Shadow is of course to recognize that aspect as part of our psyche. In that way we can learn to use that aspect when the need arises. Jung thought wholeness could be achieved by working to integrate all these aspects of your psyche, not by escaping from your Shadow, which, of course, is impossible. So the work, then, is to integrate your Shadow. And integration can often begin to take place by using active imagination. You can try to play the part of your Shadow, as if in a play. It is what I did when I worked to become Neil in my kneeling dream.

The Crow Dream

Here is an example where direct association helped the dreamer connect to and understand the source of her phobia, a fear of crows. We will discover the crow as her Shadow, and see how active imagination helped the dreamer get closer to her Shadow. A kindergarten teacher from Vancouver named Hannah met with me while visiting Montreal last summer. She dreamed a black crow was sitting on her shoulder. She said it wasn't hurting her, but she wondered if she should feel afraid. She remembers wondering if it would hurt her or not. She was trying to gently pat the crow, while at the same time sort of pushing it, hoping it would fly off. It did not, though. She awoke terribly worried. To make matters worse, a few days after she had the dream, a big black crow flew into her house. She had quite a time getting it out. The dream, coupled with this incident, made her feel sure that this was some bad omen.

Hannah shared with me that this was not the first time she had dreamed of a crow. It has been a recurring symbol in her dreams for the last three years. Pinpointing the initial reason she had this dream at that particular time was fairly simple because Hannah connected to the emotions almost immediately. I asked, "Are you currently in a situation where you feel wary about something? Do you feel unsure you can trust a person or a situation as to whether they might hurt you?"

"Yes," she explained. "I started teaching at this school three years ago. The teacher I replaced mentioned some of the mothers are difficult to please. She said some are snooty and judgmental. Over the first two years many parents complained and wondered why I was not 'doing things the old teacher's way' as they put it. It was obvious by some of the comments made to me that several mothers were talking about me behind my back. Many of the parents whose children I teach are younger than me. I tried to reassure myself. After all, I have successfully raised three children of my own while most of these women were still in school! I have now entered my fourth year of teaching there and to be honest with you, the mothers are for the most part comfortable and familiar with my program now. Recently, there is one person who has been giving me a particularly hard time. She must have awakened an old insecurity in me. Yet, hard as I try to remind myself she is only one person, I worry if I can feel safe with *all* the mothers. I find myself wondering, are they talking about me? Are they going to hurt me? Are they looking for a reason to criticize me? Are they judging me?"

"What comes to your mind when you think of a crow?" I asked. "Take your time." I added, "Let the thoughts just come to your mind."

"Crows are birds. I am very frightened of crows," she started. After a few minutes, she added, "You know what I just realized? My brother used to scare the heck out of me when we were children. He used to tell me a crow is going to come and fly off with me. Crows definitely do not represent a sense of security for me."

"There are three thoughts that occurred to me," I explained. "First, is that the symbol is recurring. When your brother teased you so long ago you learned to connect the crow with not only a sense of fear and insecurity, but your description almost added an element of mistrust. You made it sound as if when you were small, you knew to mistrust or be suspicious and watch over your shoulder because a crow could just fly in and grab you. Am I right to have that feeling?"

"Yes," she said. "You must have an older brother."

We laughed, and I do. Do you remember I mentioned how symbols can relate to a time in our life when a notion began? By using the symbol of a crow, Hannah connected back to a time when she not only felt powerless, but powerless and vulnerable because it described precisely the emotion she was feeling at the time she had this dream. She explained that she felt especially unable to protect herself around the time she started working at that school three years ago. The recurring symbol of a crow in her dreams also began three years ago. She needed to work through her insecurity. Remembering the dream, I explained, gave her an opportunity to look at the issue consciously. We "shone the light" on the dark, scared, vulnerable part of her unconscious by talking about her feelings related to the crow.

Let us talk more about this crow. When Hannah was describing her age versus the mothers' ages and the question of seniority, I admit I had the image of a pecking order.

I asked, "Isn't that what birds do?"

She agreed. "Even that woman I was concerned with was talking behind my back. Talking behind my back is like pecking too."

The Solution

Hannah had described the crow in the dream as steadfast, even though she was gently pushing at him hoping he would fly away. "Do you know what?" I asked. "The crow might be the answer to your predicament. The crow was the strength in your dream. You might need to become more like him or her." Hannah needed to adopt some of that steadfastness and not fly away so fast just because someone gave her a push (by talking about her behind her back). In the dream the crow has the control and along with it, a certain quiet confidence. The crow represents the underinvested aspect of Hannah's character she needs to tap into. The crow also represents the Shadow of herself she is uncomfortable with. As for the pecking, it was time for Hannah to try a little pecking herself! Well, at least to adopt a stance that *looks like* she has the *capability* of pecking!

We can personify the crow using two archetypal symbols. As we just saw, the crow is her Shadow in this dream. She needs to get in touch with and utilize this part of herself, which makes her uncomfortable and a little afraid, in order to help her through this situation. Hannah needs to *become* the crow. This is what I was referring to earlier when I suggested that using active imagination might help this dreamer. Remember how I had to work at becoming Neil? Well, the same principle was happening here. Hannah needed to move closer to and become more familiar with her Shadow. You know it's not just with dream-people that you will be using active imagination. You can just as easily use it to be an animal or bird, or even a brick wall whose qualities you might want to emulate. Hannah wanted to adopt that ability to peck. You see, a peck is not like giving somebody a big blow in the arm with your fist. It is more of a little prod that might have a bit of a sting to it, right? And there is another quality that the crow in Hannah's dream has. That she really isn't sure if and when he is going to peck at all! So let's say he is no easy mark. She's not sure that he'll necessarily be nice.

Hannah might do well to put out some of this energy towards the woman who is intimidating her. It is the air of the crow Hannah needs to move closer to and get comfortable with. So maybe instead of always having her ready, accommodating smile when she greets this woman, she might stand back with a certain cool guardedness. It is amazing how people back off a bit when they sense that there is only so far you will be pushed.

The Trickster

In another respect the crow is almost like what Jung describes as *the Trickster*. My understanding of the Trickster (but please do not hold me too close to this definition), is of this tricky character—some have referred to him as a buffoon or clown—showing up in your dream. Was the crow going to harm Hannah or not? He could have gone this way or that!

The Trickster might appear while you are in a reflecting

stage on a given subject or during a given period of life, like transition. It is that space that all of us experience and typically have all gone through since the beginning of human existence. It is when we arrive at a crossroads and ask ourselves, "Which way am I going to go with this? Am I going to move this way or that?" We are reflecting, and along with the reflection understandably comes indecision. Hannah's crow forced her to reflect, to ponder, deciding what action to take.

Remember the positive or negative qualities I discussed in each of the archetypes? We can see both sides operating in this crow. On one side, he frightened Hannah. But in his reflective side he held the solution to the dream. The Trickster's negative quality, which frightens Hannah, represents the same stuck part of her who was scared as a little girl when her brother would frighten her with thoughts of crows. Do you think this scared part could have also helped give her an extra push towards the reflective part? I think so. It would be the same exercise you learned when linking aspects of your dream to your past. Once you have arrived at the memory, you would reflect as an adult whether you want to remain feeling the same way now as you did then. How would Hannah get there? She might ask herself, "Why is this crow frightening me? Is it still appropriate? Am I still stuck, feeling scared and intimidated? Do I still, now, want to accept the same fear I had as a child? Do I go this way or that?" The negative scared side can lead into the reflecting side.

The two (the Trickster and the Shadow) can seem similar sometimes because they can both cause the dreamer to feel a sense of discomfort. What are you, the reader, taking away from this? What can you look for? Recognize a tricky this way or that kind of movement or joker in your dream, and maybe he will help you connect to a transition in your life. What way are you deciding about moving, and why? The appearance of the Trickster and Shadow will help you search out the ways in which they represent your habitual approach. Then you might decide to trick the Trickster in yourself, and play the new role he might be there to inspire you to!

Hannah decided to do exactly that. She needed to assimilate this part of her Shadow in her current situation, and she did! The first thing she did was to directly approach the woman who she thought was talking about her, to ask her if there was anything she would like to discuss. Hannah realized that if her direct approach didn't help to bring things out into the open, she would ultimately have to change her focus. You know, sometimes it is a healthy exercise to change the focus of your fear from what someone else thinks about *you* into what you might think of *his or her* behavior. Doing that exercise, even inwardly, you might change the rhythm of the dance, or pecking order!

So you see, Hannah, in some way *did* get to "trick the Trickster." She changed the rhythm of the dance. This is what I mean. When you reach that reflecting part of yourself, the part that wonders which way shall I go, I think this Trickster character appears *because* there will always be one way to go that feels more familiar, our habitual way that I discussed earlier in this book. And it is specifically at times of transition that the option of doing it the "other way" appears through this character. When you trick the Trickster, you search out and find which of two ways the Trickster character in your dream might go. What might he do in the dream? Which is the way that seems the most habitual for you? You'll want to investigate what might happen if you go the other way. Open your options. How are you going to choose to proceed?

By the way, in the weeks after the dream work Hannah shared with her brother, all these years later, how the image of a crow has remained with her. She finished the dream. In doing so, she grew closer to both her Shadow and the Trickster in herself.

I wonder if when we arrive at a crossroads and stand there

deciding which way to go, we don't sense some inner spiritual strength rising up from our deepest self. Maybe we are able to recognize this strength of spirit by the appearance of the Trickster or a Hero. Perhaps the mere appearance of a Trickster image is in fact a byproduct of human instinct that appears to us all, for the purpose of helping us take a stand when we need to. These characters give us strength in making choices, inspiring movement in us. If it is true that the images are spontaneous, it seems reasonable to me that the strength they impart must be spontaneous as well. But we should also be able to enhance the spontaneous appearance of these archetypal figures by tapping into their spontaneous strength. How? By connecting to the images through active imagination. How about imagining yourself as the Trickster or Hero from your dream, the way Hannah did?

Do you see the similarities of all the approaches we have talked about and how they begin to overlap each other? This idea here, about connecting to an archetypal character in your dream and applying that very connection to your waking-life experience, is another aspect of adopting the different parts of the dream, like I discussed in the Gestalt section of the book. It is the same as Karen, moving over into the pilot's seat of the plane and becoming the pilot—the same as Sarah stretching herself to react more like her aunt might. It is Deborah, deciding *not* to be like the buildings in her dream, and giving herself permission to fall apart sometimes. It is the same too as my becoming Neil, and behaving as he might if he were in my situation. It's a psychological workout, getting in touch with and utilizing all the potential you have.

Archetypal Imagery and Alchemy

Alchemy is a medieval chemical art whose principal objectives were to find a cure for all ills, a universal remedy, and to transmute base metals into gold. Jung believed the principles of alchemy mirror the process of transforming the confusion and conflict in our minds into psychological well-being. The alchemist's goal was to "unite" opposites, and in so doing create a new "wholeness" or gold. Alchemy puts a picture on the idea of bringing polarities together inside ourselves, to change ourselves into something new.

We've already learned to look for polarities through Perls' Gestalt method. Bosnak, in his "body work" approach to dream understanding, teaches us how to *feel* our polarities and their fusion through the different physical sensations we experience during a dream. So now I'd like to present a synopsis of alchemy brought to light for me when I read Robert Bosnak's *A Little Course in Dreams*, and my understanding of how Jung paralleled alchemy with psychological "wellness." I give you this particular description from Bosnak because it is helpful to recognize what stage you are at by noticing certain images that might easily appear in your dreams.

Using alchemical terms, the alchemists wanted to mix the black world, the "negredo," where the metal is lead, with the white world, the "albedo" where the metal is silver. This would bring them to the red world, the "rubedo," where they would find gold. Jung saw these images as metaphors for the different stages we move through when we are going through something. The something can be any kind of transition, any change, even the road to maturation that I have been discussing in this book. So the lead symbolizes our unconscious, the unknown, death, blackness. I call this stage depression. It is the first stage you hit when something difficult happens, when a change happens. It can show up in our dreams as death, war, graves, stink, rats, leeches, etc. Yet it also symbolizes a beginning, because from the ending comes the beginning. The end can be the end of a relationship, a sickness, a loss. It is the place where you might find yourself asking, "Where am I going from here?" Well, actually if you are at the point when you are already asking "Where am I going from here?" you are at the door to the next stage, the place where you come out of the depression or shock and begin reflecting on your situation.

The reflecting stage is where you enter the white world. Jungians call it the world of Roman Mercury, the mighty and the merciful. I am not sure I click with this Mercury stuff, except that I know it used to be in thermometers. But I do seriously connect with the idea of reflection coming soon after depression, or the shock of realizing an unavoidable change is at hand. Jungians say the reflecting Mercury is the god of our imagination, the god of transition, the god of tricks and pranks. In fact Mercury is the *Trickster*, the archetype of going this way or that. As we just saw with Hannah's crow dream, he can trick you into different paths you might follow during transition. The trick, I suppose, is that you are presented with the way you would habitually proceed, which may not, after all, be the best way to go in your given situation. The Trickster can lead you to distraction or to great deeds. He did inspire Hannah to move in a new direction, one that she was less accustomed to.

The Trickster symbolizes our ability to reflect and in turn become a healing power. The very nature of reflection is to ponder about going this way and then considering that way. Sometimes, we don't ponder and actually *do* go this way and then that! Some dream symbols of the white world or reflecting stage might, and I do mean *might* be the moon, reflecting light in the dark, drifting without direction, unsteady balance, people needing help, and helpers (nurses, doctors), and animals like owls and cats who see in the dark. I like that example of an animal that has the ability to see in the dark. It is so apropos, for isn't that exactly what we are trying to do when reflecting, see in the dark? The time for reflection is an opportunity, if one takes it, for learning and healing. And it is *through* the reflection that the transition actually takes place.

Finally, when you are through with the reflection and the indecision, you arrive at the red world, which is associated with the golden sun. The first light, it is the awakening you come to after the reflection. It is the world of fusion and marriage, where the movement takes place. The alchemists said it is the melting point where the conflicting elements fuse into a new alloy, a new quality.[9] I think of this as the "action" phase. When I have reflected and am ready to put what I have learned during the reflecting stage into action. I find the "value," the "gold," in having survived the depression and taken the time for reflection. This is what happened to Hannah when she took action and decided to stand up to the woman she was afraid of. The gold for me was when I took the decision to "fuse" together with Neil, and approach my brother honestly and maturely, unafraid. For Deborah, this final stage means asking for help and for Sarah, it means to feel deserving. The gold comes from growing closer to and getting more comfortable with your Shadow.

I mentioned earlier that when working with a Jungian analyst, the work might be to imagine yourself getting closer to the part of the dream that frightens you or what makes you feel most uncomfortable. Sometimes you find this uncomfortable spot almost immediately at the mere mention of the symbol. Other times it is the exercise of direct association that gets you there, as it did with Hannah and the crow. Once you find the uncomfortable symbol or place in your dream, your goal becomes moving closer to it. In my section on polarities back in Chapter 4, I mentioned you might have to take a stance or a new way of thinking all the way on the other extreme of a subject in order to finally arrive somewhere in the middle. I understand this to be another metaphor illustrating how we mix the black world with the white world and arrive at a new perspective. We come to the gold, the sun. Jung suggests that if we truly allow ourselves to simply experience both opposing parts, there is in the act, a new creation. He called it individuation.

Now, I don't think you are really supposed to be looking for graves, or moons, or whatever else I have described here that might clue you in to a particular place you are at during your transition. I would repeat now what I said earlier, that these symbols arrived at by Jung or by Jungians are just a very rough guideline. You'll need to go with your gut in terms of whether a dream means you are mired in depression, moving towards reflection, or getting at some kind of resolution or new creation in your current life experience. And I guess then, the question becomes *how* exactly does one listen to his gut in these situations? What kinds of questions might you ask yourself? What kind of *click* might you be looking for?

Here's a quick example that comes to my mind. Two weeks ago, I woke one morning having dreamed that I was at my brother-in-law's grave. The thing that struck me in the dream was how I had not reacted to his death until I saw his son at the gravesite. It was only then that I reacted, when I saw how sad his son was. It was a car accident. I woke feeling so sad and wondering why I dreamed my perfectly young and healthy brother-in-law had died in my dream. I never did arrive at any meaning.

Next morning I woke, dreaming I had news that my brother had died in a car accident. In my dream I ran into some cousins who wanted to go for a walk with me. I remember I was waiting for a telephone call in the dream, which was supposed to confirm if in fact it was true that my brother had died. When I saw the cousins, I told them the news and explained that I had to stop and cry before I went for a walk. I knew in my heart he had died. I woke feeling absolutely grieving, overwhelmed, freaked out, in total shock.

In both dreams my initial reaction to these deaths of my

brothers was nonexistent. Then I had a delayed reaction when I felt grief-stricken, overcome with sadness. I asked myself, "What's happening that's making you feel this intense sinking feeling?" Really, I could not connect.

Here's what I mean by following your instinct, your hunch. I said to myself, "Come on, Layne! These are dreams that get you in touch with a great, wide sadness, and the flavor of this sadness has something unexpected (car accidents) to it (given that both brothers are young and healthy)." I am saying to myself, "This is something big. Something big that you are not initially reacting to. And it is coming at you from 'all sides' (the fact that each brother is from a different side of the family)." So never mind the black stage of transition, which is a metaphor for a depression, this seems like it is pre-black stage! I haven't even hit the depression yet! I don't even know yet what in the heck I am so devastated by that comes as a surprise I am not even reacting to!

By the way, that is in fact how a depression might come up and hit you. It hits you because you are not really in touch with the sadness. You are *in the dark*, get it? Once you are in the white, or reflecting stage, you are in touch with and thinking about the feelings. That is why I maintain that it takes a certain degree of health to be at a place where you can ask for professional help and go into therapy. When you are in the black, you may not even yet be aware enough to have acknowledged the onset of a problem. I am winding back here to the earlier chapters of this book where I suggested that if a person tells you he has problems, it can be a sign for you that he has some health. Similarly, when a person professes to be so "healthy," you might stay more on guard.

So, you know what? Underneath all my self-questioning brewed the answer to my dreams. The thing is, if you take the Hero you have inside, and open yourself up fearlessly for a minute to what scariness you might find, your intuition will let you know what it is. "Don't push it aside," I said to myself. "There's time to push the fear aside later. Let's just discover for a minute here what the fear is!" So here it is. I'm forty-nine. Okay. I am not yet fifty, but I am in my fiftieth year. It's coming up on me like an unexpected car accident. While, like my brothers, I have going for me the fact that I am still "young and healthy," yet like them too, I have my mortality looming up on me.

When you read the next chapter, you'll see that the Emma-Jo Dream ultimately brings me back to my own mortality. I admit I didn't realize this until recently, while I was writing the last few chapters of this book. So I've been thinking a lot about my own death lately. But the thing is, you can think about something and even write about it, and it still doesn't hit you, emotionally. I've been writing that I know I'm going to die someday, maybe not too long from now, but it's been more like an exercise for me. Like Deborah with her falling buildings, it *hasn't even hit me* yet.

Truth is, and I know inside me, it's true, I have this undercurrent of extreme fear, panic, dread, and doomed sadness looming somewhere in the background that I have been choosing to ignore. It is, rather somewhere underneath me, getting ready to shake up my whole world like an earthquake. Yes, I'm talking about my mortality, but I mean *feeling* my mortality. While the subject is in my face right now because of my writing, I have not faced or chosen to even look that way. The way of actually *experiencing* my feelings, my emotions attached to this subject of my impeding death. The dreams both have death, and one even a cemetery setting. No, thank you. I am still, even now, not ready to get down into my feelings on this subject. But I *do* know now, there is the beginning of a new transition at hand here.

Do you think this exercise of paying attention to my intuition has helped me even though I admit I am not yet ready to get in there and face the music? It has. First of all, I stopped thinking that one of the brothers is about to have a car accident, which in itself was a relief. And second of all, I know I am at the door of an impending transition. I am, yes, going to have to look at it. Maybe there is value and some preparation in the mere knowledge of this fact. And maybe I am not even looking yet because I'm still stuck in the black, as opposed to the reflecting stage. I have found the beginning of the depressed stage, this feeling of inescapable doom. Come on, do you blame me? Whatever happens, at least now I have a sense of what this is about. All I can do today is appreciate that the process of this latest transition will at the very least not be boring! And I am confident my transition will involve change and movement along the way, for I am bound to journey at some point into the reflecting stage and away from this doom that is my undercurrent for the moment. One of life's wonderful guarantees is that change is constant. It is one of those things you can depend on. This reminds me of one more fringe benefit I have found in dream work. You get a certain practice with unexpected change here in dream work, as you must in any life circumstance—the practice of moving forward with a process actually having no idea where it is going to take you. When you engage in any dream work, from the most traditional method to the most experimental, you too have no idea at the outset where it is going to take you. Dream work is practice about life's ambiguities; getting familiar in a space that is unfamiliar. And it all ties back to having confidence in the knowledge that change is constant. It is what stops me from going off the deep end so to speak, when I realize an impending transition is coming. The knowledge is there for me even when crisis rears its ugly head unexpectedly. I need not worry there will be no end to my sadness, dismay, or misery. I can have great confidence in movement. And I believe it is that confidence that helps me flow with it. Now don't go thinking that when I arrive at crisis's door or as I have described here, transition's door, that I get there ready to face it right away. I don't. But I do have this information and knowledge with me, and as soon as the black begins to fade away and as Bosnak might say, I start getting my night vision, it is then that this knowledge is very helpful.

If you think your dream seems to indicate a stage of depression, or reflection or creation, ask yourself questions like I have shown you here and stay open to the answers. Try and hear your intuition. Trust it. It won't lie to you.

Finding alchemical parallels in your dreams can help you have more patience with yourself and a better sense of the process that we go through in order to arrive at change. And I hope you can appreciate, as I have reiterated several times throughout this book, that change is a process. It takes time, and a desire on your part. It is certainly possible, but it is not always easy. Having an awareness of this process can really help you go easier on yourself. Enjoy the journey. That's the main focus of this book; to help you not only understand the journey, but enjoy it, if only for the sheer adventure of discovery!

Michael's Dream

I planned to revisit Michael's dream in this part of the chapter because I wanted to point out how I think that Michael, like all of us who are in great pain or transition, tapped into a spiritual energy we all possess. I am astounded what synchronicity was at work this morning when I picked up the paper to find the following piece on the front page. The headline read, "Keeping God in Mind." Underneath it said, "Religious beliefs won't disappear as long as the human brain functions as it does, says a scientist [Andrew Newberg] who has traced brain activity during worship." I said to myself, "Goodness gracious! Is this not exactly the discussion I plan to begin this very morning in my current chapter? And to boot, scientific proof? Dr. Jung would be pleased!"[10]

Let's go back to Michael's dream, because I think here we will find some of the spiritual imagery inherent in our makeup that Andrew Newberg discusses in his article. Michael had what Jung referred to as a *grand dream*, one with a very universal quality to it. We generally have these dreams when we are going through a really rough time. Grand dreams might typically happen during transition or times of great stress. Michael must have been at the beginning of the reflecting stage because if you remember, Michael dreamed his late father-in-law said that one day they would find genies buried on the other side of the lake. The lake would be a symbol of the reflecting stage, and the fact that there are spiritual, magical beings on the other side infers a kind of crossing over, a movement. There is a movement over to another side, another way of being. But he says "one day," so this new way of being hasn't happened yet. Michael was crossing over to a new place in his life without drug use.

Let's isolate this crossing over. One story about crossing over immediately came to my mind. Before I went to write it in this chapter, I was so curious to see if Michael himself would have the same association, so I called him. Well, of course I kept the idea I had in mind to myself! But Michael had the same thought as mine! No matter that some years have passed since he dreamed of genies and his late father-in-law, Michael too was reminded of Moses parting the Red Sea and freeing the Jewish slaves from the Pharaoh in Egypt. Here is another example of a motif that we see again and again throughout time in our stories, the crossing over. It is a bridge.

Look how in his time of great stress, Michael brought forward these images of spirits from another realm. I think this is what Andrew Newberg means. We have this human tendency to tap into a spiritual source when we are in great need. It is a universal quality in human nature. Michael gave himself a source of strength. And didn't Moses do the same? When he couldn't convince the Pharaoh to "let his people go," Moses turned to God for help. He too asked for help from another realm. And God gave Moses a staff, which became his source of strength.

As a source of strength, Michael brought several spiritual beings into his dream. His father-in-law for one, besides being departed, was for him a kind of mythological Hero to help him cross over, to transcend his pain. I have read authors who link the appearance of a Hero in a dream to the dreamer's courage to investigate his unconscious. The Hero is the searcher of truth, the character in the dream who faces the fear or pain of developing self-awareness, which is exactly what Michael was doing here. Remember also those two men who suddenly appeared to walk with him. They said, "It's time to go." Haven't we so often heard about these beings who accompany us as we pass to the other side? Finally there are those buried genies. What do they make you think of? Michael suggested the story of Aladdin and his Lamp. In the story of Aladdin, he finds the lamp deep in a cave, also underground. And the genie grants wishes. You can see that Michael's unconscious mind is providing him with spiritual strength during his time of need.

I'll tell you, it really does make me wonder sometimes if there isn't a case of two different elements at work here. One, as Jung would have said, that these images rise up spontaneously out of our unconscious, as we need them. But two, that maybe those who have departed reappear to us when we are in need, for in fact they really aren't that far away. Gives you something to think about, doesn't it? Well, for some of us anyway. I know my Andy wouldn't want to be included with those of us who think about that!

So here we are again. Where is the learning in this chapter?

What can you go home with and do with your dreams, your
loved ones, your relationships, your problems, and your *life*?
What are the possibilities you have learned in this chapter?
What happens when you change the direction of the dance and
the choices you might make because you have connected yourself to an archetypal image or story or character? Where might
it take you? Who will react to your changes? Are you concerned
about someone's reaction? I think the answers to some of these
questions put you in a powerful position for several reasons.
One is because when you have your options and your fears out
there on the table, right in front of you, you are powerful. You
are powerful because you have created awareness. You are powerful because your awareness opens for you the door to conscious choice. And consciously choosing a plan of attack, or
more accurately put, the way you want to proceed in a given situation will definitely bring you a wonderful feeling of having
control over events and how they happen in your life. Now,
isn't that fantastic when you consider all the things in our lives
we are powerless over?

And if that isn't enough, the whole point of collective
imagery and Jungian analysis is not just the awareness of your
fears, or that it is one more tool for opening up your choices.
This way of looking at your dreams connects you to a more *spiritual* level of your existence. A Jungian framework somehow
brings your view of your fears and options to a new level, the
level we all have in common. It's not just consciously choosing
a new plan of behavior, but somehow seeing the events and relationships in your life in a different way. Take Michael, with his
new understanding of the higher forces in his dream. His father-
in-law, for example, linked him to a personality who had great
strength in rising above adversity in his life. The genies connected him to an image of characters who can only free themselves by someone else's help, and only then are they powerful.

Moses with the Red Sea helped Michael stay strong in the face of his addiction, because he was reminded how Moses before him needed help too, and asked for it. Like the genies, Michael became powerful enough to part the Sea to freedom with the help he allowed himself to ask for.

It is the same frame of mind I felt when I connected myself to the universal issue of our fear of authority. The issue I was facing was no longer me, alone. I became smaller, more a part of a bigger picture. It was less about just me, and more about the business of being a human being. Humans, even the best of them through time, have asked for help, not only of other humans, but like Michael, of spirits. And we do get the strength we need from these spiritual forces! It is in our nature, part of our make-up.

What about Karen, my sister-in-law? What greater help could she find than the image that rose up from her unconscious at such a sad time in her life? Didn't she gather strength from the knowledge that there is no end to the circle of life? Jung proposes that she, like all of us, is born with this knowledge. The knowledge that connects us in a spiritual way to all people, to all those who came before us. We have a constant resource of access to this knowledge that rises from our unconscious. All we need do is to utilize the power we already have.

I am thinking about the fringe benefit to connecting yourself with something bigger than just you. When you do this you widen the whole scope of things, your whole perception. Life and life's issues are somehow not about just me, me, me anymore when you adopt this framework. It is more about us, us, us. And then too, you open the door to seeing others in your life as also part of a bigger universe. And don't you think that by putting your relationships inside the bigger picture of things, you make the appreciation of the individual relationship, and the people in it more precious, less threatening? I do. It is not a case anymore of you against me, or of you doing something to me, or me doing something to you. It is us, doing the human experience, together. We move together through the cycle of humanity, like those before us, and those to come.

CHAPTER TEN

The Whole Self

"Thus our dream life creates a meandering pattern in which individual strands or tendencies become visible, then vanish, then return again. If one watches this meandering design over a long period of time, one can observe a sort of hidden regulating or directing tendency at work, creating a slow, imperceptible process of psychic growth—the process of individuation."

—M.-L. von Franz

This is the chapter in which I want to bring together everything we have looked at so far. Let's go back to an overview of the dream work and see if we can agree that while some is good, *any* understanding is valuable, but surely the whole is greater than the sum of the parts. I would ask you to keep in mind as you read this chapter that I have attempted not just to "bring together" everything we have looked at, but really tie it together. So, while my discussion may be still moving outward towards a universal understanding of our dreams, I want to keep tying concepts back to things you learned in the earlier chapters of this book. I have done this, not only to remind you of these frameworks and ideas, but to illustrate how this circular motion is there for you to use in all your approaches to dream work, and to life.

The Process of Discovery

In the process of doing the exercises in this book, we have learned to discover who we truly are. While I talk sometimes about the options we have for discovering something about ourselves through one exercise or another, I want to emphasize that self-knowledge doesn't lie in any particular layer or level of "deep." Self-knowledge doesn't even lie in the "deepest" layers. I think the point is to look at the whole of it, together. That brings you to the truer picture of yourself.

If we were talking about a picture in the literal sense, say we looked at a picture of only your arm. That arm is real and certainly a part of you. It may be very attractive, or maybe it isn't. Then, we might look at your forehead. Your forehead is there. It is real, and a part of you too. Say it has some lines in it. Your forehead might not look so good by itself, but what happens when you add your eyes? What about another picture still, of your feet, and another of your legs? Each may have their attributes and their flaws, but you see, all these individual parts are *not* the whole person. You really aren't getting the whole picture unless you have all the pieces and see what they look like together, because it is only then that we see the real you. It's the way you put yourself together. Your dream work, *all of it together* from the initial dream-interpretation (your immediate waking-life situation), to the Gestalt framework, to your past, to the universalist Jungian approach, is exactly that; a picture, but from the inside. It is an interior picture of how you put yourself together.

My greatest discoveries and learning about who I am came from actually going *through* the process of the dream work. That has been my personal experience. My discoveries have come from feeling that initial *click* of understanding and experiencing what it's like to do Gestalt play-acting exercises and then, taking the road back, remembering all those things from my childhood. And then, finally trying to figure out how I fit into the greater human picture.

But you don't have to take my word for it. Take a dream you had, any dream that feels interesting or important to you, and try going through the exercises in this book based on your dream. See if you feel different afterwards than you did before. Explore whether you learn something about yourself that you didn't know before.

They say a picture is worth a thousand words. Is there some way we can get a visual image of all these different thoughts and feelings right next to each other, all on the same page, so to speak? It turns out that we can. This is precisely what a mandala does. Remember the mandala from Chapter 1? That was only part of my mandala for the Emma-Jo Dream. In this chapter, I'm going to give you the entire mandala, so you can discover how it lets you see the whole, right there in front of you. The mandala allows you to discover how you can actually see right there on the table in front of you, a visual of your interior. Here I am again, back to Carl Jung, and that part of him I so love. His focus was on the whole of yourself and the art of reaching towards that end, wholeness.

The Mandala: Figure 6

Carl Jung pointed to the mandala as an archetypal image representing the Self, the whole Self. This idea of the mandala as a whole comes from way back in history, starting thousands of years ago. In his commentary to *Secret of the Golden Flower*, Carl Jung himself described a mandala. He wrote, "Mandala means a circle, more especially a magic circle, and this form of symbol is not only to be found all through the East, but also among us; mandalas are amply represented in the Middle Ages. The specifically Christian ones come from the earlier Middle Ages. Most of them show Christ in the center, with the four evangelists, or their symbols, at the cardinal points. This conception must be a very ancient one because Horus was represented with his four sons in the same way by the Egyptians . . . For the most part, the mandala form is that of a flower, cross, or wheel, with a distinct tendency toward four as the basis of the structure."[1]

Figure 6: The Emma-Jo Dream—Mandala

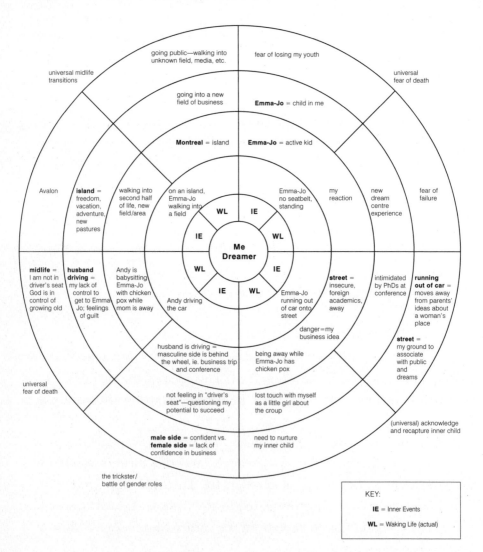

KEY:

IE = Inner Events

WL = Waking Life (actual)

In civilizations around the world, the mandala is an archetypal image often used to pull together different parts into a whole. In Eastern mythology too, mandalas were used widely to represent wholeness and balance. So whether you are talking about the Egyptian gods, or the different parts of me as represented in the Emma-Jo Dream, still the function of the mandala would be the same, to pull together these different parts of something into a whole being. Jung called it a "psychological viewfinder," a cross or circle divided into four. He said when you superimpose this viewfinder on psychic chaos, it gathers the content together and holds it inside the protective circle, reducing the confusion.[2]

I like the concept of a psychological "viewfinder." The viewfinder, as you know, is the part of the camera that you look through to see the picture. So, in the example of the Emma-Jo Dream, there's what appears to be all this confusion, with the driving and then walking along St. Catherine Street, the men following us, and then suddenly the scene with us in the car and Emma-Jo running out into the field. The whole thing seems disconnected and confusing, as dreams often are. But when you superimpose the mandala onto the confusion, somehow, you start to see order and clarity.

When a mandala image appears in your dream, it may symbolize the integration of your personality.[3] With that in mind, let us look at the mandala of my Emma-Jo Dream and see if we can find the value in seeing the whole of it together. It is interesting because actually, the first thing that I did when I thought about all the different layers of my dream *was* to focus on the individual parts. But it occurred to me that when you do that, you end up in the place Jung calls "confusion." After I had the mandala in front of me, and some time on my hands to consider its themes and implications, all the confusion fell into a shape that *did* create order. When I looked at my mandala again, it made so much sense to me. I was able to see how and why my reactions happened the way that they did. Plus I discovered something else. My understanding of the Emma-Jo Dream gives a beautiful metaphor of the movement that takes place through the different stages of a life. It is amazing to me how, as I look at the layers unfolding, I am able to see a neat breakdown of these stages. And the whole picture was set in motion by a dream! The thing that truly fascinates me though, is that this movement can be set in motion by many, many dreams that you have, if you care to take the time to analyze them. The phenomenon is right there for the picking.

If I have a dream that I do not understand at all, if the message of the dream is completely unknown to me, it is the same as a tight muscle or knot. Each connection I make, and I mean to say just the connection; the simple understanding of what the dream means, frees the anxiety tied up in the conflict. The knot starts to untie. And the more I come to know or define the issue, the more I automatically set the knot to unraveling, even if I am not yet prepared to face the inevitable—because when I can see the whole dream with all its parts together, I experience a basic shift in perception. And then some change, at some point, becomes inevitable. Let me explain.

When my older girls were small, and still now with Emma-Jo too, from time to time they would naturally come home from school feeling hurt or betrayed or humiliated by some other little girl in the class. They'd say, "Oh Mummy! She's so mean!"

"What if," I pose after hearing the events, "this little girl watched her parents fighting and totally screaming at each other at breakfast this morning before she came to school? What if it wasn't an argument between her parents, but instead they were both screaming at *her*? Here's another thought. What if it wasn't a fight? What if she has a grandmother or grandfather who is very sick, or dying and everyone in the house has been so sad and worried for weeks, that no one is spending any snuggly time with her?"

There is inevitably and immediately a change of expression that washes over my child's face as I pose these hypothetical questions. I have set the shift of perception in motion. Now the slant is already moving away from what my child feels was done to her, and rather what may have happened to her friend. I continue, "What if something like those things happened to you? Would you go to school and tell everybody about it?"

"No!" is the response I normally hear.

This may not always be true of a few of my girls, but that's another story. I bring home the point, "The thing is, though, while you might not tell anybody what happened to you, I imagine your mood would definitely show. Maybe you'd jump on someone without thinking about what you're saying, or maybe just feel generally in an unfriendly, maybe sad, or even bad mood. What do you think?" I get the nod of agreement. The door has always opened by this point in our conversation. The shift of perception has taken place. My daughter, whichever one I have had this conversation with, is already not taking her experience so personally. Instead, now she realizes that for sure there is a part of the picture hidden from her view, no matter what part that may be. And seeing the whole picture changes your attitude and your judgments, especially when you are making those judgments about yourself.

That is the experience you have when you look at the whole of your dream, when you see it with all its layers. You get the whole picture and as a result, you don't judge any one of the individual pieces too harshly, because each has had an effect, an impact on the other. And now the whole of it not only takes on a new form, but the form you see makes sense!

A Closer Look at the Mandala

The mandala can be thought of as a drawing of a kind of movement. It's like seeing a picture of the dreamer's mind, from the outside to the inside and then back out again. Think of it this way. An event or circumstance happens to you. It comes to you from the outside, and it impacts on you, the same way a stone would affect the water in a pond the minute it lands. You have a dream. The dream mirrors the impact the event has had on you. And if you take the time to analyze the dream, it will carry you slowly deeper inside yourself. At the deepest layers, as you have learned, are the universal archetypal themes, which bring you outside yourself again, connecting you to the rest of humanity. This time though, you have a new perspective. Visually, the concentric circles of the mandala have the same rippling effect you see when you toss a stone into a pond. The stone is something that comes from the outside, lands, and impacts the water. You can see the ripples start in the center and move out to the edges. But eventually the wave recoils, it turns around and comes back inside towards the center again.

I am going to discuss three aspects of the dream mandala here. First I'm going to talk about the dream story itself. When you draw a mandala of a dream, you start with the story of the dream and work outwards from there. So the dream itself becomes the inner circles of the mandala. When you turn your dream-story into a mandala, you will want to think about which parts of your dream refer to actual, waking-life experiences that you had, and which parts correspond to what I call "inner events." In other words, some parts of the dream come from things that really happened to you, but the inner events are what happen *inside* you when waking-life events occur. So really, your waking life triggers something inside you.

Take, for example, my waking experience of being away from home on business when Emma-Jo came down with the chicken pox. This triggered some feelings of guilt. Then the *inner* event around this outer event of the chicken pox became my inner conflict about male and female roles. But the waking-life experience doesn't necessarily have to be a *current* experience. How about Johnathan's dream of the dogs coming out of the bungalow? One actual, waking-life experience of his that triggered the dream was the fact that while he was growing up, his parents really did used to take in abused, abandoned dogs.

A second very important aspect of the dream-mandala has to do with the exact process you have already learned in this book, the process of discovering the different layers of meaning in your dream. A mandala is the ideal way to see these different layers and how they come together. Then when you have drawn your mandala with the dream story, the initial connections, and all the different layers of meaning in it, you put it down on the table in front of you. Now you can find the third purpose of your mandala. This is where the deeper learning happens. Finally, you can discover the themes that appear and reappear in all the different layers of your dream.

Drawing Your Mandala

Drawing a mandala can be especially helpful when you have a few smaller dreams over a short period of time, or a long dream that feels really confusing. So, here's what you do. Start by drawing a small circle and put your name in the middle. As you can see (Figure 6), that first circle corresponds to, or represents the dreamer. The next circle illustrates the dream itself, the story of the dream.

When I was doing my mandala workshop on the Emma-Jo Dream, the workshop group leader divided my dream as I told it into four main sections, the four main events of the dream. That's what you'll want to do. Pick some main scenes or sections of your dream that come out at you. The act of doing this is exactly like looking at a room that is a complete, disastrous mess and having to choose four main categories or boxes to toss each item into. Here are a few examples using dreams you are familiar with. If it was Sarah's dream about her uncle, she might choose one section about how her uncle was giving her a ring with lots of diamonds, another on how the ring was too big, a third about her awareness in the dream that he was still married to her aunt, and a fourth wondering how to refuse him. Johnathan may have chosen the first section about watching Labradors and other dogs coming out of a bungalow. He could have a second section about how the house didn't look as though it could accommodate them all. A third part of his dream could be the European couple, who were standing outside with their little child, and a fourth section might be the smiling bulldog.

Now you must be sitting there asking me what to do if your dream has only two sections. I say, "Don't get stuck. Have two? Use two!" These are not hard and fast rules. Besides, I don't want you getting a headache trying to make this fit perfectly, if, with a particular dream you had, it simply doesn't!

So now, if you were able to, you have divided your dream into four main events or scenes. For my Emma-Jo Dream mandala the workshop leader chose the following sections. Emma-Jo had no seat belt on and was standing in the car. Then she was running out of the car on to the street. Third, it was Andy who was driving the car. And finally the dream ended with Emma-Jo walking into a field. If you turn to Figure 6, you'll see how the circle of the mandala is divided into four main parts, with these different parts of the dream-story forming each part.

Now let's go back to those waking-life versus "inner events" that I talked about before. In my dream, one example of a waking-life event is how Emma-Jo really doesn't like wearing her seat belt. In fact, she was four years old around the time I had the dream and it was an ongoing issue then. This waking-life event fits into the part of the dream where she was standing in the car without her seat belt on. If you look at the inner events of the same section, you will see how Emma-Jo represents the child in me, and also how her standing with no seat belt trig-gered my feeling of being unprotected in the face of growing older. I can't strap my youth in, or hold it in place, can I? Let's look at a different part of the dream, the ending where Emma-Jo is walking into a field. You may remember from Chapter 2 that this field reminded me of an island. In my waking life, as you know, I was walking into a new field of work at the time I had the dream. Also, Montreal is an island. These events in my life triggered the inner event that comes from growing older. As I age, I am walking into a new area or field of life. In other words, I am walking into the back nine. And the back nine is a new pasture for me, no?

So, as you are drawing your mandala, you can, if you like, make a distinction between events in your dream from your waking-life, and those that I call "inner events." This is not something you have to do. I did want to do it here in the Emma-Jo Dream though, for your better understanding. Mostly I did it because I wanted you to notice how these two categories, the waking life and the inner life, operate simultaneously.

Once you have those beginning parts in place, which relate more to the dream story itself, you can begin to draw and fill in the concentric circles of the rest of the mandala. While you can feel free to use whatever part of your interpretation you'd like in each circle, I personally use the same order, or layers of the dream I used while writing this book. I begin with the dream's first level of meaning and how it relates to the dreamer's cur-rent experience. Here, for example, I dreamed that Emma-Jo was out of the car and I couldn't get hold of her, and at the first level of meaning this had to do with my being in Asheville, North Carolina, while she was at home in Montreal. I couldn't get a hold of her. In another section of the dream, Andy was driving the car because he was holding down the fort at home while I was away. He was in the driver's seat, so to speak.

I try to use the next circle of the mandala to represent how the different characters and symbols in the dream represent different parts of me. This circle illustrates the framework you learned in the Gestalt chapters about how all the parts of the dream are parts of you. Maybe you want to use one of your circles to illustrate your different parts. You can see this in my mandala where it says that Andy was driving the car to represent my male, businesslike side, which was away at a conference doing business! You can choose to use your next circle, visually moving outwards on the mandala but metaphorically moving inwards to your past, to fill in the memories your dream triggers inside you. I took this opportunity to relate the struggle I have vis-à-vis male and female roles, and the messages I understood as a young child about what those roles should and shouldn't be. As I mentioned, this inner struggle was triggered by my feelings of guilt when I heard that Emma-Jo had contracted the chicken pox and I wasn't there to mother her.

I use the outermost circle to show how your issues fit into archetypal, familiar patterns. And remember, it is those outermost reaches of the mandala, the universal part of you, that spur the recoil effect. They bring your deepest self together with the rest of the human race. You suddenly begin to see yourself as a part of a bigger picture, not so different from other people. And more importantly, the recoil begins when you find an archetypal image or story that *resonates* with you. This is the act of *literally* taking something from outside yourself and bringing it back in to impact on you personally.

As we have seen again and again, there is no "nice neat model." You will not find a mandala where each framework fits exactly into each circle. The mandala might cause anxiety for those of you who need structure. Not every section has a "Gestalt" or a "Freudian" layer, and when it doesn't, it may have several "first-layer" meanings filled in. When a section does have all the layers, I place them in the order I have described. In that case, please don't get stuck or lose your focus. The point of using the mandala is to discover emerging themes and how they impact your reactions to any layer of a situation. We are looking at the whole picture.

In the workshop, when we finished attaching meaning to my dream, we amplified symbols to a universal meaning. Someone from the back of the room suddenly called out, "She's the Trickster!" He was right. She is Trickster. Emma-Jo represents both sides of the see-saw of my own emotions and impulses: she is the source of my anxiety, but also the freedom, excitement, and fearlessness. I was questioning my authority to write this book and present my ideas about the value of understanding your dreams. Emma-Jo's in-and-out movement from the car was the picture that connected me to that archetype. Is she in the car? Then she's out! Then she's walking into a field. She's this way then that, just like the crow in Hannah's dream. I had the potential to throw my idea away because of my insecurity or forge ahead with it. It was a turning point. Would I free myself from early impressions and allow myself to move ahead?

My connection to the Trickster linked me to my midlife transition. As I sit here, writing this book four years after my Emma-Jo Dream, the archetypal issues continue to resonate with me. Back then, I was in the early stages of my midlife transition, where people often change careers. I was debating and deciding about my worth, my chances of success or failure, and which road to take. Now as I have revisited my mandala during the writing of this chapter, I am further into my midlife transition. We saw this illustrated in the dreams where my brother and my brother-in-law had died. I am on to issues concerning my mortality. This time when I looked at the mandala, I felt much more connected to the archetypal theme of losing my youth, my fear of death, and the unknown.

Looking for Themes

When you are done mapping these layers, I want you to start thinking about emerging themes. Dividing your messy room up into four main boxes is just the beginning. When you start seeing the emerging themes in your dream, you can begin to create order in the confusion. So let's talk about the process of looking for unifying themes.

In the course of exploring the four different parts of my dream, I discovered the following main theme that we've already seen in this book. It had to do with feeling inexperienced, and as a result of that inexperience, feeling insecure, and especially, afraid. I was, on several levels, not feeling in control of how the events in my life were unfolding. While there is some excitement and adventure attached to that, it still made me fearful. I was afraid of the unknown. Finally, for me this fear or insecurity came out in my own inner battle about the roles I thought the sexes should play.

Now, I don't want you under the impression that I attended the mandala workshop, got a look at the mandala of my Emma-Jo Dream, and suddenly all these themes came flooding at me. It doesn't happen like that. I definitely connected like crazy during the workshop to the professional insecurity I was feeling at the time. But as for the more general theme of fear, and how I deal with it, I only began making some connections after digesting the information for a while. I also took some time to consider and go over the mandala. So please, don't feel surprised if you draw a mandala and when at first you see it, nothing comes out at you. If you see nothing at first, you may even put it away for a day or more, and come back to it. That can sure make a difference. As you have seen in this book, there is a process. Trust it.

How might you see or notice themes? Well, there are a few ways. Try looking for the story behind the story. You can do that by asking questions similar to those you might use for free association when you are trying to link yourself to your past. In that case, you would ask yourself, "Where in my life have I felt this way before?" Here, though, you listen to the story of the dream, and then ask yourself, "What is *really* going on here?" And I'll tell you what. The reason I find this process similar to free association is because, while it doesn't *have* to be linked to feelings, I find that when I do it I usually end up attaching the answer to a feeling.

Here's what I mean. You dream a man is chasing you. In the distance you notice a door. You are picking up speed and heading for that door. While you have the sense that your pursuer is gaining ground on you, you suddenly find yourself extremely close to the door; a place you know will lead you to safety. What is the real story here? Can you see it? It is a story about pressure, intense pressure to get somewhere and to get there fast. Thing is though, there is a goal in this dream. It's not as if you have no place to run. There's the door. So the theme is feeling pressured (even panicked if you like) to get to a place very quickly, a place where you can feel safe. But most importantly, there is the sense that you will finally get there.

When you work through a mandala from this perspective, you will likely find the same themes emerging again and again. And when they do, do you know what is happening? These are your emotional reactions, your lifestyle, right there for you to see on your mandala. Here I am tying you back again to earlier chapters. It is the same framework we looked at in Chapter 7, when we talked about your lifestyle and the back nine. Let me show you eight instances where the variations on my salient theme came up one after another. See if you can find the *lifestyle* behind the story.

1. An Inner Event: My panicked reaction to Emma-Jo standing without a seat belt described how I was feeling about attending my first ASD conference, especially

because I had shared a business idea that I worried would be copied. What is the story behind the story? The dreamer is feeling unprotected and insecure.

2. A Waking-life Event: Emma-Jo without her seat belt connected me to the Dream Interpretation Center and how I was feeling *unprotected* against my fear of failure. What is the story behind the story? This story is about a person who is feeling *insecure*, because she is *inexperienced* due to the fact that her endeavor is a new one for her. As a result she is also feeling some *fear of the unknown*.

3. An Inner Event: Emma-Jo walking into the field symbolized my fear of losing my youth. What is the story behind the story? The dreamer does not know where her "inner child," her youth, is going. She is worried about *losing her child*, and she is *afraid of the unknown*. You can see by my panic in the face of this loss, that this is a story about a person who *has no control* over her aging.

4. An Inner Event: Emma-Jo running out onto the street symbolized my "newness" to the field of public dream interpretation. What is the story behind the story? This is a person who is new at something, *inexperienced*. She is right "out there" with all those academics, and feeling *insecure*. There it is again, insecurity and inexperience as a variation on the theme of fear.

5. An Inner Event: Andy driving the car is the male side of me who drives me away from home on business. My being away from home during a time when I felt that Emma-Jo needed me, created a pull between those same *male and female roles*. Notice how Andy is the one who stays in control of the situation, while in the dream I feel *panicked* and *out of control*. The pull between my male and female sides also represents two different ways I have for *coping with fear and insecurity*, and *trying to stay in control*.

6. An Inner Event: Emma's running out of the car symbolizes my running away from my parents' idea about a woman's place. Here, again, the theme that emerged from the story behind the story was my inner conflict that I experience between my *male and my female sides*.

7. An Inner Event: Andy's driving the car symbolizes my not feeling "in the driver's seat." I was questioning my potential to succeed. I *didn't feel in control*.

8. A Waking-Life Event: My having croup as a young child. That was a story of someone who must have felt very *frightened* and *not in control* of what was happening to her.

I want you to notice how the deeper the mandala reaches, and even though in some ways the discussion or picture appears to be changing, these same main themes are lying there underneath it all. There is a unity among all these different sections. They are pictures of my lifestyle, my emotional reactions. But you would not have seen them unfold repeatedly like this if we just looked at the dream in pieces.

As I have said before, there was value in attaching the dream's meaning to my current situation because it gave me a better understanding of what I was feeling at that time. But it was only when I came back to the mandala and attached my dream to the broader experiences of my life, that my sense of myself and how I was reacting to my current situation really began to take a form. And doesn't it stand to reason now, when you see the dream in the context of my whole life, how I was questioning my potential to succeed and in this regard was not feeling "in the driver's seat"? As you can see from the mandala, the fact that I was questioning my potential directly relates to issues from my past experience with male and female roles, and what I was taught they should and shouldn't be. Don't you think this discovery led me to understand and connect to the impact these messages had? And knowing that now, when you think of it, doesn't it make sense that I experienced guilty feelings about figuratively being in the passenger seat, since I was away from home during a time when I felt Emma-Jo needed me?

With this form that the dream now had, I became hopeful at arriving to some end. I began to see the form as a *process*. And process, for me, means movement. It's true. The movement does lead me to some understanding, respect, appreciation, and forgiveness for the authority figures from my childhood, who taught me what a woman should and shouldn't do. Even more important, it also helped me take responsibility for the authority figure that lives inside me, inside each of us. The process of discovering recurring themes in your mandala has the identical effect I discussed with you in Chapter 6, where we looked back to our past to see where our emotions are coming from. When I saw a visual, it helped confirm for me how my emotional reactions are rooted in my past. I see it there. I understand it. It makes sense to me. I can forgive myself for the way I operate. It is not a mystery anymore. And why do I find myself in the position of feeling forgiving not only towards myself, but towards my parents? Because I am in charge of my own destiny now. I am taking responsibility for the authority figure that lives inside me. The onus is off my parents when I have taken on the job myself.

This is the same as Annie, when she understood that her feeling of responsibility for everyone was directly a result of her childhood experience with looking after her younger siblings. She began to realize *she* has the power to choose when she wants to take the responsibility, and when she will decide to ask for help. The knowledge of a dream at this level helps you to *forgive yourself* for who you are. It helps you to shift your perspective, your judgments about yourself, and why you have reacted the way that you did in a situation. You get the opportunity to see the whole picture about why you are reacting the way you do. With that knowledge, you might open the path towards accepting yourself, while you go about the business of changing what you want to change.

The Emma-Jo Dream
Mortality as an Archetypal Theme

Let's talk again about Emma-Jo walking into a field at the end of my dream. As I said earlier, she is like me, walking into the second half of my life. This is one of the final steps we take towards true maturation, when we get ready to face the fact that we are closer to our death than to our birth. Let's look back to the mandala, where I say that I am approaching midlife. I am realizing that I have no control over growing older, for, in this matter time or *God* is in the driver's seat. You can also see in the mandala how my growing awareness that I have no control over my aging leads right to the universal human theme of facing my own death.

Why do we have so difficult a time letting go of our roles, and our childhood? Because to admit we are adult is to acknowledge our own mortality. Interestingly, when I talked about walking into a field like an island, someone from the back of the room in the mandala workshop called out, "Avalon!" I felt like I was back at one of my Jungian lectures. I said to myself, "Where is Avalon? What is Avalon?" The name sounded so familiar to me. Later, when I had the time, I looked up Avalon in the dictionary. It said, "The blessed island of medieval romance to which King Arthur was carried wounded after his last battle, and from which it was believed he would one day return to rule again."[4] Now I remembered that Lady Guinevere was unfaithful to him. I must tell you, when I read the definition, a feeling of such romantic melancholy came over me— something lost that cannot be recovered.

So, if Jung was talking about an archetype or archetypal themes reverberating or resonating within the dreamer, I caught it here. I don't know why. I did feel moved, though. It seems to me I had attached myself to that universal theme, midlife transition. And surely that would bring with it a certain melancholy too. While Emma-Jo's standing up with no seat belt well illustrates my fear of losing my youth, the deepest layer of this dream taps me into the universal issue which many people experience, my fear of death. For this inescapable eventuality, I feel I have no protection (seat belt).

And none of us does. As you move through your life with both excitement and anxiety, making decisions in whatever way you do, all of your characteristic lifestyles will emerge when you look at your dream through this "psychological viewfinder," the mandala. One example that you have seen in me is my constant inner battle between my "Andy" side and my panicky "feminine" side, and how I am always carrying with me both this admiration for, and rebellion against my parents as I go through each stage of my life. What about you? Can you think of any characteristics inherent in your make-up that continue to emerge as you face the different challenges in your life? I think this is one of the greatest helps you can have while approaching any new transition. It is easy to imagine how a nonjudgmental knowledge of your habitual reactions, an awareness of the whole picture, can help you make decisions in the future, or maybe change some aspect of your behavior or reinforce some choice you have made. Let us investigate this possibility while considering our mortality as an archetypal theme.

I am going to discuss my feelings about my mortality. And it's not just my mortality but my mortality in the context of a life, my *whole* life. I'll also ask you to consider your own feelings about mortality as you move through your life. But before I go there, I want to first illustrate to you how I got to thinking about this transition, and why I think it is no accident that it happened to me now, so that you too might recognize such a dream when you have one.

The Emma-Jo Dream is a midlife dream. How do I know that? I know it because I had it when I was forty-five years old. I know it because so many issues in the dream point to my struggle with individuating from my parents' ideas about roles. I know the dream happened during a midlife re-evaluation, because I was stepping out into a new field, as you can see by the imagery in the dream, and by my career move in waking life. People often do that at midlife, change their work. And what about my fear of walking into that unknown field? My fear of the unknown is a fear shared by most everyone, isn't it? It is a metaphor for the inescapable mortality we all must eventually face. Finally, we can see in the dream how I can't "catch my youth." My youth is getting away from me. The inevitable issue we all must face at some point and understandably, most often we begin to do so in midlife. In *Dreams That Can Change Your Life*, Alan B. Siegel sites, "Themes of children, babies, fertility, and infertility are often prominent in the dreams of women undergoing midlife crisis. One theme that appears often is that of searching for, rescuing, nurturing, or healing children, often sick or lost babies."[5] And so there it was, the rescuing theme in my Emma-Jo Dream.

As I mentioned earlier in this book, at ASD conferences, when wanting to share our impressions with the group about someone else's dream, we say, "If this were my dream it might mean . . ." Recently, I read Robert Bosnak's "confession" in describing his feelings about letting go and accepting not only his father's death, but his own mortality. I was moved. While many of these words are his, I replaced some to show you what I felt like saying, how strongly I connected to his thoughts. So I express *to you* that if this were *my* confession, I would say, "When my father was alive I lived in a world where I could always remain his little girl. We both helped perpetuate the condition of our roles. I, often leaving myself just shy of enough money for what I wanted, and he always ready to provide, to look after me. My walking into 'a new field' and starting another career is my *becoming* my father. In some way becoming him is part of letting go of him; looking after myself is accepting that he is no longer here to play the role." Bosnak wrote, "To my surprise I find that the death of my father has sharpened this homing device now that I have to go entirely my own course. The world had been my father's domain . . . his encouragement had been the voice from home that helped me find direction. Now that the worldly voice from home is silenced, my own homing device surfaces. It gives me a sense of the essential within the manifold appearances, a sense of direction through the wilderness of dreaming. It keeps me connected to the source of my being."[6]

"I can't return to the old world. The world that made sense when my father was alive, died with him. I get sick trying to hold on to the old. I need to gain flexibility, to allow for change. I'm petrified . . . The earth is black and I feel a pain in my chest. Will I die the way my father did? I'm next in line."[7] My own father died in 1991. He is gone ten years. I am almost fifty. In accepting his passing, I, as Bosnak so well puts it, must acknowledge my impending passing. Bosnak asks, "What will I become in a world where *I* am the father? I'm moving into my dead father's spot, the new authority, the next to die."[8]

And finally, I know that I am beginning to face my mortality because of my dreams! The two dreams one right after the other of my brother-in-law and then, moving even closer to me, my blood brother dying. These dreams were clearly an indication of the beginning of transition for me. As I mentioned earlier, they showed me that it is coming at me from "both sides," since these brothers are from different sides of my family. They are also on "both sides" of me because one is a few years older than me and the other a few years younger. I feel right *in the middle* of it!

And by the way, I can thank my dreams, these two nightmares in particular, for initiating me into the feelings of dread and doom and sadness. Wait a minute. I should *thank* these dreams? For making me feel "dread and doom and sadness"? Look at it this way. These dreams serve the function, not only of prodding me to look at my emotions about my mortality, but they give me the opportunity to literally practice feeling the feelings. As you learned earlier, it is one function of dreams that I compare to working out in the gym. By practicing the emotions of fear and doom in our dreams, over time we become more and more in shape, comfortable with those emotions. We become more ready for when the time really does arrive.

I am searching here for how I can fit my own awareness of death into my life so it has some meaning, some constructive meaning. I am hoping that the process you see me going through here will help you face this issue in *your* own life. I'd like you to start here thinking about your mortality too, and your awareness of mortality, as one more phase of your life. Using Adler's lifestyle framework, let me point out that some people move ahead slowly, timidly in life. Others negotiate about their fear. Some just push right through it. Others still are stuck by their fear. Each of us has a lifestyle preferential way for reacting to the major events that come up in our lives.

Listen, the crisis is going to arrive. Haven't I been honest with you so far? Trust me. The crisis arrives, no matter if you try and hide from it, face it or what. We all at some point come to think about our inevitable, impending death. And the ideas that you have about how you will react to your own death, have an impact on the way you live your life.

You can see your lifestyle in all the major decisions you make in life. Why not then in how you approach death? You can use this midlife stage to bring these choices out and put them right there on the table. Instead of ignoring this impending crisis, let's discuss it. If you understand the images in your dreams, and through them are able to determine what stage you are at, you make yourself able to take up a position toward the transition. That's what I am doing here, encouraging you to take up a position, *choose* a position! Are you going to move ahead slowly, timidly? Do you want to negotiate about your fear, or are you going to be stuck in your fear? Maybe there is a part of you who is afraid of doing things alone. That's the piece I can relate to. Not only must I face this eventuality, but worse, do I have to go through it alone?

We have come back to the issue we faced in Chapter 7, in the conflict between *lifestyle* and "playing a different game on the back nine." If you really have a typical "lifestyle" way of facing major transitions and decisions in your life, how can you choose to play it differently? So let me show you what I mean to say by bringing your lifestyle choices right out on the table, in order to possibly choose a position. For me it is that ongoing battle between my "ignore the fear and proceed" attitude (my "male" side), and the worry that if I allow my fearful, "feminine" side to take over, I might never recover. Surely I am going to have to face this dance within myself again, at the moment I realize I really am going to die someday. There is no question that how I think of death will profoundly affect how I live. I may not have the answers here, and you do appreciate I am now at the threshold of this transition, admittedly in the black stage, but here are some thoughts I have.

This is where maybe a Jungian approach, with its archetypes and its ideas of human interconnectedness, can give me some strength. And when I searched out universal, archetypal themes in my Emma-Jo Dream, it brought me right back to my midlife transition and so too my mortality. How can I truly treat death as an *archetype?* How can I turn it around and find some strength there?

I am thinking about my father. Watch how he grabbed the bull by the horns when he faced his death head on. Every now and then when I think that one day I'll be closer to leaving this world than I feel right now, I imagine that I will face death and take the jump to the other side the same way my father did. When he heard the blockage was too close to his heart for them to perform another bypass, and while doctors assured him that many people live a long life on medication, he would hear nothing of it. He said to himself (and to us), "The time has come. I am not going to be anyone's guinea pig. Take me home. I'm out of this hospital *now!*" And he just jumped into death (I mean figuratively) the same way he would have into any scary business venture. He was gone within a few days of hearing the news. When I think about how I will react to growing old and being close to death, I actually have an image of myself holding my nose, the same way as I would when jumping into a pool, and simply jumping. Doing what has to be done despite the element of panic and fear. It is my *lifestyle,* the way I am accustomed to behaving.

My father is a Hero image for me. He shows me how I want to enter the final scene. He is a Hero who I happened to know personally. What about other Heroes? Really, we can pick any character who we aspire to and see how they behaved in any story we are familiar with.

Now here, I have another thought. Maybe I can search out a frightened character to link myself to. For me that would mean allowing myself my weakness, giving myself permission to go right into that fear and sadness. I would play it differently than say, I did in the instance of forging ahead with the Dream Center. In that decision I just ignored my fears, as my father would have done. Will I decide to explore another kind of reaction to my fear of death? I pose these questions aloud for the purpose of letting you hear what the process sounds like.

I would need to become something like my mother, who was only eight years old when her own mother died right there in the room next to her. She is admittedly frightened silly in the face of death, always has been. I will need to reown that under invested aspect of my character. Have you noticed the way I keep talking about my father throughout this book, but say so little about my Mum? There is a reason for that. If my father is my fearless Hero, my mother is my Shadow, my frightened "feminine" side who does not feel in control. In fact she is the typical stay-at-home mom, who depended on my dad to look after her. My mother defined my idea of the "feminine" role growing up. It is hard enough to think about our Heroes and try to be like them, although this process can give us strength. But the hardest thing is to recognize our own Shadow and come close to it, so that we can accept it as a part of who we are.

This is what I will have to do in the face of my own mortality, if I really want to play a different game on the back nine and trick the Trickster inside me. The Trickster offers me two choices. I can play it the same as I always have, close my eyes and hold my nose and jump, while I ignore the scared woman inside. Or I can open my eyes and stare straight at her. I can feel her fear. And then, I'll have to see where I come through on the other side. I don't know where I will be. I've never done it before because I'm afraid I'll get trapped in her fear.

Emma-Jo, with her slippery, shall-I-go-this-way-or-that kind of movement in the dream, so well defines my ever-present pull between what I perceive as my masculine and feminine sides. These two sides of me are how I make choices, my way of reacting in my own life. Emma-Jo as the Trickster in my dream is the one who presents me with these different possibilities.

This Trickster is fundamentally about my masculine/feminine polarity, first in terms of opening the Dream Interpretation Center, and then in my reaction to my own mortality. So the only way to trick the Trickster is to bring these two sides together. Is there a possibility of some kind of synthesis here? Maybe a new "femininity," one that acknowledges my fear but somehow goes through and beyond the panic? But how can I do this? Interestingly, it is my "masculine" side that I might use to help me facilitate this end, for I will need courage in going to that place. I might walk *right into* that fear and sadness, ignore my fear, forge ahead and just do it! And this part of me can give me the confidence that it will work. I can think about all the times I have been like my father, and realize that I have the strength to get through this.

One thing I have learned on this most basic level of human existence—we all have the same issues and ways we can react. They not only repeat within ourselves, but repeat themselves in humans all through time. So you can become proficient in swaying towards the different archetypes or different people you know and have known. You can practice moving along with the tide, rather than staying fixed while the world is moving around you. The fact is that whatever characters and stories came before us, we can learn something from their experience. This is why I would search out universal meaning in my dreams, for it is there where I might find the images of those who have gone through life and death before me. From these pictures I can appreciate my place in the whole of the universe. My experience, my fears are not mine alone.

I have just a few final thoughts on the subject of preparing ourselves for death. As I have been engaging in this discussion, the image of Karen's circle dream keeps coming forward in my mind. The one of her dad, feet off the ground, walking around the young springtime tree. The image of the circle of life spurs me to look at another aspect of that circle. When a woman is around six months pregnant, she begins to experience contractions. While she is still far away from labor, her body begins the process of preparing her. And as the months progress closer to the birth, these contractions slowly become stronger and more frequent. So, when her labor really does begin, the woman is more prepared physically for the experience. Another very common experience women in the early stages of pregnancy have had through the ages is a panic and fear at the thought of giving birth. Yet, as the months pass the woman becomes more and more cumbersome, tired, and heavy. By the end of her term, she is *wishing* for the day labor will begin. She is ready to go through that transition and begin the next stage. So nature prepares mother for the birth of her child emotionally too.

Here's my point. The circle of life has for us all two defining moments, our birth and our death. Of course, I can't predict the future. I don't know if my death will happen suddenly and unexpectedly through illness or a car accident, but I do have some ideas about how to bring death into a life-fulfilling experience that it otherwise might not have been. I don't want to stay fixed while the world is moving around me.

Like nature prepares the mother who is going to give birth, I too can prepare myself. I must have faith and respect that as I grow older and move closer to my final days, I too will feel more ready, both physically and emotionally, to move on to the next stage of my spirit's existence. There is a process at hand here. I must trust it. Besides, does the child in its mother's womb realize that there is a whole world of people, cars, cities, happiness, joy, starvation, wars, and sadness going on right outside its existence? No. It does not. There is a whole world of things going on around that little being, and it has no vision of it, even though it is all so close. Who is to say that you and I are not like children in the womb? We may be unable to see the vast universe around us, filled with souls that continue to survive and learn, just because we can't see it all with our eyes.

Some people come to face their mortality through their religion, others by making changes in their relationships. While I take great comfort in the teachings of my faith, I have often chosen traditional therapy when facing major transitions and crises in my life. I went into therapy after giving birth to Tina, again leading up to my divorce from Murray, and for a time with my girls when Murray died. I find that asking for help during major transitions has been very beneficial for me, and imagine I may go the same route at some point through this final life stage too. For me it doesn't matter what you choose. It is simply a question of doing everything you can to live your life the way you want to live it.

However difficult change is, once you have an idea in your heart, it becomes harder and harder to ignore it. Even in the face of tremendous fear, a vision of the goal can keep you moving towards it. Keep these things in your heart, and they will spur you to change what you need to change. In *The Alchemist* by Paulo Coelho, The Sun advised the boy, " . . . Even if you pretend not to have heard what it [your heart] tells you, it will always be there inside you, repeating to you what you're thinking about life and about the world." And then Paulo Coelho's shepherd described my own experience when he said, "When I have been truly searching for my treasure, every day has been luminous, because I've known that every hour was a part of the dream that I would find it. When I have been truly searching for my treasure, I've discovered things along the way that I never would have seen had I not had the courage to try things that seemed impossible for a shepherd to achieve."[9]

What about you? Do you have a treasure, a dream? Do you want to pursue your highest goals and face your deepest fears?

Are you trying to take control of your choices, and live the life you really want to live?

We have so much in common, we human beings. That is why understanding our dreams can bring us together. If we are more in tune with our own hearts and souls, we will see we are not that different from each other. Then we will make others happy at the same time as we achieve our own happiness. Dream work can be an important step on the road to a better existence for you and for everyone.

Conclusion

Hindsight

The greatest strength I have found in working with my dreams is that the deeper I moved into the layers of the dreams, the more I moved along my own timeline of growth—growth from infancy and childhood, to separation and individuation, to maturity. A timeline that is unique to me, but that I also share with all people. This was not something I set out to do. But I discovered that we all have the opportunity of realizing not only where we stand in our view of our current situation, but how our position is couched in the context of who we are. I mean *all* of who we are. You know, when you assess your position towards any given situation, two points will inevitably color your opinion. One is who you are in the framework of your past. The other is what stage of life you are in. Don't you agree that at fifty, possibly in a midlife transition, you would not necessarily come to the same conclusions and decisions as you may have, say, at twenty, when you were separating emotionally from your parents? Having the ability to understand our dreams gives us the opportunity to be *completely in touch with our whole selves when making decisions.*

The actual process of writing this book has introduced me to all the different stages that I talk about in the context of a life. Working with my dreams throughout this book, especially my Emma-Jo Dream, has brought me through all my major life stages to the point where I am beginning to think about that last transition in our journey from birth to death. I think you too will find that if you take the time to understand your own dreams, they will show you where you have been, where you are now, and where you are going in your life. They will show the *whole* of you. And then you can move ahead from where you are now, using the power that this knowledge gives you.

For me the feeling of moving through life without a sense of who I really am would be like driving my car in a strange country without a map. I hope this book has given you a sense of the road map you might be looking for, or at least the tools to draw your own map. For me the book has been a kind of microcosm, like all maps, a sort of mini-world that I've been traveling through with you, the reader. We have been exploring it together. And after all, that's what living is for us humans, isn't it?

Besides all the other wonderful advantages to understanding our dreams, one of the most crucial is how dreams can alert us to our most serious problems. And while as Faraday assures us, most people are "perfectly capable" of exploring their own dreams, I do want to stress the importance of seeking professional help for serious problems. The fact is that when you feel unable to cope with the problems of life and you experience depression, substance abuse, serious emotional upset, instability, or other behaviors that seriously interfere with your work or your relationships, these will show up in your dreams as an indication that you need to consult outside help.

On a recent *Oprah* show, while discussing with several women how they accomplished their goal in life, Marsha Mason suggested that she sometimes felt as though she was asleep, unconscious. When she woke up to getting in touch with what will fulfill her, she was able to start down the path to her goal. Please don't quote me exactly on this but she said something like, "I believe in therapists, friends, priests, dogs, whatever it is that will help you get unleashed towards working through your fears." I like the way she said that. As you have read, when in my life I have come upon crisis, which we all do, I have always given myself the permission to seek professional help. I think it is my greatest gift to myself, my ability to ask for help.

Endnotes

Opening Quote

von Franz, M.-L. *Man and His Symbols*. Part 3. The Process of Individuation, p. 211.

Chapter 1

Opening Quote: Perls, Frederick S. *Gestalt Therapy Verbatim*, p. 87.

1 Garfield, Patricia. *The Healing Power of Dreams*, p. 22.

2 Delaney, Gayle. *In Your Dreams*, p. 7.

3 Bosnak, Robert. *A Little Course in Dreams*, pp. 14–21. ©1986 by Robert Bosnak, translation ©1988 by Shambhala Publications, Inc. Reprinted by arrangement of Shambhala Publications, Inc., Boston, *www.Shambhala.com*.

4 Garfield, Patricia. *The Healing Power of Dreams*, p. 24.

5 Delaney, Gayle. *In Your Dreams*, p. 9.

6 "Mandala means a circle, more especially a magic circle and this form of symbol is not only to be found all through the East, but also among us; mandalas are amply represented in the Middle Ages. The specifically Christian ones come from the earlier Middle Ages. Most of them show Christ in the center, with the four evangelists, or their symbols, at the cardinal points. This conception must be a very ancient one because Horus was represented with his four sons in the same way by the Egyptians. . . . For the most part, the mandala form is that of a flower, cross or wheel, with a distinct tendency toward four as the basis of the structure."

(Commentary to *Secret of the Golden Flower*, CW 13, *The Collected Works of C.G. Jung*, par. 31, mod.)

"Mandalas . . . usually appear in situations of psychic confusion and perplexity. The archetype thereby constellated represents a pattern of order which, like a psychological 'view finder' marked with a cross or circle divided into four, is superimposed on the psychic chaos so that each content falls into place and the weltering confusion is held together by the protective circle . . . At the same time they are *yantras*, instruments with whose help the order is brought into being." (*Civilization in Transition*, CW 10, *The Collected Works of C.G. Jung,* par. 803) Jung, C. G. *Memories, Dreams, Reflections.* Translated from the German by Richard and Clara Winston. Recorded and edited by Aniela Jaffé. pp. 396, 397.

7 ". . . widely used in Eastern mythology to represent wholeness and balance (the mandala), may symbolize the integration of the personality in dreams. . . ." Faraday, Ann. *Dream Power,* p. 118.

Chapter 2
Opening Quote: Stone, Oliver. *Cinema* television show, with Jack Matthews, interviewer, Nov. 1, 1997.

1 Faraday, Ann. *Dream Power,* p. 205.

2 Freud, Sigmund. *The Interpretation of Dreams,* p. 239.

Chapter 3
Opening Quote: Adler, Alfred. *The Individual Psychology of Alfred Adler,* p. 359.

1 Faraday, Ann. *Dream Power,* pp. 296.

2 Fromm, Erich. *The Forgotten Language*, p. 212.

3 Freud, Sigmund. *The Interpretation of Dreams,* p. 344.

Chapter 4

Opening Quote: Hesse, Herman, Taken from *Freud and Beyond: A History of Modern Psychoanalytic Thought* by Stephen A. Mitchell and Margaret J. Black, p. 85.

1 Jung, Carl G. *Man and His Symbols*, p. 62.

2 Fromm, Erich. *The Forgotten Language*, p. 150, also Jung, Carl G., (CW8 *The Collected Works of C.G. Jung, The Structure and Dynamics of the Psyche*, par. 509, Jung).

3 Perls, Frederick S. *Gestalt Therapy Verbatim*, p. 85.

4 Ibid., p. 31.

5 Ibid., p. 190.

6 Jung, C. G. *Memories, Dreams, Reflections,* pp. 192, 193, 196, 197.

Chapter 5

Opening Quote: Jung, Carl G. *Man and His Symbols*, p. 85.

1 Polster, Erving and Miriam. *Gestalt Therapy Integrated, Contours of Theory & Practice,* pp. 265–278.

2 Faraday, Ann. *Dream Power,* p. 150.

3 Perls, Frederick S. *Gestalt Therapy Verbatim*, p. 243.

4 Ibid., p. 49.

5 Bosnak, Robert. *Tracks in the Wilderness of Dreaming*, p. 47.

Chapter 6

Opening Quote: Shultz, Charles. *The Gazette*, 1989 United Feature Syndicate, Inc. Mon., April 30, 2001.

1 Freud, Sigmund. *The Interpretation of Dreams,* p. 192.

2 Faraday, Ann. *Dream Power,* p. 96.

3 Coelho, Paulo. *The Alchemist,* p. 28, 137.

4 Siegel, Alan B. *Dreams That Can Change Your Life,* pp. 158–159.

Chapter 7
Opening Quote: Steadman, Ralph. *Sigmund Freud,* p. 8.

Chapter 8
Opening Quote: Boznak, Robert. *A Little Course in Dreams,* p. 87 ©1986 by Robert Bosnak, translation ©1988 by Shambhala Publications, Inc. Reprinted by arrangement of Shambhala Publications, Inc., Boston, *www.Shambhala.com.*

1 Kramer, Dr. Milton. *Psychology Today,* September/October, 2000, *"Dreamspeak,"* pp. 56, 58, 60, 85.

2 Ibid., p. 58.

Chapter 9
Opening Quote: Taken from the Internet, *Perspective on Life According to George Costanza* (Seinfeld).

1 Bosnak, Robert. *Tracks in the Wilderness of Dreaming,* p. 149.

2 Jung, C. G. *Memories, Dreams, Reflections,* pp. 401, 402. Also *The Structure and Dynamics of the Psyche,* CW 8, by C. G. Jung, pp. 133 f.

3 Jung, C. G. *Man and His Symbols,* p. 75.

4 Jung, C. G. *Memories, Dreams, Reflections,* pp. 158–160.

5 Jung, Carl G. *Man and His Symbols,* p. 98.

6 Ibid., p. 56.

7 von Franz, M.-L. *Man and His Symbols,* p. 304.

8 Jung, Carl G. *Man and His Symbols*, p. 96.

9 Bosnak, Robert. *A Little Course in Dreams*, pp. 128–138. ©1986 by Robert Bosnak, translation ©1988 by Shambhala Publications, Inc. Reprinted by arrangement of Shambhala Publications, Inc., Boston, *www.Shambhala.com.*

10 Sheperd, Harvey. *The Montreal Gazette*, Monday, June 4, 2001, pp. A1 and A4.

Chapter 10
Opening Quote: von Franz, M.-L. *Man and His Symbols.* Part 3. The Process of Individuation. *"The Pattern of Psychic Growth,"* p. 161.

1 Jung, Carl. Commentary to *Secret of the Golden Flower*. CW 13, par. 31, mod.

2 (*Civilization in Transition*, CW 10, par. 803) *Memories, Dreams, Reflections.* By C.G. Jung. Translated from the German by Richard and Clara Winston. Recorded and edited by Aniela Jaffé. (New York: Random House, 1963; Vintage Books edition 1989), pp. 396, 397.

3 Faraday, Ann. *Dream Power*, p. 118.

4 *The New Lexicon Webster's Encyclopedic Dictionary of the English Language*, p. 65.

5 Siegel, Alan. *Dreams That Can Change Your Life*, p. 172.

6 Bosnak, Robert. *Tracks in the Wilderness of Dreaming*, pp. 202, 203.

7 Ibid., p. 183.

8 Ibid., p. 186.

9 Coelho, Paulo. *The Alchemist*, pp. 136–137.

Permissions

Quotations from *Tracks in the Wilderness of Dreaming* by Dr. Robert Boznak (A Delta Book, published by Dell Publishing, a division of Bantam, Doubleday, Dell Publishing Group, Inc., 1996) reprinted with permission of the author.

Quotations from *Man and His Symbols,* edited by C. G. Jung (Ferguson Publishing Company, 1969) reprinted with permission of the publisher.

Quotations from *A Little Course in Dreams* by Dr. Robert Boznak (Translation © 1998 by Shambhala Publications, Inc.) reprinted by arrangement with Shambhala Publications, Inc., Boston, *www.shambhala.com.*

Quotations from *Memories, Dreams and Reflections* by C. G. Jung, edited by Aniela Jaffe, translated by Richard and Clara Winston, © 1961, 1962, 1963 and renewed 1989, 1990, 1991 by Random House, Inc., used by permission of Pantheon Books, a division of Random House.

Quotations from *Dream Power* by Ann Faraday, © 1972 by Ann Faraday, used by permission of Coward-McCann, Inc., a division of Putnam Penguin, Inc.

Suggested Reading

I n this book I have only had time to give you a quick overview of the different schools and methods of dream analysis. For those of you who wish to learn more, these are some of the best sources of dream interpretation that I have covered in this book, along with other non-dream books related to my discussions herein.

Adlerian Dream Interpretation

Adler, Alfred. *The Individual Psychology of Alfred Adler.* (Basic Books, Inc., 1956)

Baruth, Leroy G. *Life Style: Theory, Practice and Research.* Dubuque, IA: Kendall/Hunt, 1978)

Gold, Dr. Leo. *A Contemporary View of Dream Interpretation and Therapy.* (Festschrift, 1988)

Gold, L. *Life Style and Dreams.* In Baruth & D. Eckstein (Eds.)

Children's Dreams

Siegal, Alan B., and Bulkeley, Kelly. *Dreamcatching. Every Parent's Guide to Exploring and Understanding Children's Dreams and Nightmares.* (Three Rivers Press, a division of Crown Publishers, Inc., NY, 1998)

Dream Dictionaries

Crisp, Tony. *Dream Dictionary.* (Wing Books, distributed by Random House Value Publishing Inc., N.J., 1994)

Fontana, David. *The Secret Language of Dreams.* (Duncan Baird, London, 1994)

Todeschi, Kevin J. *The Encyclopedia of Symbolism.* (The Berkley Publishing Group, N.Y., 1995)

Dream Interpretation During Illness
Garfield, Patricia. *The Healing Power of Dreams.* (Simon & Schuster, N.Y., 1992)

Freudian Dream Interpretation
Freud, Sigmund. *An Outline of Psychic Analysis.* (The Hogarth Press Ltd., 1973)

Freud, Sigmund. *The Interpretation of Dreams by Sigmund Freud*, from *The Basic Writings of Sigmund Freud,* Translated and edited, with an Introduction by Dr. A. A. Brill. (Random House Inc., N.Y., 1938)

Hall, Calvin S. *A Primer of Freudian Psychology.* (The World Publishing Company, N.Y., 1954)

Mitchell, Stephen A. and Black, Margaret J. *Freud and Beyond: A History of Modern Psychoanalytic Thought.* (Basic Books, N.Y., 1995)

Thomas, D.M. *The White Hotel.* (Printed and bound in Great Britain by Guernsey Press Co. Ltd., Guernsey, Channel Isles. This Indigo edition is an imprint of the Cassell Group, Wellington House, London, 1981)

General Dream Interpretation
Bulkeley, Kelly Ph.D. *Transforming Dreams: Learning Spiritual Lessons from the Dreams You Never Forget.* (John Wiley & Sons Inc., N.Y., 2000)

Delaney, Gayle. *In Your Dreams.* (Harper Collins, N.Y., 1997)

Faraday, Ann. *Dream Power.* (The Berkley Publishing Group, N.Y., 1980)

Fromm, Erich. *The Forgotten Language.* (Grove Press Inc. Distributed by Random House Inc., N.Y., 1980)

Sheppard, Linda. *Wake Up to Your Dreams: A Practical Self-help Guide to Interpretation.* (Blandford, London, 1994, Distributed in the United States by Sterling Publishing Co. Inc., N.Y.)

Taylor, Jeremy. *Where People Fly and Water Runs Uphill: Using Dreams to Tap the Wisdom of the Unconscious.* (Warner Books, Inc., N.Y. 1993)

Van de Castle, Robert. *Our Dreaming Mind.* (New York: Ballantine Books, 1994)

Gestalt Dream Interpretation

Perls, Frederick S. *Gestalt Therapy Verbatim.* (The Center for Gestalt Development, Highland, N.Y., 1992)

Polster, Erving & Miriam. *Gestalt Therapy Integrated, Contours of Theory & Practice* (Vintage Books Edition, Random House, N.Y., 1974)

Stevens, John O. *Awareness: Exploring, Experimenting, Experiencing.* (Bantam Books, Inc., N.Y., 1973)

Jungian Dream Interpretation

Bly, Robert, and Woodman, Marion. *The Maiden King. The Reunion of Masculine and Feminine.* (Henry Holt and Company Inc., N.Y., 1998)

Bosnak, Robert. *A Little Course in Dreams.* (Shambhala Publications Inc., Boston, MA, distributed by Random House, Inc., N.Y., 1988)

Bosnak, Robert. *Tracks in the Wilderness of Dreaming.* (Dell Publishing, N.Y., 1996)

Hall, James A. *Jungian Dream Interpretation: A Handbook of Theory and Practice.* (Inner City Books, Toronto, Canada, Printed and bound in Canada by University of Toronto Press Incorporated, 1983)

Jung, Carl G. *Man and His Symbols.* (Doubleday & Company Inc., N.Y., 1964)

Jung, Carl G. *Memories, Dreams, Reflections.* Translated from the German by Richard and Clara Winston, Recorded and edited by Aniela Jaffé. (New York: Random House, 1963; Vintage Books edition 1989). From the Glossary: Commentary to *Secret of the Golden Flower*, CW 13, *The Collected Works of C.G. Jung,* par. 31, mod and also *Civilization in Transition*, CW 10, *The Collected Works of C.G. Jung,* par. 803.

Sharp, Daryl. *Jungian Psychology Unplugged.* (Inner City Books, Toronto, Ontario 1998)

Woodman, Marion. *Addiction to Perfection.* (Inner City Books, Toronto, Canada, 1982)

Psychic and Precognitive Dream Interpretation

Bro, Harmon H. *Edgar Cayce on Dreams.* (Warner Books, N.Y., 1988)

Magallon, Linda Lane. *Mutual Dreaming.* (Pocket Books, Simon & Schuster, N.Y., 1997)

Ryback, David. *Dreams That Come True.* (Doubleday, Dell Publishing Group, N.Y., 1988)

Sexual Dreams

Delaney, Gayle. *Sensual Dreaming: How to Understand and Interpret the Erotic Content of Your Dreams.* (Formerly titled *Sexual Dreams.*) (A Fawcett Columbine Book, Ballantine Books, N.Y., 1994)

Hinshaw Baylis, Janice, Ph.D. *Sex, Symbols and Dreams.* (Sun, Man, Moon, Inc., Seal Beach, CA, 1997)

Spiritual Dream Interpretation

Coburn, Chuck. *Reality Is Just an Illusion.* (Liewellyn Publications, St. Paul, MN, 1999)

Hoffman, Edward. *The Way of Splendor: Jewish Mysticism and Modern Psychology.* (Shambhala Boulder & London, 1981)

Monford, Harris. *Studies in Jewish Dream Interpretation.* (Jason Aronson Inc., Northvale, N.J., 1994)

Pike, Diane Kennedy. *Life as a Waking Dream.* (The Berkley Publishing Group, N.Y., 1996)

Transition

Sheehy, Gail. *Passages. Predictable Crisis of Adult Life.* (Bantam Books Inc. N.Y., 1974)

Siegal, Alan B. *Dreams That Can Change Your Life.* (The Berkley Publishing Group, N.Y., 1996)

Spencer, Sabina A., and Adams, John D. *Life Changes. Growing Through Personal Transitions.* (Impact Publishers, San Luis Obispo, CA, 1990)

Other Reading

Bradshaw, John. *Bradshaw On: The Family: A Revolutionary Way of Self-Discovery.* (Health Communications Inc., Deerfield Beach, FL, 1988)

Chopra, Deepak. *The Seven Spiritual Laws of Success.* (Amber-Allen Publishing, and New World Library, Novato, CA, 1994)

Coelho, Paulo. *The Alchemist.* Translated by Alan R. Clarke. (HarperCollins Publishers Inc. 1994) This book is an English version of *O Alquimista*, the Portuguese original edition, published by Editora Rocco Ltd. (Rio de Janeiro, Brazil), 1988 by Paulo Coelho. This edition was prepared by Alan R. Clarke in consultation with Paulo Coelho.

Redfield, James. *The Celestine Prophecy.* (Warner Books, N.Y., 1996)

Steadman, Ralph. *Sigmund Freud.* (Firefly Books Ltd., Ontario, Canada, 1997)

Articles and Magazines

Kramer, Dr. Milton. *Psychology Today*, September/October, 2000, *"Dreamspeak."*

Rochen, Aaron, Ligiero, Daniela, Hill, Clara E., and Heaton, Kristen J. University of Maryland. *Preparation for Dreamwork: Training for Dream Recall and Dream Interpretation. The Association for the Study of Dreams.* Fourteenth International Conference. Abstracts. June 17–21, 1997. Warren Wilson College, Asheville, North Carolina.

Shultz, Charles. United Feature Syndicate, Inc. *The Gazette*, Montreal, Monday, April 30, 2001.

Sheperd, Harvey, as reported by in *The Gazette*, Montreal, Monday, June 4, 2001, pp. A1 and A4.

Zadra, Antonio. 1996, *Recurrent Dreams; Their Relation to Life Events and Well Being.* (ed.) D. Barrett. *Trauma and Dreams*, pp. 231–247, Cambridge, Harvard University Press.

Index